英汉对照·国际汉语教师发展丛书

汉语二语字词教学

Teaching Chinese as a Second Language: Character and Word Acquisition and Instruction (Second Edition)

[美] 沈禾玲（Helen H. Shen）著

（第2版）

北京语言大学出版社
BEIJING LANGUAGE AND CULTURE UNIVERSITY PRESS

图书在版编目 (CIP) 数据

汉语二语字词教学 / (美) 沈禾玲著 . — 2 版 . —
北京 : 北京语言大学出版社, 2020.7
(英汉对照 · 国际汉语教师发展丛书)
ISBN 978-7-5619-5591-8

Ⅰ. ①汉… Ⅱ. ①沈… Ⅲ. ①汉语—词汇—对外汉语教学—教学研究 Ⅳ. ①H195.3

中国版本图书馆 CIP 数据核字 (2019) 第 289008 号

汉语二语字词教学（第 2 版）
HANYU ERYU ZI CI JIAOXUE （DI 2 BAN）

排版制作：华伦图文制作中心
责任印制：周 燚

出版发行：北京语言大学出版社
社 址：北京市海淀区学院路 15 号，100083
网 址：www.blcup.com
电子信箱：service@blcup.com
电 话：编辑部 8610-82303647
发行部 8610-82303650/3591/3648
北语书店 8610-82303653
网购咨询 8610-82303908
印 刷：北京中科印刷有限公司

版 次：2020 年 7 月第 1 版 印 次：2020 年 7 月第 1 次印刷
开 本：710 毫米 × 1000 毫米 1/16 印 张：19.25
字 数：343 千字
定 价：66.00 元

Preface

In recent decades, scholars in the field of second language acquisition have paid increasing attention to research on vocabulary instruction, as vocabulary knowledge is proved to be a strong predictor for reading comprehension (Jeon, 2012; Jiang, 2016; Kuhn & Stahl, 2003). This observation holds true in learning Chinese as a second language (CSL). Students' character recognition accuracy had a moderate to high correlation with reading comprehension among lower-level learners regardless of differences in learning environment and first language backgrounds (Shen & Jiang, 2013). And advanced students' depth and size of vocabulary knowledge contribute significantly to reading comprehension for reading complex texts (Zhang & Yang, 2016). It is reported that character recognition is a strong predictor for reading fluency (Xue et al., 2013). It is also reported that an increase of one percent of new words in a reading material could decrease reading comprehension in a fixed reading time by 2–4 percent (Shen, 2005). Without a doubt, vocabulary acquisition plays a key role in successful reading comprehension. Within this context, for CSL, we noticed that learners' written vocabulary acquisition is a slow developmental process. One study indicated that American students with 26 credit hours learning in Chinese language, acquired, on average, only about 2,229 words from the 8,500 high-frequency words listed in the *Modern Chinese Word Frequency Dictionary* (《现代汉语频率词典》, Beijing Language Institute Press, 1986). The acquisition of active vocabulary was only about 59% of the 2,229 words (Shen, 2009).

Why is learning Chinese characters so difficult to western learners? One major difficulty can be attributed to the fundamental differences in phonology, orthography, and morphology between Chinese and the students' native languages. Phonologically, Chinese is a tonal language with four lexical tones. Chinese characters do not have a sound-to-script correspondence, which creates difficulty in memorizing the sound of characters. Although there are phonetic radicals that cue the sound of compound characters, the accuracy rate of phonetic radicals cuing the pronunciation of compound characters is only about 26% without considering the tonal difference (Fan, Gao, & Ao, 1984). Phonetic radicals are independent characters. According to statistics, there are about 1,348 Chinese characters serving as phonetic radicals for 6,542 commonly used compound characters (周有光, 1978). This means that students first need to learn the pronunciation of the 1,348 characters before they can use them effectively as phonetic radicals for learning compound characters. Orthographically, characters are composed of strokes and there are no fixed rules regarding the number of strokes and composition of individual characters. Morphologically, overwhelming majority of Chinese characters are free morphemes. A Chinese character itself can be a word, but with other characters, it can also form two-character or multi-character words. Chinese words have no inflections and there are no visible space boundaries between words. All of these require a cognitive restructuring for students who have acquired a western language as their native language to learn this unique language. Western learners will encounter at least two major cognitive difficulties in learning the Chinese language. The first difficulty is to establish a new cognitive mechanism that is suitable for learning a logographic language; the other difficulty is to overcome the interference from the existing cognitive structure used to process their first language. Due to these difficulties, western learners need to spend about three-fold more time to learn Chinese to reach an equivalent proficiency in learning a western language (Everson & Xiao, 2009).

Without a doubt, these cognitive difficulties have brought challenges to character/word/vocabulary instruction in Chinese. Understanding learners' cognitive processes in character learning and exploring effective character/word/vocabulary instruction approaches have been a strategic effort among educators. The purpose of this book is to present theoretical models on Chinese character/word/vocabulary acquisition and instruction coupled with examples of theory-guided and research-based instructional methods.

This book consists of six chapters. Chapter 1 defines important terms used in this book to allow readers to share a common understanding of these terms with the author while reading this book. Chapter 2 addresses studies on learners' orthographic knowledge acquisition and how instruction can facilitate this acquisition. Chapter 3 presents unique cognitive and psycholinguistic models for Chinese word acquisition to help readers understand the general process of word acquisition and how instruction should keep in line with the learner's learning process. Chapter 4 addresses five cognitive theories from an information process perspective and their application in Chinese word instruction to maximize learning effects. Chapter 5 discusses the identification of good character and word learning strategies and how to train learners to use effective learning strategies during learning. Grounded on the discussion in these five chapters, Chapter 6 proposes CSL character/word instruction frameworks for both beginners and advanced learners.

The intended readers for this book are CSL educators (including middle school teachers), graduate students who are seeking careers in teaching CSL, and researchers in CSL acquisition and instruction, particularly in character/

word instruction.

Educators who wish to know more Chinese character/word learning methods guided by the theories presented in this book may also read the accompanying book, *Teaching Chinese as a Second Language: Theory-Based Character and Word Instruction.*[①]

① The book introduces 45 character and word teaching methods, and will be published by the Beijing Language and Culture University Press.

前　言

近几十年来，在二语习得领域，学者们对词汇教学研究给予了越来越多的关注。大量研究证明，词汇知识对阅读理解具有强有力的预测作用。（Jeon，2012；Jiang，2016；Kuhn and Stahl，2003）这个发现在汉语二语学习领域中也得到了证实。Shen 和 Jiang（2013）的研究表明，低水平汉语学习者汉字认读的准确度与阅读理解之间具有越来越强的相关性，而且这种相关不受学习者学习环境和母语背景的影响。Zhang 和 Yang（2016）的研究表明，高水平汉语学习者词汇知识的深度与广度直接影响他们对复杂文本的理解。Xue 等人（2013）的研究还显示，汉字认读流利度是阅读流利度的有力预测因子。在阅读时间固定的前提下，阅读材料中每增加1%的新词就会导致阅读理解率下降2%~4%（Shen，2005）。毫无疑问，阅读理解若想成功，词汇的习得至关重要。但是，汉语二语学习者的书面词汇习得是十分缓慢的。Shen（2009）的研究表明，以北京语言学院出版社1986年出版的《现代汉语频率词典》中列出的 8,500 个常用词为参照，已修完26个汉语课程学分的美国学生平均掌握的词汇数量是 2,229个，其中积极词汇只占59%。

为什么汉字对于西方学习者来说这么难掌握呢？一个主要的困难在于汉语与学习者的母语在语音、缀字法、构词法等方面存在着根本性的差异。从语音方面说，汉语是有四个声调的有声调语言，但汉字的音形之间没有直接的联系，这让记忆汉字字音变得十分困难。汉字中的合体字虽然有声旁，但是在不考虑声调差异的情况下，声旁表音的正确率只有 26%左右（Fan，Gao，and Ao，1984）。声旁都是一个个独立的汉字。据统计，现代汉语中常用的 6,542 个合体字中大约有 1,348 个（周有光，1978）由汉字充当的声旁，这意味着学生要先学会这 1,348 个汉字的发音才能很好地利用它们来学习合体字。从缀字法方面看，汉字是由笔画组成的，而且每个汉字的笔画数和字形构成是没有规律可循的。从构词法方面说，绝大多数汉字是自由语素，可以独立成词，也可以同其他字组合成词。汉语词没有词形上的变化，书写时词与词之间也没有明显的界线。这些差别使以西方语言为母语的学习者在学习汉语这种独特的语言时必须在大脑中进行认知结构的重组。他们在学习汉语时至少要面临两重认知困难：第一重困难是，他们必须重新建立一种适合于认知汉字这种表意文字的新机制；第二重困难是，他们必须克服加工第一语言过程中形成的认知结构对汉语学习的干扰。这些困难使得西方学习者必须花费比学习一种新的印欧语言多三倍的时间来学习汉语才能达到同等的流利水平。（Everson and Xiao，2009）

毋庸置疑，上述提到的这些认知困难也给汉语二语字词教学带来了挑战。了解汉语二语学习者字词习得的认知规律，探索行之有效的字词教学途径，将是汉语教师今后相当长一段时间内的研究方向。本书旨在探讨汉语二语字词习得和教学的理论模式，并提供以理论为指导的和以研究为基础的教学方法。

本书共六章。第一章先对本书涉及的几个重要概念加以界定，使读者在阅读本书时对这些概念的理解能与作者达成共识；第二章阐述了学习者缀字知识的习得过程，并探讨教学如何能促进其习得；第三章描述了汉语词语习得的独特认知模式和心理语言学模式，使读者了解词语习得的一般过程，以及教学应该如何顺应学习者的词语习得认知规律；第四章从信息加工的角度讨论了五种认知理论及其在词语教学上的应用；第五章介绍了有关字词学习策略的研究，以及如何帮助学习者找到好的学习策略并进行训练。基于上述五章的讨论，作者在第六章提出了面向低水平和高水平汉语学习者的汉语二语字词教学模式。

本书主要面向汉语二语教育者（包括中学教师）、正在寻找汉语二语教学方向工作的研究生，以及汉语二语习得领域的研究者，尤其是对汉语字词教学感兴趣的学者。

读者如需了解更多的本书理论指导下的适用于不同水平学习者的汉语二语字词教学方法，请参阅与本书配套的《汉语二语字词教学方法》[①] 一书。

References 参考文献

周有光. 1978. 现代汉字中声旁的表音功能问题[J].中国语文（3）：172–177.

Everson M E, Xiao Y. 2009. Teaching Chinese as a foreign language: theories and applications[M]. Boston: Cheng & Tsui Company.

Fan K Y, Gao J L, Ao X P. 1984. Pronunciation principles of Chinese characters and alphabetic writing scripts[J]. Chinese character reform, 3: 23–27.

Jeon E H. 2012. Oral reading fluency in second language reading[J]. Reading in a foreign language, 24 (2): 186–208.

Jiang X. 2016. The role of oral reading fluency in ESL reading comprehension among learners of different first language backgrounds[J]. The reading matrix: an international online journal, 16 (2): 227–242.

Kuhn M R, Stahl S A. 2003. Fluency: a review of developmental and remedial practices[J]. Journal of educational psychology, 95(1): 3–21.

Shen H H. 2005. Linguistic complexity and beginning-level L2 Chinese reading[J]. Journal of Chinese language teachers association, 40(1): 1–28.

Shen H H. 2009. Size and strength: written vocabulary acquisition among advanced learners[J]. Chinese teaching in the world, 23(1): 74–85.

Shen H H, Jiang X. 2013. Character reading fluency, word segmentation accuracy, and reading comprehension in L2 Chinese[J]. Reading in a foreign language, 25 (1): 1–25.

① 《汉语二语字词教学方法》一书即将出版，该书将详细介绍本书所述理论指导下的45种字词教学方法。

Xue J, Shu H, Li H, et al.. 2013. The stability of literacy-related cognitive contributions to Chinese character naming and reading fluency[J]. Journal of psycholinguistics research, 42(5): 433–450.

Zhang D, Yang X. 2016. Chinese L2 learners' depth of vocabulary knowledge and its role in reading comprehension[J]. Foreign language annals, 49 (4): 699–715.

Contents 目录

Chapter 1 第一章

Chinese Characters, Radicals, Words, and Word Knowledge

汉字、部首、词和词语知识的概念

1.1 What are Chinese characters? 什么是汉字?

A Chinese character is an individual written unit separated by a space boundary, with each character corresponding to one oral syllable. Most of Chinese morphemes are monosyllabic. Each morpheme is represented by a character in written form. Each Chinese character also represents one syllable. Therefore, there exists a general one-to-one correspondence between morphemes and Chinese characters (施春宏, 2018). Unlike the case in English where most morphemes are bound morphemes in words, most of Chinese characters are free morphemes. They can stand alone to be a word. Only a very small number of characters lacking independent meanings are required to combine with other characters to form two-syllable morphemes such as 蟋蟀 (xīshuài) *cricket*. Characters are constructed by individual strokes. In general, there are seven basic strokes. The different combinations of the seven basic strokes yield another 24 types of strokes (张静贤, 1992: 31–32). These 31 types of strokes are used to create about 50,000 Chinese characters, of which only

5,000–8,000 are in common use. Of them, 3,000–4,000 are commonly used in daily communication. Please refer to Appendix A for the seven basic strokes and 24 types of combined strokes.

汉字是书写单位，每个汉字对应一个音节。汉语语素大部分是单音节的，在书面上用一个汉字表示，而每个汉字代表一个音节，因此语素和汉字之间大体上是一一对应的。（施春宏，2018）在英语中，大部分语素是黏着语素；而在汉语中，大部分汉字是自由语素，可以独立成词，只有极少数汉字没有独立的意义，需要跟其他汉字结合在一起组成双音节语素，如蟋蟀（xīshuài）。汉字由笔画构成。张静贤（1992：31—32）认为，基本笔画有7种，这7种笔画通过不同组合又派生出24种笔画（请参见附录 A）。这31种笔画的不同组合形成了约50,000个汉字，其中只有5,000～8,000个是常用汉字。在这些常用汉字中，只有3,000～4,000个是日常交际中频繁使用的。

Chinese characters can be classified into two categories in terms of their physical structure: simple characters and compound characters. A simple character such as 日 (rì) *sun* or 月 (yuè) *moon* is composed of a number of strokes and cannot be decomposed into meaningful orthographic units. A compound character consists of two or more orthographic units such as 明 (míng) *bright,* which contains 日 and 月. How are these two categories of Chinese characters formed? In the study of the composition of Chinese characters, a traditional theory known as 六书 (liùshū) *six writings*, explains that six types of characters are developed based on the characteristics of their formation. The six types of characters are termed pictographs, indicatives, ideographs, phonetic-semantic compounds, mutual explanatory (characters), and phonetic loans (谢光辉, 1997). Precisely speaking, the last two are not methods of creating new characters, because "mutual explanatory" is a way of explaining the meaning of a character through comparison with another existing character of similar meaning. Phonetic loans are ways of borrowing existing characters to represent new ideas. That is, to give an existing character a new meaning. Neglecting these two types for the moment, let us take a close look at the other four methods of character creation.

根据汉字的结构，我们可以将其分成两类：独体字和合体字。独体字由一定数量的笔画构成，不能拆分成有意义的缀字部件，如“日”（rì）、“月”（yuè）。合体字则由两个或两个以上的缀字部件构成，如“明”（míng）由“日”“月”构成。那么这两类汉字又是如何形成的呢？传统的“六书”理论介绍了六种汉字造字法，它们是象形、指事、会意、形声、转注和假借。（谢光辉，1997）确切地说，后两种不属于造新字的方法，因为转注是借用已有汉字注释另一个汉字，假借是借用已有汉字表示与其音相同或相近的另一个意义不同的字。除去这两种，我们来仔细考察一下前四种造字法。

The first type is the pictograph, in which each graph depicts an object. For example, 日(rì) and 月(yuè) originate from the pictographs of ⊖ and ☽ . Pictographs are based on the external forms of objects, so it is difficult to express abstract ideas. This probably is the reason why the use of pictographs is very limited. Approximately, 1,700 pictographs are identified from the oracle bone inscriptions (韩鉴堂, 2005:20). Nonetheless, pictographs showed us that Chinese characters are rich in meaning-shape connection in origin. Due to the simplification and standardization of Chinese characters over history, pictographs in modern script have been obscured because the cursive strokes are all straightened.

第一种是象形，也就是描摹事物的形状代表该事物。例如，现代汉字“日”和“月”的象形古字就是 ⊖ 和 ☽。因为象形字只能描绘出事物的外形，所以它很难表达抽象的概念，这大概就是象形字使用非常有限的原因。目前，我们已从甲骨文中考证了大约1,700个象形字（韩鉴堂，2005：20）。虽然数量还比较少，但象形字揭示了汉字的起源，告诉我们最早的汉字义形之间是有着紧密联系的。由于历史上汉字的不断简化和标准化，汉字的笔画已从曲线型发展为直线型，所以现代汉字中象形字的痕迹已经不明显了。

The second type is the indicative, which refers to the way of forming abstract characters using indicative symbols. There are two subtypes of indicatives. One is created by adding an indicative marker to a pictograph. For example, 刃 (刃, rèn, *blade*) is composed by adding a dot to a knife, which 刀 to indicate that part of a knife, which is the knife-edge. The character 本 (本, běn, *root*) is constructed by adding a horizontal stroke to the pictograph 木 (木, mù, *tree*). The other subtype is created by using symbolic signs to represent abstract ideas. For example, ⌣ (上, shàng, *above*) indicates that an object is above the cursive line; ⌢ (下, xià, *underneath*) indicates that an object is underneath the cursive line.

第二种是指事。指事是使用指示符号创造抽象字的造字法，具体包括两种造字方式。第一种是在原有的象形字上加指示符号。例如，刃（刃，rèn，*blade*）是在 刀 字上加一点表示刀锋，本（本，běn，*root*）是在 木（木，mù，*tree*）字下边加一笔表示树的根。第二种是用象征符号表示抽象概念。例如，⌣（上，shàng，*above*）表示一个物体在中线的上面，⌢（下，xià，*underneath*）表示一个物体在中线的下面。

The third type, the ideograph, is composed of two or more existing pictographs. For example, a single pictograph 𣎳 (木, mù) means *tree*. By adding another 木 to it, the character becomes 林 *woods*. Putting three 木 pictographs together, which is 森, gives the meaning *forest*.

第三种是会意。会意字一般由两个或两个以上的象形字组成。例如，象形字 𣎳（木，mù）表示"树木"，再加上一个"木"，两个"木"在一起就是"林"，三个"木"就是"森"。

The fourth type is the phonetic-semantic compound, which refers to a character consisting of a semantic component and a phonetic component. The semantic component of the compound character indicates the meaning category of the character while the phonetic component signifies its pronunciation. Here are two examples: 根 gēn (*root*) and 花 huā (*flower*). For the character 根, the left component 木 is a semantic component indicating that this character is semantically related to a tree. The right component 艮 gèn cues the sound of the character without considering the tonal difference. For the compound character 花 huā, the top component 艹 (ΨΨ) signifying the meaning category "plant" and the bottom component 化 huà cuing the sound of the character although the tone of 化 is different from that of 花. Here, we would need to point out that the semantic component in a compound character shows only the meaning category of the character, but not its specific meaning. For a phonetic component, due to the phonological changes in the history, only about 26% of phonetic components in the phonetic-semantic compounds can reliably indicate the sounds of the characters, even though tonal differences are ignored (Fan,

Gao, & Ao, 1984).

第四种是形声。形声字都是合体字，每个字包含一个表音部件（称为“声旁”）和一个表义部件（称为“形旁”）。形旁标明该字的意义类属，声旁则标明该字的发音。例如，“根”（gēn，*root*）和“花”（huā，*flower*）这两个字都是形声字。“根”左边的“木”是形旁，代表这个字与树木有关；右边的“艮”（gèn）是声旁，虽然声调不一致，但它标示“根”字的发音 gēn。“花”的上部“艹”（ψψ）代表该字与植物有关；下部“化”（huà）标示“花”字的发音，虽然声调不同。需要特别指出的是：形旁只标示该字的意义类属，给不出确切的字义；声旁虽然表音，但由于历史上汉语语音的演变，在不考虑声调差异的情况下，形声字声旁表音的正确率只有 26% 左右（Fan，Gao，and Ao，1984）。

From the above description, we can understand that pictographs and indicatives are simple characters, while ideographs and phonetic-semantic compounds are compound characters. According to the *Dictionary of Chinese Character Information* (《汉字信息字典》, 1988), about 7,462 of the commonly used 7,785 characters are compound characters. Among these compound characters, the phonetic-semantic compounds are the predominant compounds.

从上面的描述中我们可以推知，象形字和指事字基本上都是独体字，会意字和形声字基本上都是合体字。根据《汉字信息字典》（1988）的统计，在 7,785个常用汉字中，7,462个是合体字，而且绝大部分合体字是形声字。

1.2 What are radicals? 什么是部首？

In the previous section, we have mentioned that pictographs and indicatives are simple characters, and the majority of compound characters are phonetic-semantic compounds. Each consists of semantic and phonetic components within. Traditionally, we refer to semantic components as radicals. What does radical mean and who invented the term? In the Eastern Han Dynasty, a scholar named Xu Shen 许慎 (c. AD. 58-147) classified 9,353 compound characters into 540 categories based on the common simple characters they contained. He used the common simple character as their heading and referred to each common simple character as a "radical." The radicals that Xu Shen identified are semantic radicals. Each radical signifies the meaning of the compound character containing the radical. For example, as characters 松,柳, and 杨 all share the same semantic radical 木 (*tree*), we can guess that the meanings of these characters are all related to a tree. This groundbreaking method—classifying characters based on their shared radicals, allowed Xu to compile the first Chinese dictionary《说文解字》*Character and Word Annotations* (Shen, Wang, & Tsai, 2009) to index characters based on their common components—radicals. Later scholars further analyzed the characters and reduced the number of semantic radicals. In the *Modern Chinese Word Dictionary*《现代汉语词典》(2016) published in China's mainland, we usually find 201 radicals in the radical index section. However, a few of the 201 radicals are not semantic radicals, but rather strokes that serve as index for searching integral characters in the dictionary. In addition to semantic radicals, another concept "bujian" (部件 *component*) is also used to refer the units within a compound character. However, "bujian" in a compound character does not signify the meaning of a compound character. "bujian" is a perception unit. We will explain "bujian" in detail in the following section.

前面我们提到了，象形字和指事字基本上都是独体字，而合体字大部分都是形声字。每个形声字都由表义部件和表音部件组成。传统上，我们一般将表义部件称为“部首”。部首是什么意思？谁发明了这个词？东汉年间，一个叫许慎（约公元 58—147 年）的学者将 9,353 个合体字按照它们包含的常用独体字进行了整理和归类，分成了 540 部，并把每部汉字中的常用独体字拿出来作为该部的标识，列为一部之首，称为“部首”。许慎所归纳的部首标明了汉字的意义类属。例如，“松”“柳”“杨”的部首都是“木”，我们据此可以推断，这些汉字的意思都跟“木”有关。根据这一具有历史开创性的汉字分类法，即根据汉字的共有部件对汉字进行分类，许慎编纂了中国第一部用部首检索汉字的汉语字典——《说文解字》。（Shen，Wang，and Tsai，2009）后来的学者在许慎研究的基础上进一步减少部首的数量，到目前为止，《现代汉语词典》（2016）“部首目录”中列出的部首是 201 个。需要指出的是，这 201 个部首中有几个是笔画而不是表义部首，这些笔画列在“部首目录”中是为了方便检索独体字。除了表义部首之外，还有一个概念——“部件”也用来指汉字合体字中的构字成分。但是，“部件”在合体字中不表义，它是一个知觉单位。我们将在下文中继续介绍“部件”这一概念。

As we mentioned above, a semantic component indicates the meaning category of a compound character and a phonetic component signifies the pronunciation of the compound character. For pedagogical convenience, many CFL teachers also refer to the phonetic component as “phonetic radical” in English. Thus, hereafter, phonetic component and phonetic radical are interchangeable in the English text of this book. In addition to the semantic and phonetic radicals, we refer to character components that provide neither semantic nor phonetic cues to the compound character as perceptual components. A perceptual component in a compound character plays a perceptual role. Visually it is an integral unit and is separated by a visibly diminutive space from other components. In the compound character 瞥(piē, *to glance at*), for example, the upper part 敝 is a stand-alone character that serves as the phonetic radical. The bottom part 目 is the semantic radical. Visually, 瞥 consists of three components 㡀, 攵, and 目, which we refer to as perceptual components. This means that the phonetic radical 敝 in this character consists of two perceptual components 㡀 and 攵. Although 攵 itself is a semantic radical and has its own pronunciation (pū), it has lost its semantic and phonetic functions in the compound 瞥. The perceptual components do not cue either meaning or sound of the compound character, but they are important cognitive components. Cognitively, if students can perceive a compound character as a combination of radicals rather than a pile of strokes, this will greatly reduce their memory load. Therefore, learning perceptual components is part of character learning. A perceptual component is called 部件(bùjiàn) in Chinese. Scholars have different opinions on the definition and categorization of perceptual components. One study defines it as "it is larger or equal to a stroke and smaller or equal to a character" (费锦昌, 1996). That study analyzed 3,500 commonly used characters and identified 384 perceptual components. These 384 perceptual components were further classified into two categories: 290 basic components and 94 commonly used compound components. For the basic components, they were further divided into two groups: single-stroke components (a total of 8) and multi-stroke components (a total of 282). This classification method is relatively new in the field. We will be open-minded for any classification criteria which may help reduce the complication in linguistic study, computer information processing, and classroom instruction. We hope that scholars can reach consensus for perceptual-component categorization in the future as this will bring greater convenience to the second language instruction.

我们在前面提到，合体字的表义部件和表音部件分别标示其意义类属和发音。为了教学方便，很多汉语教师在用英语教学时将表音部件直接译为“声旁”。因此，本书英文文本中的“表音部件”与“声旁”是可以互换的。除此之外，我们称那些既不表音也不表义的成分为“知觉部件”。知觉部件在合体字中主要提供知觉信息。从视觉上看，知觉部件是一个完整的知觉单位，部件之间由微小的空间隔开。例如，在合体字“瞥”（piē, *to glance at*）中，上面的“敝”本是一个独立的汉字，但在这里是声旁；下面的“目”也是一个独立的汉字，但在这里是形旁。从视觉上看，“瞥”由“㡀”“攵”“目”三个部件构成，我们就称这三个部件为“知觉部件”。也就是说，声旁“敝”由两个知觉部件组成——“㡀”和“攵”。虽然“攵”本身是一个形旁，读音为 pū，但是在“瞥”这个合体字中，它失去了作为形旁的音和义。知觉部件虽然不能标示合体字的音和义，但它是重要的认知单位。从认知的角度看，如果学生能把一个合体字从知觉上分解为一组部件而不是一堆笔画，那么其记忆负荷量就会大大地减少，因此知觉部件学习是汉字学习的重要组成部分。我们这里所说的“知觉部件”其实就是汉语中的“部件”[①]。学者们对部件的界定和划分有不同见解。费锦昌（1996）将它定义为“大于或等于笔画，小于或等于汉字”的构字单位。他分析了 3,500 个现代汉语常用字，并从中确定了 384 个部件。这 384 个部件进一步被划分为两大类：基本部件（290 个）和常用复合部件（94 个）。其中，基本部件又被划分为 8 个单笔部件和 282 个多笔部件。这种分类方法很新颖。如果新的分类方法有利于降低语言学习、计算机信息加工和课堂教学的复杂度的话，我们是非常欢迎的。我们希望学者们能在不久的将来就部件的分类问题达成共识，这会给汉语二语教学带来诸多方便。

---

① 汉语中的部件也是有大有小的，有的部件可以切分为更小的部件。根据部件能否切分为更小的部件，我们可以将部件分为单一部件和复合部件。这里所说的“知觉部件”，严格来说其实是指汉语中的单一部件。

1.3 What are words? 什么是词？

"Word," according to the *Modern Chinese Word Dictionary*《现代汉语词典》(2016:212), is "the smallest, meaningful unit in the language, which can be freely used." We mentioned earlier that most characters are free morphemes and that can serve as words. Most individual characters have multiple meanings and can combine with other characters to form new words. Therefore, a character can serve as a word when it is stand-alone; it can also serve as a component of words when combined with other characters to express meaning. According to the *Modern Chinese Frequency Dictionary*《现代汉语频率词典》(1986), single-character words comprise about 27% of the daily use corpus, while two-character words account for 65%. Therefore, two-character words are predominant in the Chinese vocabulary corpus.

《现代汉语词典》(2016：212）将"词"定义为"语言里最小的、可以自由运用的单位"。前面我们提到，绝大部分汉字是自由语素，能单独成词。大部分汉字都有多种意思，可以跟其他汉字组合成新的词。因此，汉字可以单独成词，但当它们与其他汉字组合成词时，这些汉字则成为词中的一个语素。根据《现代汉语频率词典》(1986）的统计，在日常使用的词汇中，单字词大概占 27%，双字词占 65% 左右，因此双字词在汉语词汇中占了绝大部分。

1.4 What is the scope of word knowledge? 怎么界定词语知识的范围？

In the classroom, what do we expect students to learn about words? That is, to what extent do we consider that a student has learned a word? In word knowledge acquisition, we use the term "breadth" and "depth" to measure a person's word knowledge. Breadth refers to how many words a person can recognize. However, recognition of a word does not mean that a learner has a full knowledge of the word. Thus, we need the term "depth" to determine how much a learner knows about a word.

在课堂教学中，我们希望学生掌握词的哪些知识呢？换句话说，学生要学到何种程度我们才认为他们掌握了一个词呢？在词语知识习得中，我们从"广度"和"深度"这两个方面衡量一个人的词语知识。广度是指一个人能认读多少词，但能认读词并不意味着这个人对该词有了全面的了解，因此我们还要从深度这个方面衡量一个人对词的掌握程度。

Read (2004) proposed a construct for defining the depth of vocabulary knowledge for an alphabetic language. The construct consists of three components: precision of meaning, comprehensive word knowledge, and network knowledge. This construct cannot be directly applied to the Chinese language as it is designed for an alphabetic language. Based on this knowledge, we propose a construct defining the depth of Chinese word knowledge that consists of five components: definition knowledge, extended semantic knowledge, syntactic knowledge, pragmatic knowledge, and network knowledge.

Read（2004）提出了一个确定字母语言词汇知识深度的构想。这个构想包含三个部分：对词义掌握的准确度、词语知识的丰富性，以及词汇网络知识。但这一构想并不能直接应用在汉语教学中，因为它只适用于字母语言。在这一构想的基础上，我们提出了一个确定汉语词语知识深度的构想，它包含五个部分：词的定义知识、词的引申义知识、词的句法知识、词的语用知识和词的网络知识。

The term **definitional knowledge** refers to the knowledge of a word as an isolated item, that is, the sound, shape, and basic meaning of the word. The learner knows the pronunciation of a particular word which includes its tonal variation (such as 任 can be read as rèn and rén), different readings (such as 解 can be read as jiě and xiè), and multiple meanings as defined in the dictionary. The term **extended semantic knowledge** refers to understanding the multiple meanings of a word. As we mentioned earlier, many Chinese words have multiple meanings—basic meanings and extended meanings. Some extended meanings can only be interpreted in context. For example, the basic meaning of the word 洗澡 is defined as using water to clean one's body (*Modern Chinese Word Dictionary*, 2016:1405). However, in the sentence 你应该给你的思想洗澡了(*you should give a bath to your brain*), the meaning of 洗澡 is different from its basic meaning. It means that one should inspect or criticize one's own thoughts. This extended meaning of 洗澡 is not provided in the dictionary. The term **syntactic knowledge** involves knowledge of grammar, collocation, and constraints for using the word. Grammar knowledge includes part of speech. How many parts of speech a word can serve in a sentence? For example, 工作 is a noun in the sentence 我有一个很好的工作 (*I have a very good job*), but it also can be a verb in another sentence such as 我每天都工作 (*I work every day*). Grammar knowledge also includes the knowledge of sentence components and the position of a word in a sentence. For example, 工作 can serve as the predicate in the sentence 我已经工作了八个小时 (*I have worked for eight hours*), but it may also serve as an attribute in another sentence such as 工作的性质决定着工资待遇 (*The type of the job determines the salary scale*). Collocation knowledge includes how a particular word can be regularly used together with another word in a sentence. For example, in the sentence 他的声音里含着脉脉深情 (*His voice embodies deep feelings*), the word 声音 cannot be used together with 脉脉深情 as 脉脉 is used to convey a feeling with the eyes but not with a voice (李芳杰, 1993:212). The constraints of using words refer to customary use of words. For example, we say 两个人 but not 二个人; we say 二人转 but not 两人转. The term **pragmatic knowledge** refers to word usage in oral and written communication that fits a social setting or environment, such as using 年纪 to ask an elder person's age but 几岁 to ask a young child's. The term **network knowledge** refers to knowledge of possible relationships between words, such as knowledge of synonyms, antonyms, coordinate and subordinate relationships.

词的定义知识是指词作为单独项时的音、形、义方面的知识。学习者应该知道词的读音，包括一字多调（如“任”可以读成 rèn 或 rén）和一字多音（如“解”可以读成 jiě 或 xiè），以及词典中列出的关于词的多个义项。前面我们提到过，汉语中很多单字词和多字词都是多义的，它们有基本义和引申义。**词的引申义知识**指词在不同语境中所代表的不同意思。有些词的引申义在词典中没有列出，只能在上下文中理解。例如，“洗澡”的基本义是“用水洗身体，除去污垢”（《现代汉语词典》，2016：1405），但是在句子“你应该给你的思想洗澡了”中，“洗澡”的意思显然跟词典中的基本义不同。它在句中的意思是“自我反省”或“检讨自己的思想”，这个引申义在词典中是没有列出的。**词的句法知识**包括语法、词语搭配和词语使用限制等方面的知识。语法知识包括词性，即词在句中能有多少种词性。例如，“工作”在句子“我有一个很好的工作”中是名词，但在句子“我每天都工作”中是动词。语法知识还包括句子成分和词在句中的位置。例如，“工作”在句子“我已经工作了八个小时”中是谓语，但在句子“工作的性质决定着工资待遇”中是定语。词语搭配知识是指词在句中通常与哪些词搭配使用。例如，在句子“他的声音里含着脉脉深情”中，“声音”不能跟“脉脉深情”搭配，因为“脉脉”是指用眼神传达的情感，而不是用声音传达的。（李芳杰，1993：212）词语使用限制是指词的习惯用法。例如，我们说“两个人”，但不说“二个人”；说“二人转”，但不说“两人转”。**词的语用知识**是指在进行口头和书面交流时，为使词语的使用适合交际的场合和环境而需掌握的知识。例如，用“年纪”询问年长者的年龄，而用 “几岁”询问年少者的年龄。**词的网络知识**是指对词与词之间可能存在的关系的认识，如同义（近义）关系、反义关系、并列关系或从属关系。

In this chapter, we first briefly discussed the linguistic features of Chinese characters and words. By doing so, we wish to highlight that Chinese is a non-alphabetic writing system which is drastically different from European languages in terms of its orthography. Therefore, learning Chinese characters requires unique cognitive process which we will address in detail in the subsequent chapters. Next, we discussed that the scope of word knowledge consists of five aspects. It should be pointed out that the accumulation of the five aspects of word knowledge is not hierarchical or linear; rather, it is interactive and spiral. A learner who has not acquired all necessary definitional knowledge of the target word may possess certain pragmatic knowledge. The development of these five aspects of knowledge is not synchronous either. One aspect of knowledge may increase faster than others, which is determined by learners' cognitive factors, curriculum factors, instructional factors, and environmental factors. We also need to bear in mind that the development of the five aspects of word knowledge takes time, but our appropriate instruction can facilitate the developmental process. We need to keep in mind that word knowledge accumulation is incremental; it may take life-long accumulation. Therefore, trying to explain a certain word exhaustively in a single teaching session is not a wise strategy. Students may not process the knowledge that exceeds their comprehension span. We will discuss effective character and word instruction in detail in the subsequent chapters.

在这一章，我们先简要地讨论了汉字和词的语言学特征，这样做是为了强调汉字是一种非字母书写系统，有着与欧洲语言完全不同的缀字法。因此，学习汉字需要经历独特的认知加工过程，我们在后面的章节中会详细论述这一过程。接下来，我们讨论了衡量词语知识深度的五个层面。需要指出的是，这五个层面的知识积累不是呈阶梯形或直线形递增的，而是在交互中螺旋式递增的。学习者还没完全掌握目的词的定义知识时，有可能已经掌握了目的词的某些语用知识。词语知识这五个层面的增长也不是同时的，某一层面知识的增长可能会快于其他层面，这取决于学习者的认知因素、课程因素、教学因素和环境因素。我们要知道，词语知识这五个层面的发展是需要时间的，但是适当的教学指导能促进其发展进程。也就是说，词语知识的积累是渐进的，也许需要一生。因此，教师在一节课上就把一个词的全部知识都教给学生并不是一个明智的教学策略，因为当知识的难度超过学生的理解跨度后，学生就会停止对知识的加工。我们会在下面的章节中进一步探讨有效的字词教学策略。

In this chapter, we discussed the definition of Chinese characters and words. We recognize the overlap and the difference between characters and words. Since individual characters can serve as single-character words, for convenience, in the English sections of the following chapters, the term "word" also includes "character" unless it is otherwise specified.

在这一章，我们对汉语中的字和词的概念进行了界定，发现字和词在概念上有交叉又有不同。因为在汉语中单字可以成词,所以为了方便起见，此后章节中英文部分提到的“word”也包括字，除非特别指明。

References 参考文献

北京语言学院语言教学研究所. 1986. 现代汉语频率词典[M]. 北京：北京语言学院出版社.

费锦昌. 1996. 现代汉字部件探究[J]. 语言文字应用（3）：20–26.

韩鉴堂. 2005. 汉字文化图说[M]. 北京：北京语言大学出版社.

李芳杰. 1993. 汉语语法和规范问题研究[M]. 武汉：武汉大学出版社.

上海交通大学汉字编码组，上海汉语拼音文字研究组. 1988. 汉字信息字典[M]. 北京：科学出版社.

施春宏. 2018. 汉语纲要・下册[M]. 北京：北京语言大学出版社.

谢光辉. 1997. 常用汉字图解[M]. 北京：北京大学出版社.

张静贤. 1992. 现代汉字教程[M]. 北京：现代出版社.

中国社会科学院语言研究所词典编辑室. 2016. 现代汉语词典（第7版）[M]. 北京：商务印书馆.

Fan K Y, Gao J L, Ao X P. 1984. Pronunciation principles of Chinese characters and alphabetic writing scripts[J]. Chinese character reform, 3: 23–27.

Ramsey S R. 1987. The languages of China[M]. Princeton, NJ: Princeton University Press.

Read J. 2004. Plumbing the depths: how should the construct of vocabulary knowledge be defined? [M]. Bogaards P , Laufer B. Vocabulary in a second language: selection, acquisition and testing. Amsterdam: John Benjamins Publishing Company, 209–227.

Shen H H, Ke C. 2007. Radical awareness and word acquisition among nonnative learners of Chinese[J]. The modern language journal, 91: 97–111.

Shen H H, Wang P, Tsai C-H. 2009. Learning 100 Chinese radicals[M]. Beijing: Peking University Press.

Chapter 2 第二章

The Acquisition and Instruction of Orthographic Knowledge
缀字知识的习得与教学

2.1 Phonological awareness in character recognition and Pinyin learning 语音意识在汉字认读与拼音学习中的作用

Chinese characters have no sound-to-spelling correspondence. Can readers recognize the meaning of a character without knowing pronunciation? During reading, when a learned character is visually presented, how do CSL readers recognize the meaning of the character? Do they need to recall the sound of the character in order to recall the meaning of the character or the reverse?

汉字没有直接的音形联系，那么读者能否不知音而知其义呢？在阅读过程中，当一个学过的汉字出现在汉语二语学习者面前时，他们是怎么识别字义的？他们是否需要先识别字音再识别字义，或是相反？

The dual-route theory initially proposed by Baron and Strawson (1976) and then further developed by Coltheart, Curtis, Atkins, and Haller (1993) addresses the activation of phonological knowledge in word recognition in

English. This theory assumes that a reader can employ two routes to recognize a word. One is the direct route in which the reader could sound out the word by using sound-to-spelling correspondence knowledge, thereby activating the meaning of the word. The other is the indirect route, where the reader looks at the whole word and retrieves the sound of the word previously stored in the memory which in turn helps access the meaning of the word. No matter which route is used, in general, scholars accept that phonological knowledge plays an important role in recognizing the meaning of a word in English.

双通道理论最初是由Baron和Strawson（1976）提出的，Coltheart 等（1993）又进一步发展了该理论。该理论阐述了英语词语认读中语音知识的激活过程。这一理论假设读者对词的认读经由两条通道：其一是直接通道，读者见到词形后运用音形对应知识读出该词的发音，由此激活词义；其二是非直接通道，读者见到词形后从大脑中提取出先前存储的该词的发音，并在这一过程中激活词义。不管采用哪条通道，学者们一般都承认，在英语中语音知识对词义识别起了重要作用。

In Chinese writing, there is no sound-to-spelling correspondence. What then is the role of phonological knowledge in character recognition? Bulk of studies has been conducted on this topic. Some studies have showed that the time course of character recognition is from orthography to sound, to meaning (Perfetti & Zhang, 1991; Perfetti & Tan, 1998). Other studies have reported that both orthographic and phonological information function interactively to activate the meaning of a character (Zhou & Marslen-Wilson, 1999, 2000). Although scholars hold different views with regard to the time course of activating the phonological information in character recognition, they have reached a consensus that phonological information plays an important role in character recognition and learners' phonological knowledge is a strong predictor of character recognition. This conclusion applies to schoolchildren and adults (Chan & Siegel, 2001; Chow, McBride-Chang, & Burgess, 2005; Feng et al., 2001; Myers, Taft, & Chou, 2007; Pan et al., 2011).

汉字没有直接的音形联系，那语音知识在汉字认读中起什么作用呢？这方面已有大量的研究。一些研究认为，汉字认读的过程是从字形到字音再到字义的（Perfetti and Zhang，1991；Perfetti and Tan，1998）；还有一些研究认为，字形信息和字音信息相互作用最终达到对字义的激活（Zhou and Marslen-Wilson，1999，2000）。学者们虽然对汉字认读过程中字音激活的时间和顺序存在不同看法，但是他们一致认为，语音信息在汉字认读中起着重要作用，语音知识是学习者汉字认读过程中的有效预测因子。这个结论既适用于学龄儿童，也适用于成人。（Chan and Siegel，2001；Chow，McBride-Chang，and Burgess，2005；Feng等，2001； Myers，Taft，and Chou，2007；Pan等，2011）

What does research say about the role of phonological information in character recognition among CSL learners? Studies from the classroom learning perspective, however, have shown the connections between phonological knowledge and character recognition. One study (Everson, 1998) on word recognition among English-speaking college students who were beginning CSL learners was conducted in the United States. In that study, students were asked to write out Pinyin for the sound and character meaning in English for 46 disyllabic words. A strong correlation was noted between being able to correctly pronounce the character and being able to correctly recall the meaning of the character. This result was confirmed by a later study conducted in Beijing

(赵果, 2003). In that study, the participants were all beginning level students at Beijing Language and Culture University; all participants' first languages were Indo-European languages. Participants were first asked to write out Pinyin for 102 characters, and then they were asked to use the target characters to form a new word or sentence to show whether they understood the meaning of the target characters. A strong correlation was found between knowing the sound and knowing the meaning. Another interesting study (江新, 2003) was conducted in Beijing among college CSL learners who had different linguistic backgrounds. A strong correlation was again found between knowing the sound and knowing the meaning of a character for learners with English as their first language. A moderate correlation was detected for learners with Indonesian as their first language.

那么在这一问题上，汉语二语研究又告诉了我们什么呢？课堂学习方面的一些研究也显示了语音知识与汉字认读之间的相关性。Everson（1998）在美国的母语为英语的大学初级汉语二语学习者之间进行了一项关于汉字认读的研究。在该研究中，参与者需要写出46个双音节词的拼音和英文意思。结果表明，正确写出拼音与正确写出词义之间存在高度相关性。这个结论在之后赵果（2003）的研究中得到了进一步的证实。在赵果的研究中，参与者都是北京语言大学的汉语初级水平的学生，他们的第一语言都属于印欧语系。参与者首先需要写出102个汉字的拼音，然后用所给汉字组词或造句，以此检查学生是否理解了这些汉字的意思。结果表明，正确写出拼音与正确理解字义之间存在高度相关性。江新（2003）在北京的大学汉语二语学习者之间进行了一项相关研究，不过参与者的语言背景各不相同。其研究结果也表明，对于母语[①]为英语的学习者来说，知音与知义之间存在高度相关性；对于母语为印尼语的学习者来说，知音与知义之间存在中度相关性。

① 本书中所说的"first language"即母语。

In summary, albeit lacking sound-to-spelling correspondence in Chinese writing, for CSL learners, the availability of phonological knowledge is crucial for character recognition. Therefore, phonological awareness, or the awareness of the sound structure of a language is important for character recognition. In an alphabetic writing system, phonological awareness refers to the ability to conceive of spoken words as sequences of smaller units of sound segments such as syllables, onsets, rimes, or phonemes (Siok & Fletcher, 2001). In modern Chinese, we adopt Pinyin, phonetic alphabet system, to help pronounce characters. Therefore, phonological awareness in Chinese can be defined as the ability to perceive syllables, to detect initial and final sounds of a syllable, and to differentiate tones. Next, we will discuss how to increase students' phonological awareness in our daily instruction.

综上所述，尽管汉字缺乏音形之间的直接联系，但语音知识对汉字认读仍至关重要。因此，对于汉语二语学习者来说，是否具备语音意识或语音结构意识对汉字认读非常关键。在字母书写系统中，语音意识是指将口语词分解为音节、音段或音素等更小语音序列片段的能力。（Siok and Fletcher，2001）在现代汉语中，我们采用拼音这种音标系统来帮助发音，因此，汉语的语音意识可以定义为感知音节，识别音节中的声母、韵母，以及区别不同声调的能力。下面我们来讨论一下如何在日常教学中增强学生的语音意识。

Pedagogical suggestions for developing students' phonological awareness
关于增强学生语音意识的教学建议

• Introducing Pinyin prior to formal Chinese character learning
拼音教学先于正式的汉字教学

Most of the institutes in western countries adopt Hanyu Pinyin as a Mandarin phonetic alphabet. In general, two practices are used for introducing Pinyin. A traditional practice is to introduce characters simultaneously while learning Pinyin and speaking. A different practice is that character learning lags behind Pinyin learning. Pinyin is introduced first. Students learn speaking and also learn to read Pinyin text and use Pinyin for writing, which will not only reinforce Pinyin learning but also make Pinyin learning meaningful (Shen, 2015). Scholars who support the latter argue that once students have got familiar with the basics of pronunciation and have gained a certain level of oral proficiency, character learning would be facilitated (Walker, 1984).

在西方国家，大部分学校都将汉语拼音作为汉语的音标。一般来说，汉语拼音教学以两种方式展开。一种是传统的教法，即拼音教学与汉字教学、口语教学同步进行。另一种是拼音教学在先，汉字教学滞后的方式。学生在学习如何发音的同时，也进行拼音读写，这不仅能强化拼音学习的效果，还可以使拼音学习变得有意义。（Shen，2015）支持第二种教学方式的学者认为，学生具备了一定的发音基础和口语能力后再学习汉字，会加快汉字学习的进程。（Walker，1984）

Although the two practices coexist in today's classroom teaching, for adult CSL learners who are non-Asian language speakers, we strongly favor having a good knowledge of Pinyin prior to formal character learning. Thus, an intensive Pinyin learning period should be scheduled in the curriculum prior to formal character learning. This proposition is supported by empirical studies. Hayes (1988) reported that during character recognition, non-native readers were not certain about the pronunciation of characters, thus, they would also need to rely on visual skills to recognize Chinese characters. Pinyin learning first can provide the student with a strong phonological foundation in the spoken language prior to working with characters. Likewise, with strongly developed phonological skills, students will not have to dwell excessively on the graphic features of the characters during character recognition. A year-long longitudinal study on the comparison of the two approaches (characters introduced at the very beginning of the course vs. characters introduced three weeks after the course) for beginning learners also supports this notion (Packard, 1990). Another study on character learning yields that presenting Pinyin together with new words helps learners to retain the words better, but only if the learners had reached the level of automatic Pinyin reading (Lee & Kalyuga, 2011). So far the empirical studies have shown that for students whose first language is an alphabetic language, Pinyin learning prior to character learning is a more effective way of learning.

虽然这两种教学方式同时存在于当前的课堂教学中，但是对母语非亚洲语言的成人进行汉语二语教学，我们主张学习者在正式学习汉字之前应该先打好拼音基础。因此，在设置汉语课程时，我们应该在正式的汉字教学之前安排一个阶段进行集中的拼音强化训练。这一主张是基于实证研究结果提出的。Hayes（1988）的研究显示，在认读汉字时，非汉语母语者在无法确定字音时需要依赖视觉技巧识别字音。先学习拼音，学生就可以利用语音知识识别字音。同样，有了强大的语音技能，学生在认读汉字时就不需要过多关注字形了。Packard（1990）对汉语初学者的追踪研究比较了两种教学方式的教学效果：一种是课程开始时拼音教学和汉字教学同时进行；另一种是先进行拼音教学，三个星期后再开始汉字教学。一年后的学生学习效果也显示，第二种教学方式要优于第一种。Lee和Kalyuga（2011）关于汉字学习的研究表明，只有学生的拼音认读达到了自动化的程度，汉字教学与拼音教学同时进行才能帮助其更好地记忆汉字。迄今为止，实证研究结果告诉我们，对第一语言为字母型语言的学生来说，拼音教学先于汉字教学是一种更为有效的教学方式。

However, our emphasis on learning Pinyin prior to character learning does not mean that characters should not be introduced during Pinyin learning. It means that the focus of learning is on Pinyin rather than on characters. We may introduce characters in order to learn Pinyin in a meaningful way, but students are not quizzed on character recognition or production during the period of Pinyin learning. The linguistic and cognitive arguments for doing so are presented below.

我们强调拼音教学在先并不是说在教拼音时不能出现汉字，而是说应将教学的重点放在拼音上，而不是汉字上。为了让拼音学习更有意义，我们可以在学生学习拼音的同时介绍些汉字，但是并不要求他们进行汉字认读和听写测验。这样做的语言学和认知心理学依据如下：

First, students from non-Asian language backgrounds have been introduced to the Roman alphabet, which is the alphabet we used for the Pinyin system. The merit for this is that students do not need to learn a new set of written symbols in order to learn Pinyin. The cognitive difficulty is that students need to try hard to resist the negative transfer or interference from the pronunciation of the alphabetic language that they have reached high degree of automaticity when learning the new Pinyin sounds. Introducing characters would demand extra cognitive resources from the working memory, which may cause cognitive overload to the students, hence, it would take longer time for them to master Pinyin. Second, introducing Pinyin prior to character learning allows students to master Pinyin in a short time, and to use it as an aid for pronouncing unknown characters. Therefore, they will be able to learn new characters that they may encounter after class even at the very beginning stage of learning. Third, at the initial stage of learning, if Pinyin is not fully introduced, then students can use only very limited characters in their spoken and written communication. This may dampen students' learning enthusiasm if they feel that they cannot communicate effectively with others. With Pinyin assistance, students can communicate with Pinyin to get message crossed even though they have not fully mastered the corresponding characters. Lastly, it is a common practice for students to use Pinyin input methods for typing in Chinese. Without a solid Pinyin knowledge, students will have substantial difficulty in efficiently using word processors. In sum, early exposure to Pinyin allows of a better mastery of the phonological knowledge that aids character learning.

首先，来自非亚洲语言背景的学生在学习汉语前已经掌握了罗马字母，而且它的书写形式跟汉语拼音字母的是一样的。这样，学生学习拼音时就不必再学一套新的字母书写系统了；但是由于学生的字母型母语的发音已经达到了高度自动化的程度，学生在学习拼音时必须在认知上努力克服字母型母语的发音造成的负迁移和干扰。如果在这个时候引入汉字，那学生势必会从工作记忆中获取额外的认知资源。学生认知负荷过重，他们只有花更长时间才能掌握拼音。其次，先学习拼音可以帮助学生在短时间内掌握拼音，学生可以以拼音为辅助去认读新的字音。这样，即使是在学习的初始阶段，学生也可以借助拼音去学习那些课堂上没有见过的生词。再次，在学习的初始阶段，如果不把全部的拼音都教给学生，那么学生只能用数量非常有限的汉字进行口头的和书面的交流。如果交流常常受阻，学生的学习积极性就很容易受到打击。如果允许学生使用拼音，那么他们想不起汉字时就能借助与之对应的拼音进行交流。最后，对于学生来说，用拼音输入法打字是一种常见的做法。学生如果没有一个坚实的拼音基础，那在使用拼音输入法时就会遇到很多困难。总而言之，学生越早学会拼音，就能越早利用语音知识学习汉字。

• Topic-based Pinyin instruction
基于话题的拼音教学

We encourage the introduction of Pinyin prior to introducing characters but we discourage teaching Pinyin without context, as it makes learning monotonous and inefficient. We propose topic-based Pinyin instruction, an approach to learning Pinyin that is based on language context. By adopting this approach, Pinyin is introduced together with words and sentences, and is practiced in a meaningful language situation. Practicing Pinyin in a meaningful language situation not only increases efficiency of memory, but also helps students accumulate spoken words and sentences during Pinyin learning, which in turn helps them learn characters. Please see Teaching Example 1 for the topic-based Pinyin instruction.

我们鼓励拼音教学先于汉字教学，但是并不鼓励没有语境的、孤立的拼音教学，因为它会让学习变得单调和低效。我们认为，拼音教学应该以话题为依托。也就是说，拼音学习应该在语境中进行。采用这种方法进行拼音教学，可以使拼音学习与词语、句子的学习相结合，还可以让拼音练习在有意义的语境中进行。这不仅能提高学生的记忆效率，而且能帮助学生在学习拼音的同时积累口语词和常用表达，从而促进学生的汉字学习。具体的教学方法请参照“教学示例 1”。

Teaching Example 1 Topic-based Pinyin instruction: Thanksgiving holiday

教学示例 1 基于话题的拼音教学：感恩节

Content 教学内容

Lesson 8 前鼻韵母 an, en, in, ün, ian, uan, üan, uen (un) of *Introduction to Standard Chinese Pinyin System* (Helen H. Shen, Chen-Hui Tsai, & Yunong Zhou, Beijing Language and Culture University Press, 2006).

《汉语拼音入门》第8课，前鼻韵母 an，en，in，ün，ian，uan，üan，uen（un）。（Helen H. Shen，Chen-Hui Tsai，Yunong Zhou. 汉语拼音入门［M］. 北京：北京语言大学出版社，2006.）

Targeted learners 教学对象

Beginners

汉语初学者

Teaching objectives 教学目标

Learn the eight front nasal Pinyin sounds.

学习并掌握8个前鼻韵母的发音。

Review previously learned vowels and consonants.

复习已学过的元音和辅音。

Teaching approach 教学方法

Learn Pinyin sounds in vocabulary and sentence patterns around the topic "Thanksgiving Holiday."

围绕着与"感恩节"相关的词汇和句型进行拼音学习与操练。

Teaching steps 教学步骤

Step 1: Introduce the theme and learn pronunciations of eight Pinyin sounds

第一步：引入主题，学习8个前鼻韵母的发音

(1) an, en, ün

① Introduce the Chinese pronunciation of "Thanksgiving"and drill an, en, ün by using pictures.

引入主题"感恩节"（Gǎn'ēn Jié），讲解前鼻韵母an，en，ün的发音并结合图片进行操练。

② Ask the question"Whom do you give thanks to?" and practice relevant vocabulary by answering this question.

通过提问"你想感谢谁？"引出相关词语，并操练其发音。

感谢gǎnxiè	我们wǒmen	你们nǐmen	他们tāmen
爸爸bàba	妈妈māma	哥哥gēge	姐姐jiějie
弟弟dìdi	妹妹mèimei	爷爷yéye	奶奶nǎinai
老师lǎoshī	很多hěn duō	很多人hěn duō rén	一群人yì qún rén

③ Review the three Pinyin sounds by using the sentence pattern: "Gǎn'ēn Jié, wǒ yào gǎnxiè yì qún rén/hěn duō rén, yǒu…."

通过操练句型"感恩节，我要感谢一群人/很多人，有……"复习前鼻韵母an，en，ün。

(2) in, ian, uan

① Introduce in, ian, uan by using pictures.

讲解in，ian，uan这三个前鼻韵母的发音并结合图片进行操练。

② Practice the following words by answering the question "Why do you want to give thanks to…?"

通过提问"你为什么想感谢……？"操练下列词语的发音：

wèi shénme（为什么）	yīnwèi (因为)	qián (钱)
guānxīn (关心)	hěn hǎo(很好)	

③ Students group in pairs. They review the three Pinyin sounds by creating dialogues and using learned words such as "Nǐ yào gǎnxiè shéi, wèi shénme? Wǒ yào gǎnxiè …, yīnwèi…."

学生两人一组，通过互相问答"你要感谢谁，为什么？我要感谢……，因为……"复习in，ian，uan的发音。

(3) üan, uen(un), and all the eight sounds in one sentence

练习üan，uen（un）的发音，然后在句子中复习8个前鼻韵母

① Learn the pronunciations of üan, uen(un) by using pictures.

讲解前鼻韵母üan，uen（un）的发音，并结合图片进行操练。

② Show a photo to students and ask students to answer questions based on the photo. Questions may include "Where is it? Who are they? What are they doing? What do you think of the family?" Students answer the questions by using the following words:

向学生出示一张全家福，通过提问诸如"这是哪儿？他们是谁？他们在做什么？这是一个什么样的家？"等问题引出下列相关词语：

家jiā	爸爸bàba	妈妈māma	爷爷yéye
奶奶nǎinai	和hé	孙子sūnzi	孙女sūnnǚ
吃饭chī fàn	温暖wēnnuǎn	团圆tuányuán	

③ Review the eight Pinyin sounds by saying the following sentences and practicing them in a relay game：Jīntiān shì Gǎn'ēn Jié. Wǒmen yī qún rén chī tuányuán fàn. Wǒ shì sūnzi/sūnnǚ.

学生通过句子接龙“今天是感恩节。我们一群人吃团圆饭。我是孙子/孙女”练习8个前鼻韵母。

Step 2: Comprehensive review activities

第二步：综合性复习活动

Activity 1: Thanksgiving Dinner

活动1：感恩节晚餐

Question: What did you have for the Thanksgiving dinner?

问题：感恩节你吃的什么？Gǎn'ēn Jié nǐ chī de shénme?

Food pictures are presented to students via PPT (see the vocabulary list below); each student has one of the pictures in hand to indicate this is the food he/she had for the Thanksgiving dinner. One student comes to the front of the class without showing his/her photo to the class. Other students in the class take turns to guess the content of this student's picture. After a correct guess is made, the student in the front needs to say whether he/she likes the food or not.

教师通过PPT展示食物的图片（见参考词汇），每名学生手中都有一张，代表他/她感恩节所吃的食物。一名学生走到讲台前，但不要让其他人看到他/她手中的图片，其他学生轮流猜他/她手中的图片上是什么食物。其他学生一旦猜中，拿图片的学生就要说出自己是否喜欢这种食物。

Vocabulary to be used in the activity 参考词汇

晚餐wǎncān	蛋糕dàngāo	玉米面包yùmǐ miànbāo
汉堡包hànbǎobāo	米饭mǐfàn	干果gānguǒ
火鸡huǒjī	南瓜派nánguā pài	点心diǎnxin
意大利面Yìdàlì miàn		

Sentence patterns to be used in the activity 参考句型

感恩节你吃的是……吗？Gǎn'ēn Jié nǐ chī de shì…ma?

不是，感恩节我吃的不是……Bú shì, Gǎn'ēn Jié wǒ chī de bú shì…

是的，感恩节我吃的是……Shì de, Gǎn'ēn Jié wǒ chī de shì…

你喜欢不喜欢吃……Nǐ xǐhuan bù xǐhuan chī…?

我很喜欢/不喜欢吃……Wǒ hěn xǐhuan/bù xǐhuan chī…

Activity 2: Thanksgiving Travel Plan

活动2：感恩节旅游计划

Each student receives a task sheet giving information such as an identity as a family member, supposed arriving time and destination of the trip during the Thanksgiving break. Students need to ask each other to find whether they belong to "one family" (those members who are planning a trip to arrive in the same destination on the same day). The "family" team reuniting in the shortest time wins the game.

每名学生手里都有一张感恩节假期旅游任务单，这张任务单上写有你的家庭成员身份、旅游时间和旅游地点。学生通过互相询问找到和自己同一天去同一个地方的"一家人"。在最短时间内完成家庭"团圆"的那组获胜。

Sentence patterns to be used in the activity 参考句型

你好，我是……（爸爸/妈妈/爷爷/奶奶……）Nǐ hǎo, wǒ shì…（a family member）

你打算什么时候去旅游？Nǐ dǎsuàn shénme shíhou qù lǚyóu?

你打算去哪儿旅游？Nǐ dǎsuàn qù nǎr lǚyóu?

我打算……月……号（感恩节假期内的一天）去旅游。Wǒ dǎsuàn…yuè…hào qù lǚyóu.

我打算去……（美国城市名）旅游。Wǒ dǎsuàn qù…（city name

in the U.S.）lǚyóu.

我们是一家人，打算……月……号去……旅游。Wǒmen shì yì jiā rén, dǎsuàn… yuè… hào qù… lǚyóu.

Step 3: Assessment

第三步：评估

Students are required to take a quiz involving reading and writing the words and sentences by using the eight newly or previous learned Pinyin sounds based on the pictures presented to them.

拼音测验：学生要根据教师提供的图片，用刚学到的8个前鼻韵母或之前学过的拼音说出或写出词语和句子。

(Teaching Example 1 is contributed by Fengping Yu, Texas A & M University)

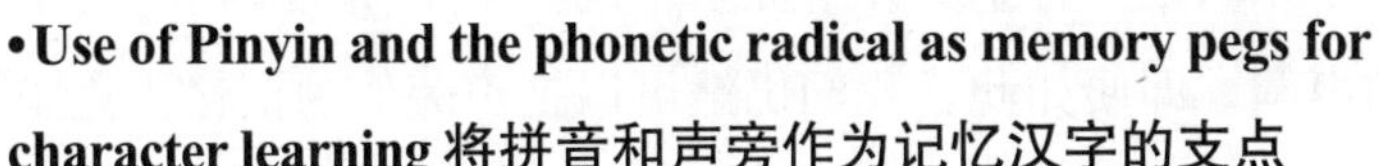

• Use of Pinyin and the phonetic radical as memory pegs for character learning 将拼音和声旁作为记忆汉字的支点

An excellent way to increase students' phonological awareness during character learning is to use the Pinyin of the character and the phonetic radical of the character as memory pegs. We discourage guessing the sound of a new character by using the phonetic radical within because this is a random guessing game. One reason as we mentioned earlier is that phonetic radicals have only 26% reliability in cuing the sounds of compound characters and there are no regularities or patterns in terms of phonetic radicals cuing the sounds of the compound characters. Another reason is that a phonetic radical itself does not carry the lexical tone. Even though students can guess the sound correctly based on phonetic radicals, they still cannot figure out the tone. However, phonetic radicals are very useful in aiding character memorization if we use them as memory pegs. When a new character is introduced, students should be encouraged to make connections with previously learned characters having the same sound as the new character. Once this type of connection is established, the sound for the new character is no longer new to the students. If the new character is a compound character, encourage students to find out its phonetic radical and its relationship to the pronunciation of the new character. If the phonetic radical can be used to cue the sound of the new character, then the student can effortlessly memorize the sound of the new character, because the phonetic radical will serve as a memory peg for the new character.

增强学生语音意识的另一个好方法就是将拼音和声旁作为记忆汉字的支点。我们不建议学生一遇到新字就利用其声旁猜测字音，因为这就好像是一个随机游戏。其中一个原因我们在前面提到过，就是现代汉语中如果不考虑声调差异的话，声旁表音的正确率只有26%，而且声旁表音没有规律可循。另一个原因是声旁本身并不标示声调。学生即使猜对了音节，也不知道准确的声调。即便如此，我们仍然可以把声旁作为记忆支点来帮助我们记忆新字。当我们把一个新字教授给学生时，我们要鼓励学生回想以前学过的同音字，并将新字与学过的同音字联系起来。这种联系一旦建立，学生对新字的发音就不再感到陌生，记忆起来就会变得非常容易。如果新字是一个合体字，教师可以引导学生找出该字的声旁，并讲解声旁与该字之间的表音关系。如果声旁能标示新字的发音，学生可以直接将声旁作为记忆支点，不费吹灰之力就能记住该字的发音。

• Practicing oral reading in the classroom
在课堂上运用朗读法

Within a short period of intensive study of the Pinyin sounds at the initial stage of learning, students can fluently read Pinyin and syllables, but this does not mean that they can also accurately and fluently read characters. It takes time to make a connection between the Pinyin sound and the shape of the character. After initial Pinyin instruction, instructors should adopt the oral reading method during normal classroom teaching sessions, especially in the beginning level class. Oral reading means to ask students to read lessons out loud. Oral reading is a traditional teaching method rooted in its linguistic, cultural, and social grounds (Tao & Zuo, 1997). Some scholars have concerns that oral reading may turn into a form of rote memorization, but this is a misconception. Oral reading can be meaningful if used appropriately. Reading a text orally can benefit students' character learning and memorization in several ways. First, it helps students to make sound-graph connections. From a cognitive perspective, Chinese script lacks sound-to-graph correspondence, which causes great difficulties for students when it comes to memorize the sounds of individual characters. Reading aloud allows them to hear the sounds of individual characters repeatedly. This aural effect will help build connections in the student's brain between a particular sound and its corresponding character. In addition, as we mentioned earlier, since phonetic radicals bear no lexical tones, the best method for reading a character with the accurate tone is to say it out loud frequently. Second, it allows instructors to identify students' problems in character learning through miscue analysis (Gillet & Temple, 1994). Oral reading miscues such as character substitution, omission, insertion, reverse character order, mispronunciation and tonal errors allow the instructor to detect problems easily and correct them in a timely manner. A third benefit is that, due to the drastic differences between Chinese and English orthographies and the complexity of the physical structure of Chinese characters, beginning learners often make character-writing errors. Reading aloud will force students to keep their eyes on every character in the text as they sound it out loud. It increases visual exposure to the physical structure of characters. Accordingly, it facilitates the memorization of the graphic structure of characters (Shen & Jiang, 2013).

在初始阶段进行短期的拼音强化学习后，学生基本上能流利地认读拼音和音节；但这并不意味着他们就能准确、流利地认读汉字，学生还需要一些时间建立字音和字形之间的联系。因此，在初始的拼音教学结束之后，教师应该在正式的课堂教学中，尤其是在初级汉语课上，采用朗读法进行教学。朗读法就是让学生将课文读出声来的一种教学法，是一种传统的汉语教学方法，有着深厚的语言学、文化学和社会学理论基础。（Tao and Zuo，1997）有些学者认为朗读会导致机械记忆，这种看法是片面的。如果运用恰当，朗读也可以是有意义的。在课堂上运用朗读法有助于学生的汉字学习和记忆，具体体现在以下几方面：第一，帮助学生建立汉字音形之间的联系。从认知的角度看，汉字字形无法直接标示字音，这给学生记忆汉字字音造成了很大困难。出声朗读能让学生重复听到每个字的发音，这种听觉效应有助于学生在大脑中建立汉字音形之间的联系。除此之外，正如我们在前面提到过的，很多声旁本身不标示声调，因此要准确地记住汉字的声调，最好的办法就是反复听读。第二，有助于教师通过对学生汉字误读情况的分析发现学生汉字学习上的问题。（Gillet and Temple，1994）在学生朗读时，教师能很容易地察觉出学生对汉字的误读，如读成另一个汉字、跳过某个汉字、增加某个汉字、互换双音节或多音节词中汉字的位置、汉字发音错误或声调错误等等，并且能及时纠错。第三，帮助学生辨认汉字字形，减少书写错误。汉语与英语在缀字法上大相径庭，再加上汉字字形结构复杂，所以汉语初学者常常会犯汉字书写错误。朗读能促使学生把注意力集中在每个汉字上，加强学生对汉字字形的视觉感知，从而有利于其对汉字字形结构的记忆。（Shen and Jiang，2013）

Repeated oral reading could risk reducing learning interests. How can we make oral reading more meaningful? Variation in methods is important. There are many methods to promote meaningful read-aloud; below are a few:

1. Individual expressive reading: Students read with prosody to convey their own feelings and understanding of the text.

2. Paired reading: Two students take turns to read. During the reading, they ask and answer reading comprehension questions of each other.

3. Role-based reading: Students read in small groups and each student takes a role in the text.

4. Question-directed reading: The teacher asks a question and the student answers the question by reading out loud a relevant sentence or a paragraph.

5. Error-detecting reading: One student reads while the other student listens. After the reading, the listener evaluates the reader's oral reading quality based on predesigned criteria.

6. Demonstration reading: The teacher can ask students to recommend good oral readers to read the text in class to demonstrate the best oral reading manner.

重复朗读会让学习变得单调乏味，让学生失去学习兴趣。怎样才能使朗读变得有意义？关键是要学会变换方法。有很多方法可以使朗读变得有意义，下面是其中几种：

1. 个人有感情地朗读：学生有韵律、有节奏地朗读，并在朗读中融入自己的感受和对课文的理解。

2. 组对朗读：学生两人一组轮流朗读，并就课文内容理解问题互相问答。

3. 分角色朗读：学生分小组进行朗读，每名学生扮演课文中的一个角色。

4. 问题导入式朗读：教师就课文内容进行提问，学生回答问题时只朗读与答案有关的句子或语段。

5. 错误发现式朗读：学生两人一组，一人朗读，另一人仔细听。其中一名学生朗读完毕后，另一名学生要根据既定的评分标准评估该学生的朗读质量。

6. 示范性朗读：教师让学生自己推荐出优秀朗读者在班上进行示范性朗读。

2.2 Orthographic awareness and character learning 缀字意识与汉字学习

Orthographic awareness refers to the awareness of the graphic construction of the language. For English, this is about the awareness of how a word is constructed and spelled. For Chinese, it is the awareness of how a character is constructed, which includes two aspects: one is the awareness of the graphic structure of a character such as how a simple character is constructed by strokes and how a compound character is constructed by components, as well as the patterns of how these components are positioned, such as left-right, top-down, half-enclosure, and full-enclosure. The other is the awareness of the function of components in a compound character such as how they signify the sound and meaning of the compound character. We will discuss these two aspects separately below.

缀字意识是指对语言图形结构（即书写形式）的认识。对英语来说，缀字意识是指对词的构成和拼写的认识。而对汉语来说，它是指对汉字的构成的认识，具体包括两方面：一方面是对汉字字形结构的认识，包括独体字是由哪些笔画组成的，合体字是由哪些部件组成的，以及合体字中部件的组成结构，如左右结构、上下结构、半包围结构和全包围结构；另一方面是对部件在合体字中的作用的认识，如它们是如何标示合体字的字音和字义的。下面我们将分别讨论这两个方面。

2.2.1 CSL learners' awareness of the graphic structure of Chinese characters 汉语二语学习者的字形结构意识

When do CSL learners start to develop their awareness of graphic structure of compound characters? Studies on CSL learners' awareness of perceptual component within a compound character (Wang, Perfetti, & Liu, 2003; Wang, Liu, & Perfetti, 2004) showed that adult English-speaking beginning Chinese learners showed strong evidence of quickly acquiring the orthographic structure of Chinese compound characters. Students could master the structural complexity and compositional relationship of the perceptual components within a compound character even with very little knowledge of Chinese perceptual components, very limited character knowledge, and no explicit instruction on the orthographic structure of characters. This observation is firmly supported by a later study (Shen & Ke, 2007) in which the authors reported that English-speaking CSL learners' ability of decomposing unknown compound characters into perceptual components and reproducing the compound characters by perceptual components emerged at the very beginning stage of learning—after only a few weeks of exposure to characters. The authors attributed this to two factors: one is the learners' cognitive maturity in perceptual organization which allows them to detect the diminutive space boundaries between units within a compound character; the other is the learners' experience with the graphic structure of Chinese, although very brief, because when new characters are introduced, instructors generally demonstrate to students how the character is constructed by components and then write out the characters by components following the stroke order. Those studies hint that adult beginning CSL learners are cognitively ready for perceiving the internal structure of compound characters. Instruction and practice play a key role in facilitating awareness of the graphic structure of Chinese characters.

汉语二语学习者是什么时候开始发展其合体字字形结构意识的？针对汉语二语学习者知觉部件意识的研究（Wang，Perfetti，and Liu，2003；Wang，Liu，and Perfetti，2004）表明，母语为英语的成人初级汉语学习者在学习初始阶段就能很快地掌握合体字的缀字结构。即使学生知觉部件知识和汉字知识十分有限，也没有接受过汉字缀字结构方面的正规学习，他们也能很快理解合体字中知觉部件的复杂性和部件之间的组合关系。这一结论在Shen 和 Ke （2007）稍后进行的研究中也得到了证实。Shen 和 Ke 的研究发现，母语为英语的汉语学习者在学习的初始阶段——只接触了几个星期的汉字后就能够把不认识的合体字分解为知觉部件，并能按部件写出合体字。Shen 和 Ke 认为，这是由两个因素决定的。一个因素是学习者对知觉结构的认知成熟度。学习者对知觉结构的认知达到一定的成熟度后，能察觉到合体字中部件之间的微小空间界限。另一个因素是学习者的汉字学习经历，即使这种经历非常短暂。合体字是由部件组成的，在教学中教师一般都会向学生示范如何写汉字，学生在观看教师示范的过程中，可以了解到合体字是怎样由部件组合而成的，又是怎样以部件为单位按笔顺书写的。上述研究的结果告诉我们，在学习的初始阶段，成人汉语二语学习者就已经具备了认知合体字内部结构的能力。但在汉字字形结构意识培养中，教学和练习仍起着非常关键的促进作用。

Several studies have also reported students' error patterns when they reproduce characters. One study (杜同惠, 1993) reported eight types of errors: (1) miswriting character components such as writing 刀 as 九; (2) switching character positions within a character such as writing 和 as 口禾; (3) missing character components such as writing 些 as 此; (4) adding or missing strokes such as writing 丸 as 九; (5) changing the shapes of strokes such as writing 见

as 贝; (6) changing the structures of characters such as changing the top-down structure 宿 to the left-right structure 佰; (7) homophone substitution such as using 坐 for 座; and (8) substituting sound-alike characters such as writing 听 as 请. Another study (范可育, 1993) identified eight types of errors which were largely similar to the patterns reported by 杜同惠. It should be pointed out that the character writing-error patterns (1)–(6) reported by 杜同惠, belong to graphic errors which relate to how students perceive the graphic structure of the characters. The error patterns (7) and (8), the substitution errors, such as homophonic character substitution or substituting a target character with another irrelevant character, did not result from students' inaccurate recall of the physical structure of characters, but rather were caused by inaccurate perception of the meaning of the character (if not caused by carelessness). Therefore, a substitution error (别字) is related to students' knowledge of characters, especially the size and depth of character knowledge. Another study (江新 & 柳燕梅, 2004) showed that students with the more character knowledge made fewer character structural errors.

还有一些研究总结了学生汉字书写中出现的一些错误。杜同惠（1993）的研究总结了学生汉字书写中的8种错误类型：（1）字素混淆，如将“刀”写成“九”；（2）字素易位，如将“和”写成“口禾”；（3）字素遗失，如将“些”写成“此”；（4）笔画增损，如将“丸”写成“九”；（5）笔画变形，如将“见”写成“贝”；（6）结构错位，如把上下结构的“宿”写成左右结构的“佰”；（7）音同字错，如用“坐”替代“座”；（8）混音错字，如把“听”写成“请”。范可育（1993）的研究也总结了学生书写的8种错误类型，其中大部分类型与杜同惠总结的一致。值得注意的是：杜同惠总结的（1）—（6）类错误属于书写结构性错误，与学生对汉字字形结构的感知有关；但是（7）（8）类属于替代性错误，例如学生在书写中用同音字或其他不相关的字替代目的字，它们的出现不是因为学生对汉字字形结构的错误感知，而是因为学生对汉字字义的不敏感或错误理解（假如不是粗心导致的话）。因此，替代性错误（写别字）跟学生的汉字知识有关，尤其是汉字知识的广度和深度。江新、柳燕梅（2004）的研究结果也表明，学生掌握的汉字知识越多，他们在书写汉字时犯的结构性错误就越少。

In summary, the graphic errors in writing characters can be divided into two types. One is miswriting strokes or components within a character; the other is configuration error—the components within a character are incorrectly positioned. This raises a pedagogical question that the instructor may want to ask: Should students follow the fixed standard order of strokes to practice handwriting characters? With the increasing popularity of computer technology, increasingly more students are interested in using a Chinese word processor for character writing instead of handwriting. CSL educators have been debating the amount of time and effort that students should devote to handwriting characters (Shen, 2015). Due to the fact that the Pinyin input methods are widely used for typing characters, students do not need to have a knowledge of stroke order to type in Chinese characters. Consequently, some instructors and students consider the knowledge of stroke order to be no longer crucial and that practicing handwriting of characters is not very necessary. We consider that practicing handwriting of characters is indispensable in learning Chinese language at the beginning stage, even though the computer may replace handwriting in most tasks. We support the notion that students should be taught about the order of strokes for writing characters. The reason behind this is that studies show that the order of stroke writing can serve as a cue for retrieval of characters during character recognition, namely the order of stroke writing is an important feature of the orthographic and lexical representations of characters in memory. Chinese learners store the information about the order of writing the strokes of a character, especially the beginning strokes of a character, as motor schema that are internalized as a code in memory. When the character is recalled, the sequence of strokes is likely to be activated as a useful retrieval cue for the memory representation of that character (Flores d'Arcais, 1994). Another study (Ke, 1996) on Chinese character recognition and production among English-speaking beginning CSL learners showed a moderate correlation between character recognition and production. Although this study did not directly investigate the role of stroke order in character memorization, the result of correlation analysis indicated that the stroke writing order might also serve as a retrieval cue for character recognition. A later experimental study (Guan et al., 2011) also provided evidence that practicing character writing led to better performance on word recognition and on character-meaning links.

综上所述，学生的汉字书写结构性错误可以分成两大类：一类是笔画或部件错误，另一类是间架结构错误。这里又引出了一个教学法上的问题：学生必须按照规定的笔顺练习写汉字吗？随着计算机技术的普及，越来越多的学生喜欢用中文输入法打字代替手写汉字，汉语二语教师也对学生应该花多少时间和精力练习手写汉字展开了讨论。（Shen，2015）有些教师和学生认为，现在电脑打字一般都采用拼音输入法，学生不需要知道正确笔顺就能打出汉字，笔顺知识对汉字学习并不是那么重要了。我们认为，虽然电脑打字可以代替我们大量的手写工作，但在汉语学习的初始阶段，让学生练习手写汉字绝对是有必要的，学生应该学习汉字的书写笔顺。Flores d'Arcais（1994）的研究证实，汉字的书写笔顺可以成为汉字认读时的提示线索。也就是说，汉字的书写笔顺可以成为大脑对该汉字的记忆表征。学习者在练习汉字书写时，会自动地把笔画的书写顺序作为一种编码存储在大脑中，尤其是汉字的起始笔画。当学习者进行汉字认读时，笔画顺序就会成为其中一条提示线索被激活，帮助其正确认读汉字。Ke（1996）关于母语为英语的汉语初学者的汉字认读与书写关系的研究表明，汉字认读与书写之间存在中度相关性。虽然这一研究没有特别调查汉字笔顺在汉字记忆中的作用，但根据汉字认读与书写的中度相关性我们可以推断，汉字笔顺很可能是汉字认读过程中的重要提示线索。Guan等人（2011）的后续实验研究也证明了，练习汉字书写有利于学习者进行汉字认读，并在大脑中建立汉字字形和字义之间的联系。

Although we consider that to practice handwriting and learning character stroke order are necessary at the beginning stage of character learning, we do not encourage students to spend excessive amounts of time on practicing handwriting characters. Rather, our instruction should strive for meaningful and effective practice by avoiding excessive time spent on handwriting characters. This would allow students to have more time to improve other language skills. As we have entered a digital age, paperless reading and writing have become regular practice in literacy education and in daily-life communication, thus computer writing will gradually replace handwriting. A study showed that for educated Chinese native speakers, nearly 50%–100% of their daily writing was done electronically (Allen, 2008). Modern technology has made it possible for Chinese learners to write with Chinese characters without memorizing how to write them. Thus, our instruction should take full advantage of it to make character learning no longer a stumbling block for Chinese reading and writing. We will discuss this topic further in later sections.

我们虽然承认练习汉字书写和学习汉字笔顺在初始阶段中的必要性，但并不鼓励学生花过多时间在练习汉字书写上。我们的教学应该努力寻找有意义、有效的汉字练习方法，减少学生汉字书写的时间，让学生把更多的时间用在提高其他语言技能上。当今，我们已经进入数字化时代，无纸化读写将成为课堂教学和日常沟通中的常规形式，电脑打字也将逐渐取代手写汉字。Allen（2008）的研究表明，在受过教育的汉语母语者中，约有50%～100%的人的日常写作都是通过电子化手段完成的。现代技术让汉语学习者不需要记忆汉字书写笔顺就能写出汉字成为可能，我们的汉字教学也要充分利用现代技术的优势，让汉字学习不再成为汉语读写的拦路虎。我们会在下面的章节中继续讨论这个问题。

Pedagogical suggestions for reducing errors in character writing
关于减少汉字书写错误的教学建议

• Accurate perception of strokes and accurate execution of stroke order 准确感知汉字笔画，正确把握汉字笔顺

Character writing practice should follow the sequence of strokes→components→characters. Before practicing components, students' skill of stroke execution should reach automaticity. Thus, when they are working on components and characters, they can pay full attention to the graphic configuration of the character rather than to the individual strokes. In general, students should follow the conventional rules of executing strokes in character writing. 张静贤 (1992:38-39) summarized this into six basic rules and eight supplemental rules (refer to Appendix B for details). During character writing practice, individual students may deviate from the standard stroke order in executing strokes. Two major practices are implemented in our instruction to reduce this kind of deviation: traditional paper-based practices and computer-supported online programs. A study (Tsai et al., 2012) compared the two handwriting character practices. For the traditional paper-based practices, the stroke order for a character is indicated in the exercise sheet and students are asked to hand copy the character following the indicated stroke order. For the computer-supported online programs, each character is illustrated with animated stroke order. Students watch the animated stroke order first and then copy the character on the computer following the stroke order. After completing each character, students can hit the submit button and receive immediate error-specific feedback for the copying result. The result of the study showed that under the multimedia condition, novice learners with no prior character writing experience and learners with six-month character learning experience all performed better on the precise production and awareness of conventional stroke sequence. According to the authors, as the online exercises provide animated visual demonstration, the students were enabled to incorporate the strokes' directionality and the components in a vividly successive manner. This offered continuous and detailed input for the visuospatial sketchpad in the short-term memory to better prepare for the kinesthetic exercise that followed immediately. Furthermore, the online feedback on the character-copying results provided immediate guidance for correctly writing each character. A later study (Hsiao et al., 2015) on designing and developing a Chinese character handwriting diagnosis and remedial instruction (CHDRI) system to improve CSL students' ability to write Chinese characters further proved that the e-system enhanced the students' ability to write Chinese characters and to understand the graphic structure of Chinese characters. Moreover, the e-remedial instruction reduced the amount of time the teacher spent in coaching learners to write characters. Based on the above research evidences, we strongly encourage instructors to design or use available technology in helping students learn handwriting characters to achieve better effects.

汉字书写练习应该按照“笔画→部件→整字”的顺序进行。在练习书写部件之前，学生对基本笔画的书写应该达到自动化的程度。这样，他们在书写部件和整字时，才可以将全部的注意力集中在整字的间架结构上，而不是单个笔画上。一般来说，学生应该遵循传统的笔顺规则书写汉字。张静贤（1992：38—39）总结了6条基本规则和8条补充规则（具体请参看附录B）。在汉字书写练习中，个别学生会因为违反笔顺规则书写而出现错误。为了减少这种类型的错误，我们在课堂教学中可以采用以下两种练习方式：一种是采用传统的纸质汉字练习本在纸上练习，另一种是采用电脑软件在在线平台上练习。Tsai等人（2012）的研究比较了这两种练习方式。传统纸上练习的具体步骤是：教师先给学生汉字练习本，练习本上标示了汉字的书写笔顺，然后学生按照标示的笔顺抄写汉字。电脑在线平台练习的具体步骤是：学生先观摩汉字的动态笔顺书写；然后在电脑上按提示的笔顺练习汉字书写；每个汉字写完后，学生可以按下提交按钮提交所写的汉字，之后会收到即时的纠错反馈。研究结果表明，没有学过汉字的初学者和学了6个月汉字的学习者，在使用多媒体练习后，其在汉字书写的准确性上和对笔画顺序的认知上都要优于线下练习。该研究的作者认为，线上练习的动态笔顺书写因其形象性和连续性能使学生将笔画的走向与部件结合起来，同时能在学生的短时记忆中为视觉空间系统提供一种连续的、详细的信息输入，让学生为接下来的动觉书写练习做好准备。另外，线上即时的纠错反馈还能指导学生及时改正书写错误，并在之后的汉字书写中少犯或不犯错误。Hsiao等人（2015）为了进一步提高汉语二语学习者的汉字书写能力而进行的一项如何设计和改进汉字书写错误诊断与纠正的教学系统的研究也证实了，学生使用在线平台进行汉字书写练习可以提高汉字书写能力，增强对汉字间架结构的理解，有效减少书写错误，同时节省教师指导学生书写汉字的时间。基于上述研究结果，我们积极鼓励教师利用现有的技术开发各种合适的在线汉字练习方式，帮助学生更高效地练习汉字书写。

• Knowledge of components and character configurations 汉字部件及间架结构知识

As we mentioned earlier, compound characters are composed of two or more components either semantic, phonetic, or perceptual components. For beginning learners, studies have indicated the pedagogical feasibility of introducing high-frequency semantic, phonetic, and perceptual components. A study (张旺熹, 1990) analyzed 1,000 high-frequency characters from the book《常用字和常用词》published by the Beijing Language Institute Press and classified components into two categories: the perceptual components which cannot serve as independent characters; and the semantic or phonetic components that can serve as independent characters. In total, the author identified 42 perceptual components and 76 independent characters that served as phonetic or semantic components. Another study (崔永华, 1997) analyzed 801 characters which comprised 1,033 Level 1 words (甲级词) listed in the《汉语水平词汇与汉字等级大纲》and identified 330 perceptual components based on the 578 perceptual units classified by the National Language Reform Committee. Classroom teachers may wish to use the research results of these products or other similar studies to incorporate them into character writing instruction. This will aid to foster students' orthographic awareness of components, simple characters, and compound characters.

我们在前面提到过，合体字一般由两个或两个以上的表义部件、表音部件或知觉部件构成。对于汉语初级学习者来说，先给他们介绍一些高频部件在教学上是可行的。张旺熹（1990）对北京语言学院出版社出版的《常用字和常用词》一书中的以1,000个高频汉字进行了分析，他把这1,000个汉字中的高频部件分成了两类：一类是不能单独成字的非成字部件，共42个；另一类是可以独立成字的表音或表义部件，共76个。崔永华（1997）分析了构成《汉语水平词汇与汉字等级大纲》1,033个甲级词的801个字，从这801个汉字中确定了330个部件，这些部件是国家语言文字工作委员会归纳出的578个部件中的一部分。教师可以吸收上述研究或相关研究的成果，并融入自己的汉字教学中，培养学生对汉字部件、独体字和合体字的缀字意识。

Although compound characters are in the thousands, in terms of graphic structures, they are formed based on certain regulations. Traditionally, we classify compound character structures into four basic categories: left-right structures (和, 河), top-down structures (男, 雷), half-enclosure structures (庆, 压) and full-enclosure structures (国, 回). Each category has several variations. Please refer to Appendix C for the variations. Students should be introduced to these basic patterns of graphic structures and should learn to identify the structure of newly introduced characters for efficient memorization.

虽然汉字中的合体字有几千个，但从间架结构看，其构成也是有规则的。传统上，我们根据汉字部件的组合规律把合体字的间架结构大致分为四类：左右结构（和、河）、上下结构（男、雷）、半包围结构（庆、压）和全包围结构（国、回）。每一类还可以划分为更小的类，具体请参看附录C。我们应该把这些知识介绍给学生，让学生自己学会分析新字的间架结构，从而帮助其更有效地识记汉字。

• Amount of meaningful practice
有意义练习的量

Introducing knowledge of strokes, components, and graphic structures of characters are the first step in character writing instruction. Sufficient amounts of meaningful practice should follow to enable accurate character writing.

Here, we emphasize "meaningful practice" rather than mechanical practice. Meaningful practice includes two dimensions: meaningful learning and meaningful copying. There are several ways to promote meaningful learning. One is that when introducing a new character, if possible, inform students about how a character is formed so that they understand the etymology of the character. The other is giving students the freedom to create their own story for memorizing the character structure. For example, one student commented on how to memorize the character 背, saying "two persons sit back to back on the moon." This is an individualized, meaningful way of interpreting and chunking during processing a new character. A study showed that this type of learning enhanced immediate character memorization and retention (Xu & Padilla, 2013). Another way is to create opportunity for students to be repeatedly exposed to the new character. If a new character can be presented in a single teaching unit by using different methods for six times, it would greatly enhance memorization (Nation, 2001). For meaningful copying, we encourage using methods such as asking students to recall the image of a character prior to writing it (柳燕梅 & 江新, 2003), or asking students to report strokes, components, and graphic structures of a character before copying it. These activities require students to devote more cognitive effort in memorizing characters rather than just mechanically copying them. We understand that students' character writing speed and accuracy are also directly influenced by the way of character learning and teaching. We will address character instruction in detail in the later chapters.

介绍汉字的笔画、部件和间架结构知识只是汉字教学的第一步，紧接着，教师应该给学生设计足够丰富的有意义练习，让学生能够准确地书写汉字。在这里，我们强调的是“有意义练习”，而不是机械练习。有意义练习包括两个方面：有意义地学汉字和有意义地抄写汉字。有意义地学汉字方法有很多，我们在这里只举几例：一是让学生学习汉字的字源知识。二是让学生自己想出来一种识记汉字的独特方式。例如，有个学生说他是用“两个人背靠背坐在月亮上”这种形象化的方式记忆汉字“背”的。这种记忆方式表明个体对汉字进行了个性化的、有意义的加工。Xu 和 Padilla（2013）的研究表明，这种学习汉字的方式能强化学生对汉字的瞬时记忆，并让汉字在学生大脑中保持更长时间。三是为学生创造反复接触目的字的机会。Nation（2001）的研究表明，如果目的字在一个教学单元中能以不同的方式出现6次，学生的记忆效果就能明显地得到加强。为了让学生有意义地抄写汉字，我们建议他们在抄写汉字前先回想一下汉字的字形，（柳燕梅、江新，2003）或者先说一下汉字的笔画、部件和间架结构。这些活动都需要学生运用更多的认知资源去记忆汉字，而不只是机械地抄写它们，因此能帮助学生加强汉字的记忆效果。我们必须认识到，学生汉字书写的速度和准确度与汉字的教与学的方式直接相关。在后面的章节中，我们会详细讨论汉字教学的问题。

2.2.2 CSL learners' awareness of components in learning compound characters 汉语二语学习者合体字学习中的部件意识

Component awareness is defined as functional understanding of the role of component in forming Chinese characters and the ability to consciously use this knowledge in character learning. To be specific, this component awareness relates to knowing and using Chinese orthographic knowledge at three levels: (1) understanding that Chinese compounds are formed of components rather than clusters of arbitrary strokes and being able to visually decompose unfamiliar compounds into component units and to reproduce unfamiliar compounds in terms of component units; (2) possessing a good knowledge of semantic components—knowing the sounds, shapes, and meanings of semantic components; and (3) understanding the orthographic structure of phonetic-semantic compounds, namely the role of semantic and phonetic radicals in a phonetic-semantic compound character, and being able to use this knowledge in learning new phonetic-semantic compound characters.

部件意识是指理解部件在合体字中的作用和功能，并能有意识地运用这一知识学习汉字的能力。具体地说，部件意识与了解和运用汉语缀字知识有关，它包括三个层面：（1）理解合体字是由部件构成的，而不是由笔画随意堆砌而成；能在视觉上把不熟悉的合体字分解成部件，并能按部件顺序书写合体字。（2）对表义部件有很好的了解，即知道表义部件的音、形、义。（3）了解形声字的构成，知道形声字中声旁和形旁的不同作用，并能运用声旁和形旁的知识学习新的形声字。

Component awareness is important for learning compound characters. A few studies have been conducted in this regard. One study (Williams, 2013) examined the effects of semantic and phonetic components on Chinese character decoding by high-intermediate level CSL learners. The results showed that the learners had developed a semantic pathway in recognizing characters in which the semantic components cuing the meaning of a character. Though the phonological pathway was an unreliable means of character identification because it did not measurably improve homonym recognition. Learners still used it as their default recognition strategy. Another study (Tong & Yip, 2015) investigated adult CSL learners' sensitivity of the position of semantic and phonetic components in a compound character as well as using a semantic or phonetic cue in learning compound characters (note: the participants' Chinese proficiency level was not reported). The results showed that learners tended to choose the options with correct components in correct positions more than the ones with correct components in incorrect positions when no cue was provided.

Also, the learners chose semantic components in correct positions more than phonetic components in correct positions. The results showed that the learners employed orthographic, phonological, and semantic knowledge of components in encoding novel characters in a manner largely similar to that of native Chinese readers.

部件意识对学习合体字十分重要。一些学者已在这方面进行了相关的研究。Williams（2013）考察了中高级汉语二语学习者的表义部件意识和表音部件意识对汉字解码的影响，结果显示，学习者能根据表义部件正确地猜出表义透明度高的合体字的意思，但是根据表音部件猜测同音异义词的读音的准确率不高。但是，学习者仍然把根据表音部件猜测合体字的发音当作一种习惯性的学习策略。Tong 和 Yip（2015）调查了成人汉语二语学习者对表义部件和表音部件在合体字中的位置的敏感性，以及其在学习合体字时对使用表义或表音的提示性线索的敏感性（注：作者没有提及学习者的汉语水平），结果显示，在没有提示的情况下，学习者倾向于选择那些表义部件和表音部件都在正确位置上的合体字，而不是那些在不正确位置上的合体字；学习者对表义部件的位置比对表音部件的位置更敏感。这些研究结果表明，汉语二语学习者在对新字进行编码时，运用了部件缀字知识、语音知识和语义知识，且其编码方式基本上与汉语母语者一致。

Several studies particularly investigated learners' awareness of phonetic components in compound character learning. For example, one study reported that beginning learners were found to be well aware of using phonetic radicals to pronounce compound characters. Their performance in using phonetic components for accurate pronunciation of compound characters was affected by word frequency and the regularity of the phonetic radicals cuing the sounds of compound characters. They performed better on high-frequency characters, and made fewer mistakes with phonetically transparent characters (陈慧, 2001; 陈慧 & 王魁京, 2001). Another study reported that intermediate and advanced western CSL learners performed significantly better on the sounds of characters that contained reliable phonetic radical, which indicated that learners were using phonological cues to pronounce compound characters. As the grade level increased, learners' awareness of the limitations of phonetic radicals cuing the sounds of compound characters was also increased (江新, 2001).

有几项研究专门调查了学习者在合体字学习中表音部件意识（即声旁意识）的发展。陈慧（2001）和陈慧、王魁京（2001）的研究结果显示，汉语初级学习者已经意识到可以利用声旁来发合体字的音，但是这种发音的准确度受汉字使用频率和声旁表音透明度的影响。使用频率高、声旁表音透明度也高的合体字，学习者的发音准确度也高。江新（2001）关于汉语二语学习者声旁意识的研究发现，西方的汉语中高级学习者对表音透明度高的合体字的发音掌握地比透明度低的合体字好，这说明学习者是运用表音线索学习合体字的发音的。随着汉语水平的提高，学习者也越来越意识到声旁表音的局限性。

Some other studies focused on students' semantic component knowledge and Chinese character learning. A study on semantic component and character learning among English-speaking adult CSL learners showed that beginners could apply semantic component knowledge in learning new semantic transparent characters. Students with good semantic component knowledge performed significantly better on the recognition and production of these characters (Shen, 2000). Shen and Ke (2007) investigated semantic component awareness and character learning among English-speaking adult learners who had completed first- and second-year Chinese courses, respectively. It showed there was a moderate correlation between semantic component awareness and character learning.

还有一些研究特别调查了表义部件知识与汉字学习的关系。Shen（2000）的研究就探讨了母语为英语的成人汉语二语学习者的表义部件知识[①]与汉字学习的关系，结果表明，初级学习者能利用表义部件知识猜出表义透明度高的合体字的字义；学生表义部件知识掌握得越好，合体字的认读和听写效果就越好。Shen 和 Ke（2007）分别调查了母语为英语的初级和中级汉语学习者的表义部件意识与汉字学习的关系，结果显示，学生的表义部件意识与他们的汉字学习情况存在中度相关性。

During character recognition, do learners recognize the character as a whole or do they identify components and strokes prior to character recognition? Studies (张武田 & 冯玲, 1992; 彭聃龄 & 王春茂, 1997) on processing units in character recognition among native Chinese speakers reported that readers used both strokes and components as visual processing units. As readers got more familiar with components, they tended to use components as processing units, as reported in a study on character recognition among skilled native Chinese speakers (Chen, Allport, & Marshall, 1996). Components were found to be functional units in character recognition and readers identified the components within compound characters, which then led to recognition of the characters. Similar evidence was also observed among beginning CSL college-level learners, whose awareness of orthographic structure demonstrated implicit knowledge of the semantic components in recognizing compound characters.

① Shen（2000）和 Shen、Ke（2007）的论文中均将“表义部件知识”或“表义部件意识”译为“semantic radical knowledge”或“semantic radical awareness”，本书统一为“semantic component knowledge”或“semantic component awareness”。

After receiving explicit instruction, the learners' performance on using semantic components in learning compound characters significantly improved (Wang, Liu, & Perfetti, 2004). Another study on component knowledge development among beginning English-speaking CSL learners reported that an overwhelming majority of the beginning learners (93%) considered semantic component knowledge to be a help in learning characters. Students reported that this knowledge helped them learn the meanings, sounds (when a semantic component served as a phonetic radical), and the graphic structure of characters (Shen, 2010). Another study showed that adult CSL learners were able to successfully apply semantic component knowledge to figure out the meanings of unfamiliar compounds containing the target semantic components (Nguyen et al., 2017). Cognitively, if learners are able to perceive components in the compound characters and use components as memory units instead of strokes, it will save memory space and increase recall speed and efficiency.

在进行汉字认读时，学习者是整体认读汉字，还是先识别出部件和笔画再认读汉字？在这个问题上，我们先看看汉语母语者的汉字认知加工情况。张武田、冯玲（1992）和彭聃龄、王春茂（1997）对汉字识别加工单位的研究表明，读者同时将笔画和部件作为汉字的视觉加工单位。随着读者部件知识的增长，他们会更倾向于将部件作为汉字的加工单位。（Chen，Allport，and Marshall，1996）部件是功能性的加工单位。在对合体字加工时，读者先识别出合体字中的部件再认读合体字。同样的情况也发生在大学初级汉语二语学习者中，他们的汉字缀字结构意识表明了他们在认读合体字时运用了隐性的表义部件知识。当学习者经过显性的表义部件知识训练后，他们利用表义部件知识学习合体字的能力也得到了显著的提高。（Wang，Liu，and Perfetti，2004）Shen（2010）研究了母语为英语的大学初级汉语二语学习者部件知识的发展情况，发现绝大多数（93%）初级学习者认为表义部件知识对汉字学习很有帮助，能帮助他们学习汉字的义、音（当表义部件在某些汉字中也充当声旁时），理解汉字的间架结构。Nguyen等人（2017）的研究结果显示，成人汉语二语学习者能有效利用学到的表义部件知识猜测包含该表义部件的陌生合体字的字义。从认知的角度看，如果学习者能识别出合体字中的部件并把部件作为记忆单位而不是笔画，那将会大大节省学习者的记忆空间，提高学习者提取汉字的速度和效率。

Pedagogical suggestions for increasing component awareness
关于增强部件意识的教学建议

• Practicing decomposition of compound characters into perceptual components 练习把合体字分解成知觉部件

We understand that a character can be decomposed into perceptual components and that a perceptual component can be further decomposed into strokes. After learning certain types of perceptual components, exercises that require students to identify perceptual units from compound characters or decompose compounds into perceptual units should be incorporated into character learning, because this type of exercises will help students to reach automaticity in perceptual component recognition, and hence, facilitate character recognition. Below are two examples of this type of exercises (cited from the workbook of *Learning 100 Chinese Radicals,* Lesson 11, by Shen, Wang, & Tsai, Peking University Press, 2009):

我们知道，汉字是由知觉部件构成的，而知觉部件是由笔画构成的。当学生学了一定数量的知觉部件后，我们应该在汉字教学中引入一些让学生识别合体字中的知觉部件或让学生把合体字分解成知觉部件的练习，因为这种练习能帮助学生对知觉部件的认知达到自动化，促进汉字认读。下面我们列举两个具体的例子（均引自《汉字部首教程：练习册》第11课，沈禾玲、王平、蔡真慧编著，北京大学出版社2009年出版）：

---

1. Please identify the components you have been introduced to, and copy the components into the brackets on the right. 请找出你学过的部件并把它们抄写在右边的空格中。

谢 [ ][ ][ ]　　新 [ ][ ][ ]　　砸 [ ][ ][ ]

2. Please find the component shared by the three characters in the list below and copy the component into the brackets. 请找出三个字中的共有部件并把它抄写在左边的空格中。

[ ] 巨 医 区　　[ ] 时 封 导　　[ ] 嘴 武 些

• Systematically introducing high-frequency semantic radicals 系统介绍高频表义部首

High-frequency components are the components that have higher combinability with other components to form compound characters. The existing bilingual (English-Chinese) textbook, *Learning 100 Chinese Radicals*(Shen, Wang, & Tsai, 2009) is an example of using high-frequency semantic components (radicals) to compile a radical textbook. According to the authors, the 100 high-frequency radicals were identified by analyzing 9, 999 characters from the *Modern Chinese Word Dictionary*《现代汉语词典》(2005, Please see Appendix D for details). We hope there will be more radical textbooks compiled with incorporation of modern technology in the field. Instructors may wish to use this type of radical textbook for systematic introduction to component knowledge.

高频部件是指那些组字能力极强的部件。现有的双语（英语—汉语）教材《汉字部首教程》（Shen，Wang，and Tsai，2009）就是一本高频部首教材。该教材系统介绍了100个汉语高频表义部首，这100个部首（请参看附录D）是根据《现代汉语词典》（2005）列出的9,999个汉字中的部首的出现频率而筛选出来的。我们希望这个领域里能出现更多的结合现代技术的部首教材，那样教师就可以使用这类教材向学生系统地介绍汉字部件知识了。

We strongly favor systematically introducing semantic radicals to students at the initial stage of character learning for three reasons. First, almost all semantic radicals that originated from pictographs are root characters. Introducing these semantic radicals with connecting pictograph origins will help students effectively memorize the radicals or root characters. A study (Chan et al., 2007) reported that native Chinese students recognized characters having direct meaning connections with pictographs (such as 马) faster and more accurately than the characters with no direct meaning connection with their pictographs (such as 南). From a cultural learning perspective, learning high-frequency radicals will expose students to the rich culture behind the characters, which will increase their learning interest. Second, since high-frequency radicals will appear more frequently in the commonly used compound characters, it will greatly alleviate the difficulty level of learning compound characters. Third, quite a number of semantic radicals also serve as phonetic radicals, such as the component 土 in character 吐. Thus, mastery of these high-frequency radicals helps students process not only the meanings of compound characters, but also their sounds. Therefore, we strongly suggest that students should have a solid knowledge of the high-frequency semantic radicals by the end of beginning level learning. Namely students should be able to read, handwrite, and fully understand the meanings of semantic radicals. This will be sure to lay down a solid foundation for further character learning.

我们十分赞成在汉字学习的初始阶段就向学生系统地介绍表义部首，原因有三：第一，几乎所有的表义部首都起源于象形字，除了极个别的失去了独立性之外，其他的都是基本字。将这些部首的学习与相应的象形字的学习结合起来能帮助学生有效记忆这些部首或基本字。Chan 等人（2007）的研究显示，母语为汉语的学生识别那些直接起源于象形字的汉字（如“马”）比识别那些与象形字无直接联系的汉字（如“南”）要快和准确。从文化学习的角度看，学习高频表义部首可以让学生了解汉字背后蕴含的深厚文化，提高学生的学习兴趣。第二，高频表义部首经常出现在常用合体字中，学生学了高频表义部首之后就能大大减轻学习常用合体字时的负担。第三，有相当一部分表义部首同时也在合体字中充当声旁，如“土”在“吐”中起表音作用，因此掌握这些高频表义部首不仅能帮助学生理解合体字的“义”，也能帮助其记住合体字的“音”。因此，我们强烈建议学生在汉语学习的初级阶段就打下坚实的高频表义部首知识的基础。也就是说，对于高频表义部首，学生要会读，会写，并且理解其义。这能为学生今后的汉字学习打下坚实的基础。

How should character components be introduced? Should we introduce them as component lessons, separate from regular lessons, or should we introduce them based on their appearance in the new characters of a regular lesson? We consider that both strategies have their advantages and disadvantages. Introducing semantic components prior to compound character learning allows students to direct their attention to character component learning, as most of semantic and phonetic components can serve as independent characters; therefore, students are also learning simple or root characters. Proceeding from simple character to compound character learning conforms to learners' cognitive processing. Furthermore, this focused learning can help students quickly and effectively learn components, which provides a strong foundation for compound character learning. The disadvantage, however, lies in the subsequent lesson learning; it is not possible to have characters in the new lesson containing all previously learned components, especially if the lessons are theme-based rather than orthograph-based. Consequently, students may forget the previously learned components if they do not appear sufficiently often in the subsequent lessons. Introducing semantic components as they appear in the lesson will help to build strong connections between a component and a compound character of the component within. This will produce an immediate effect on facilitating the character memorization. Especially during introduction of a new character (Taft & Chung, 1999)[①]. However, if components are introduced based on appearance of components in the lesson, it may take a much longer time to learn high-frequency components as the lesson organization is not component-based, thus each lesson may contain very few new components or even no new components. Instructors will have to decide which method is better based on learning reality and curriculum goals.

我们应该如何向学生教授汉字部件呢？是单独开设汉字部件课进行教授，还是在部件随生字出现时随课进行教学？我们认为两种方法各有优缺点。部件教学先于合体字教学，能使学生将全部的注意力集中到部件学习上，而且大部分表义和表音部件本身就是汉字，学生在学习部件

① Taft、Chang（1999）论文原文中将“部件”表述为“radical”，本书统一为“component”。

的同时也学习了汉字中的独体字或基本字。从独体字过渡到合体字也符合学习者由简单到复杂的认知规律。除此之外，这种有重点的强化学习还能帮助学生在短时间内快速、有效地习得部件，为合体字的学习打下坚实的基础。但其缺点在随后的课文学习上。如果教材是以话题为纲而不是以缀字知识为纲进行编排的，那么学过的部件有可能不再在后续课文中出现。如果学过的部件没有在后续课文中充分地再现，学生很可能就会忘记先前学过的部件。在部件随生字出现时就随课进行教学，能够帮助学生建立起部件与包含该部件的合体字之间的紧密联系，进而帮助学生更有效地记忆所学的合体字，尤其是在学习新字时。（Taft and Chung，1999）这种教学方法的缺点是，学生需要花费比较长的时间才能学完高频部件，因为课文不是以部件为纲进行编排的，每课中包含的新部件可能很少，甚至没有新部件。教师必须根据教学实际和课程目标选取合适的部件教学方法。

• Emphasizing component knowledge application
强调部件知识的应用

A study among beginning to advanced English-speaking CFL learners (Shen & Ke, 2007) revealed that students' ability to apply semantic component knowledge in learning compound characters was not synchronous with the development of component knowledge[①]. Component knowledge increased steadily from year 1 to year 3 of the study, but the ability for accurate application of the semantic component knowledge in learning characters did not show a significant increase until the end of the second year of study. Thus, a gap exists between knowledge gained and knowledge application. We understand that, cognitively, it takes time to transfer knowledge into skills. Nonetheless, this gap

① Shen、Ke（2007）论文原文中是“radica knowledge”，本书统一为“component knowledge”。

could be narrowed if our instruction paid attention to component knowledge application after the components are introduced. Exercises such as requiring students to guess the meaning of a new compound character based on its known semantic component or to choose an appropriate component for an uncompleted character based on its meaning or sound given are all helpful in facilitating component knowledge application. Below are a few examples of this type of exercise (cited from the workbook of *Learning 100 Chinese Radicals*, Lesson 11, by Shen, Wang, & Tsai, Peking University Press, 2009):

Shen 和 Ke（2007）的一项关于母语为英语的汉语二语学习者表义部件知识的应用的研究表明，从初级阶段到高级阶段，学习者表义部件知识应用能力的发展与部件知识的增长并不同步。学生从一年级到三年级，部件知识每年都在稳步增长，但是准确应用表义部件知识学习汉字的能力直到二年级学习结束后才有明显的提升。可见，知识的习得与应用之间是存在缺口的。我们都知道，从认知的角度看，将知识转化为技能是需要时间的。虽然如此，但如果教师能在教学中重视部件知识的应用，那么部件知识的习得与应用之间的缺口是可以缩小的。例如，教师可以让学生根据已知的表义部件推知新字的意思，或让学生根据字义或字音给一个缺少部件的汉字选择适当的部件，这些练习都可以促进部件知识的应用。下面我们具体列举几种这类练习（均引自《汉字部首教程：练习册》第11课，沈禾玲、王平、蔡真慧编著，北京大学出版社2009年出版）：

---

1. Based on your understanding of each component's meaning, please choose the appropriate meaning from the list and fill in the brackets on the left:

根据你对部件的理解，为汉字选择适当的意思并填入左边空格：

[ ] 甜　　a. sad　　b. sweet　　c. broken

[ ] 房　　a. room　　b. waist　　c. ring

2. Based on the sound of each component you have learned, please choose the correct Pinyin for the characters from the list to fill in the brackets on the left:

根据所学部件的发音，为汉字选择适当的读音并填入左边空格：

[ ] 沪　　a. hù　　b. luàn　　c. xiàng

[ ] 址　　a. chōng　　b. zhǐ　　c. láo

3. Based on the sounds and meanings of components that you have learned, please match the characters on the left to their sounds and meanings on the right with a line:

根据所学部件的音和义，为汉字找到相应的音和义并用线连起来：

a. 趾	gōng	bow
b. 护	cūn	village
c. 躬	zhǐ	toe
d. 村	hù	protect

After introducing a semantic component, having students analyze a group of characters sharing the same semantic components helps develop component awareness. A study reported that this type of semantic-component-based character grouping consistently led to better recall and better component generalization than learning in distribution (Xu, Perfetti, & Chang, 2014). Apart from classroom learning, using mobile devices to develop e-learning programs is an excellent way of extending component learning beyond the classroom walls. A study (Chen et al., 2013) reported a comparison between the traditional learning method and the e-platform learning in learning components and component-embedded characters. In the study, students were required to learn a component followed by learning a group of characters containing the target component. The results showed that students used the e-learning platform achieved better learning results in character learning and component awareness than the students who used traditional learning approach. The possible reason was that the e-learning platform allowed students to apply the learned component knowledge in learning the group of new characters embedded with the newly learned component through multimedia-supported interactive and hands-on activities, which make learning more meaningful and interesting. We suggest that in addition to providing meaningful exercises, when introducing new characters, students should be asked to analyze the characters and identify the relationship between the character and the component within. These are all excellent ways to encourage students to apply learned component knowledge in learning new characters.

介绍完一个表义部件后，紧接着让学生分析一组含有同一部件的汉字能促进学生部件意识的发展。Xu、Perfetti和Chang（2014）的研究表明，相较于分散学习，这种方法能让学生更有效地识记汉字并对汉字部件进行更全面的概括。除了在课堂上提供有意义的练习之外，教师还可以运用移动电子设备开发学习程序，将部件学习延伸到课堂之外，让学习不受地点、环境的限制。Chen等人（2013）比较了两种学习方法——用部件衍生汉字电子平台学习与传统课堂部件学习的效果，他们要求两组学生学完一个部件后，紧接着自学一组字义与该部件有直接联系的合体字。三个星期后的评测结果表明，用部件衍生汉字电子平台学习的学生在记忆汉字与部件意识发展方面均优于传统方法组。这可能是因为部件衍生汉字电子平台能为学生提供多种可操作性强的多媒体互动活动，使学习变得更有意义，更能激发起学生的学习兴趣。我们建议教师在教授新字时，除了提供有意义的练习外，还要让学生自己尝试分解汉字，找出部件与汉字之间的内在联系。这些都是鼓励学生应用部件知识学习新字的有效方法。

References 参考文献

陈慧. 2001.外国学生识别形声字错误类型小析[J]. 语言教学与研究（2）：16-20.

陈慧，王魁京. 2001. 外国学生识别形声字的实验研究[J]. 世界汉语教学（2）：75-80.

崔永华. 1997. 汉字部件和对外汉字教学[J]. 语言文字应用（3）：49-54，62.

杜同惠. 1993. 留学生汉字书写差错规律试析[J]. 世界汉语教学（1）：69-72.

范可育. 1993. 从外国学生书写汉字的错误看汉字字形特点和汉字教学[J]. 语文建设（4）：28-31.

费锦昌. 1996. 汉字部件探究[J]. 语言文字应用（2）：20-26.

国家对外汉语教学领导小组办公室汉语水平考试部. 1992. 汉语水平词汇与汉字等级大纲[M]. 北京：北京语言学院出版社.

江新. 2001. 外国学生形声字表音线索意识的实验研究[J]. 世界汉语教学（2）：68-74.

江新. 2003. 不同母语背景的外国学生汉字知音和知义之间关系的研究[J]. 语言教学与研究（6）：51-57.

江新，柳燕梅. 2004. 拼音文字背景的外国学生汉字书写错误研究[J]. 世界汉语教学（1）：60-70.

柳燕梅，江新. 2003. 欧美学生汉字学习方法的实验研究——回忆默写法与重复抄写法的比较[J]. 世界汉语教学（1）：59-67.

彭聃龄，王春茂. 1997. 汉字加工的基本单元：来自笔画数效应和部件数效应的证据[J]. 心理学报（1）：8-16.

上海交通大学汉字编码组，上海汉语拼音文字研究组. 1988. 汉字信息字典[M]. 北京：科学出版社.

谢光辉. 1997. 常用汉字图解[M]. 北京：北京大学出版社.

张静贤. 1992. 现代汉字教程[M]. 北京：现代出版社.

张旺熹. 1990. 从汉字部件到汉字结构——谈对外汉字教学[J]. 世界汉语教学（2）：112-120.

张武田，冯玲. 1992. 关于汉字识别加工单位的研究[J]. 心理学报（4）：379-385.

赵果. 2003. 初级阶段欧美留学生识字量与字的构词数[J]. 语言文字应用（3）：106-

112.

中国社会科学院语言研究所词典编辑室. 2005. 现代汉语词典（第5版）[M]. 北京：商务印书馆.

Allen J R. 2008. Why learning to write Chinese is a waste of time: a modest proposal[J]. Foreign language annals, 41(2): 237–251.

Baron J, Strawson C. 1976. Use of orthographic and word-specific knowledge in reading words aloud[J]. Journal of experimental psychology: human perception and performance, 2: 386–393.

Chan C C H, Leung A W S, Luo Y-J, et al.. 2007. How do figure-like orthographs modulate visual processing of Chinese words? [J]. Cognitive neuroscience and neuropsychology, 18(8): 757–761.

Chan C K K, Siegel L S. 2001. Phonological processing in reading Chinese among normally achieving and poor readers[J]. Journal of experimental child psychology, 80: 23–43.

Chen H-C, Hsu C-C, Chang L-Y, et al.. 2013. Using a radical-derived character e-learning platform to increase learner knowledge of Chinese characters[J]. Language learning and technology, 17 (1): 89–106.

Chen Y P, Allport D A, Marshall J C. 1996. What are the functional orthographic units in Chinese word recognition: the stroke or the stroke pattern? [J] The quarterly journal of experimental psychology, 49A(4): 1024–1043.

Chow B W-Y, McBride-Chang C, Burgess S. 2005. Phonological processing skills and early reading abilities in Hong Kong Chinese kindergarteners learning to read English as a second language[J]. Journal of educational psychology, 97(1): 81–87.

Coltheart M, Curtis B, Atkins P, et al.. 1993. Models of reading aloud: dual-route and parallel-distributed-processing approaches[J]. Psychological review, 100(4): 589–608.

Everson M E. 1998. Word recognition among learners of Chinese as a foreign language: investigating the relationship between naming and knowing[J]. Modern language journal, 82(2): 194–204.

Fan K Y, Gao J L, Ao X P. 1984. Pronunciation principles of Chinese characters and alphabetic writing scripts[J]. Chinese character reform, 3: 23-27.

Feng G, Miller K, Shu H, et al.. 2001. Rowed to recovery: the use of phonological and orthographic information in reading Chinese and English[J]. Journal of experimental psychology: learning, memory, and cognition, 27(4): 1079-1100.

Flores d' Arcais G B. 1994. Order of strokes writing as a cue for retrieval in reading Chinese Characters[J]. European journal of cognitive psychology, 6(4): 337-355.

Gillet J W, Temple C. 1994. Understanding reading problems: assessment and instruction[M]. 4th ed. New York: Harper Collins.

Guan C Q, Liu Y, Chan D H L, et al.. 2011. Writing strengthens orthography and alphabetic-coding strengthens phonology in learning to read [J]. Journal of educational psychology, 103(3): 509-522.

Hayes E B. 1988. Encoding strategies used by native and non-native readers of Chinese mandarin[J]. The modern language journal, 72(2): 188-195.

Ho C S-H, Bryant P. 1997. Phonological skills are important in learning to read Chinese[J]. Developmental psychology, 33(6): 946-951.

Hsiao H-S, Chang C-S, Chen C-J, et al.. 2015. The influence of Chinese character handwriting diagnosis and remedial instruction system on learners of Chinese as a foreign language[J]. Computer assisted language learning, 28 (4): 306-324.

Jiang N. 2004. Semantic transfer and its implications for vocabulary teaching in a second language[J]. The modern language journal, 88: 416-432.

Ke C. 1996. An empirical study on the relationship between Chinese character recognition and Production[J]. The modern language journal, 80: 340-350.

Koda K. 1996. L2 word recognition research: a critical review[J]. The modern language journal, 80 (4): 450-460.

Lee C H, Kalyuga S. 2011. Effectiveness of on-screen pinyin in learning Chinese: an expertise reversal for multimedia redundancy effect[J]. Computers in human behavior,

27(1): 11-15.

Myers J, Taft M, Chou P. 2007. Character recognition without sound or meaning[J]. Journal of Chinese linguistics, 35(1): 1-57.

Nation I S P. 2001. Learning vocabulary in another language[M]. Cambridge: Cambridge University Press.

Nguyen T P, Zhang J, Li H, et al.. 2017. Teaching semantic radicals facilitates inferring new character meaning in sentence reading for nonnative Chinese speakers[J]. Frontiers in psychology, 8: 1-12.

Packard J L. 1990. Effects of time lag in the introduction of characters into the Chinese language curriculum[J]. The modern language journal, 74: 167-175.

Pan J, McBride-Chang C, Shu H, et al.. 2011. What is in the naming? A 5-year longitudinal study of early rapid naming and phonological sensitivity in relation to subsequent reading skills in both native Chinese and English as a second language[J]. Journal of educational psychology, 103(4): 897-908.

Perfetti C A, Tan L H. 1998. The time course of graphic, phonological, and semantic activation in Chinese character identification[J]. Journal of experimental psychology: learning, memory, and cognition, 24(1): 101-118.

Perfetti C A, Zhang S. 1991. Phonological processes in reading Chinese characters[J]. Journal of experimental psychology: learning, memory, and cognition, 17: 633-643.

Pollatsek A, Tan L H, Rayner K. 2000. The role of phonological codes in integrating information across saccadic eye movements in Chinese character identification[J]. Journal of experimental psychology: human perception and performance, 26(2): 607-633.

Ramsey S R. 1987. The languages of China[M]. Princeton, NJ: Princeton University Press.

Read J. 2004. Plumbing the depths: how should the construct of vocabulary knowledge be defined? [M]. Bogaards P, Laufer B. Vocabulary in a second language:selection, acquisition and testing. Amsterdam: John Benjamins Publishing Company, 209-227.

Shen H H. 2000. Radical knowledge and character learning among learners of Chinese as a foreign language[J]. Proceedings of the international conference on Chinese pedagogy, 85–93.

Shen H H. 2010. Analysis of radical knowledge development among beginning CFL learners[M]. Everson M E, Shen H H. Research among learners of Chinese as a foreign language. Honolulu, HI: University of Hawai'i, National Foreign Language Resource Center, 45–65.

Shen H H. 2015. Chinese L2 literacy debates and beginner reading in the United States[M]. Bigelow M, Ennser-Kananen J.The routledge handbook of educational linguistics. New York: Routledge, 276–288.

Shen H H, Jiang X. 2013. Character reading fluency, word segmentation accuracy, and reading comprehension in L2 Chinese[J]. Reading in a foreign language, 25 (1): 1–25.

Shen H H, Ke C. 2007. Radical awareness and word acquisition among non-native learners of Chinese[J]. The modern language journal, 91: 97–111.

Shen H H, Wang P, Tsai C-H. 2009. Learning 100 Chinese radicals[M]. Peking: Beijing University Press.

Siok W-T, Fletcher P. 2001. The role of phonological awareness and visual-orthographic skills in Chinese reading acquisition[J]. Developmental psychology, 37(6): 886–899.

Spinks J A, Liu Y, Perfetti C A, et al., 2000. Reading Chinese characters for meaning: the role of phonological information[J]. Cognition, 76 (1): B1–B11.

Taft M, Chung K. 1999. Using radicals in teaching Chinese characters to second language learners[J]. Psychologia, 42(4): 243–251.

Tao L, Zuo L. 1997. Oral reading practice in China's elementary schools: a brief discussion of its unique roots in language, culture, and society[J]. The reading teacher, 50 (8): 654–665.

Tong X, Yip J H Y. 2015. Cracking the Chinese character: radical sensitivity in learners of

Chinese as a foreign language and its relationship to Chinese word reading[J]. Reading and writing, 28(2): 159–181.

Tsai C-H, Kuo C-H, Horng W-B, et al.. 2012. Effects on learning logographic character formation in computer-assisted handwriting instruction[J]. Language learning & technology, 16 (1): 110–130.

Wade-Woolley L. 1999. First language influences on second language word reading: all roads lead to Rome[J]. Language learning, 49(3): 447–471.

Walker G LR. 1984. “Literacy” and “reading” in a Chinese language program[J]. Journal of Chinese language teachers association, 19(1): 67–84.

Wang M, Liu Y, Perfetti C A. 2004. The implicit and explicit learning of orthographic structure and function of a new writing system[J]. Scientific studies of reading, 8(4): 357–379.

Wang M, Perfetti C A, Liu Y. 2003. Alphabetic readers quickly acquire orthographic structure in learning to read Chinese[J]. Scientific studies of reading, 7(2): 183–208.

Williams C, 2013. Emerging development of semantic and phonological routes to character decoding in Chinese as a foreign language learners[J]. Reading and writing, 26(2):293–315.

Xu X, Padilla A M. 2013. Using meaningful interpretation and chunking to enhance memory: the case of Chinese character learning[J]. Foreign language annals, 46(3): 402–422.

Xu Y, Perfetti C A, Chang L-Y. 2014. The effect of radical-based grouping in character learning in Chinese as a foreign language[J]. The modern language journal, 98(3): 773–793.

Yang J. 2000. Orthographic effect on word recognition by learners of Chinese as a foreign language[J]. Journal of the Chinese language teachers association, 35: 1–18.

Zhou X, Marslen-Wilson W. 1999. Phonology, orthography, and semantic activation in reading Chinese[J]. Journal of memory and language, 41(4): 579–606.

Zhou X, Marslen-Wilson W. 2000. The relative time course of semantic and phonological activation in reading Chinese[J]. Journal of experimental psychology: learning, memory, and cognition, 26(5): 1245–1265.

Chapter 3 第三章

Cognitive and Psycholinguistic Models for Chinese Word Acquisition
汉语词语习得的认知模式与心理语言学模式

How do students learn new words? What are the processes that students go through from initial perception of words to the final mastery of words? How can instruction facilitate a student's word acquisition process? These questions are important for us to understand the nature of word learning and instruction. This chapter will provide answers to these questions by presenting several cognitive and psycholinguistic models on Chinese word acquisition and the corresponding pedagogical measures.

学生是如何学习新词的？从对词的最初感知到对词的最终掌握，他们历经了哪些认知过程？教学是怎样推进学生的词语习得过程的？要理解词语习得与教学的本质，我们必须先解答以上问题。这一章我们会介绍汉语词语习得的认知模式和心理语言学模式，以及相应的教学措施。

3.1 Cognitive processing models for word acquisition 词语习得的认知模式

We first discuss the two cognitive models. One is the cognitive model of five-stage word acquisition and the other is the multilevel interactive-activation word identification cogin. The former provides a general outline of the cognitive stages of word acquisition; the latter specifically describes individual word identification during reading.

我们先介绍两种认知模式：一种是五阶段词语习得认知模式，另一种是多层次交互激活词语认读模式。第一种模式从总体上介绍了词语习得的认知过程，第二种模式则具体描述了阅读过程中单个词语的认读过程。

3.1.1 Cognitive model of five-stage word acquisition 五阶段词语习得认知模式

From a cognitive processing perspective, in the classroom environment, what stages do learners go through in acquiring words and where should the focus of instruction be placed to accelerate word learning at each developmental stage? Based on the characteristics of cognitive processing of Chinese words, we propose a cognitive model that involves five stages of word acquisition: perception, association, comprehension, internalization, and generation. We discuss this five-stage model in detail below.

从认知加工的角度看，学生在课堂环境中习得词语要经过哪些阶段？为了加快学生的词语习得，每个阶段的教学重点又应该放在哪里？基于汉字认知加工的特点，我们提出了五阶段词语习得认知模式。这五个阶段分别是感知阶段、联结阶段、理解阶段、内化阶段和生成阶段。下面我们详细介绍一下这一认知模式。

Stage 1: Perception. When a new word is presented to learners, they perceive the sound, shape, and meaning of the word. At this stage, learners will register the information of the word in their brains as a mental photo. Therefore, attracting students' attention to the target words and leaving them with a deep impression of the features of the target words are the key points to ensure that information will be successfully retained in learners' short-term memory for further processing. Instructional effort should focus on how to present the new word to catch learners' attention and arouse their intellectual curiosity for making a vivid impression of the new word in learners' brains. When introducing new words, we usually present the written form of the new word, the Pinyin for the word, and its L1 (the first language) translation. How should this information be presented, and in which order, for the best retention? A study (Chung, 2002) compared four types of presentation conditions for beginning English-speaking CSL learners. Condition 1 was a simultaneous presentation of character–Pinyin–English (translation), after which students were asked to look at the character and read the Pinyin. Condition 2 was a simultaneous Pinyin–English–character condition, in which students were asked to say the sound of the character. Condition 3 was character, delayed Pinyin–English condition, in which students were asked to look at the character first as soon as it was presented, then 5 seconds later the Pinyin and English translation were also presented. The teacher then asked the students to say the sound of the character. Condition 4 was Pinyin–English, delayed character condition, in which the Pinyin and English translation were presented first, and 5 seconds later, the character was presented. The teacher then asked the students to say the sound of the character. At the end of the experiment, a character recognition test was administered. Of the two simultaneous conditions, the character–Pinyin–English condition resulted in better character recognition. Of the two delayed conditions, Condition 3 had significantly better results than Condition 4. Among the four conditions, condition 3, character, delayed Pinyin–English condition had the best results for character recognition. The reason was thought to be that presenting the character first without Pinyin and English helps learners to direct their attention solely to the character. It also prompts their curiosity about the sound and the meaning of the character, which in turn helps them pay attention to the Pinyin and English presented 5 seconds later. Similarly, if we present the three items at the same time, students would need to pay attention to all three items and their attention to each item is divided and diffused, which leads to poor perception.

第一阶段：感知阶段。当一个新词呈现在学习者面前时，学习者会感知到该词的音、形和义。在这一阶段，学习者会把新词的信息注册到大脑中，这样大脑中就形成了该词的心理图像。因此，为了使目的词信息成功地保持在学生的短时记忆系统中等待进一步加工，关键是要将学生的注意力吸引到目的词上并使之对目的词的特征留下深刻印象。教学的重点应放在如何呈现目的词才能引起学生的注意，唤起他们的求知欲，让目的词在他们大脑中留下鲜活的印象上。在教授新词时，我们通常会向学生展示新词的书写形式、拼音以及对应的母语翻译。这些信息以什么方式和什么顺序呈现才能最大化地利于学生对信息的保持？Chung（2002）比较了母语为英语的汉语初级学习者的四种不同信息呈现方式的效果：第一种方式，同时呈现“汉字—拼音—英文翻译”，之后要求学生看汉字读拼音；第二种方式，同时呈现“拼音—英文翻译—汉字”，之后要求学生说出汉字的发音；第三种方式，先呈现汉字，5秒钟后再呈现拼音和英文翻译，然后要求学生说出汉字的发音；第四种方式，先呈现拼音和英文翻译，5秒钟后再呈现汉字，然后要求学生说出汉字的发音。实验结束前的汉字认读测验结果显示：比较前两种同时呈现的方式，第一种呈现顺序，即“汉字—拼音—英文翻译”的效果要优于第二种；比较后两种间隔呈现的方式，第三种呈现顺序的效果要优于第四种。在四种呈现方式中，第三种，即先呈现汉字，5秒钟后再呈现拼音和英文翻译的汉字认读效果最好。原因可能是，汉字先呈现的话，因为没有拼音和英文翻译的干扰，学习者可以将全部注意力都集中在汉字上。这同时也能引起学生对该字字音和字义的好奇心，这种好奇心驱使他们对5秒钟后出现的拼音和英文翻译更加关注。同理，如果我们把新词的音、形、义同时展示给学生，学生的注意力就会被分配到三个信息源上。学生注意力分散了，对词的感知也会变差。

Stage 2: Association. Once the information of the sound, shape, and meaning of the word is available, the working memory (short-term memory) will start to process the word, which includes establishing the association between the sound, shape, and meaning within the word and the association of this word with related words learned previously. At this stage, instruction should direct students to pay attention to the internal relationship of the word, such as asking students to analyze radicals within the character to find out connections between the character and the radicals within as well as analyzing the morphemes within the word to understand the relationship between the word and the morphemes within. Instruction should also help students to find connections of the new words with previously learned relevant words. This step is important as this will help students to integrate the new word into the existing cognitive schema in their brains.

第二阶段：联结阶段。当目的词的音、形、义信息储存到大脑中后，这些信息立刻就会被传递到工作记忆系统（即短时记忆系统）中进行加工。加工过程包括建立目的词内部音、形、义之间的联结，以及目的词与先前学过的词语之间的联结。这一阶段的教学重点是引导学生关注词语内部的联系。例如，教师可以让学生分析词中汉字所包含的部首，并找出部首与汉字之间的联系；还可以让学生分析词中的语素，并理解语素与词之间的联系。教学还应该帮助学生建立新词与相关旧词之间的联系。这一步骤很重要，因为它能帮助学生把新词融入他们已有的认知结构中去。

Stage 3: Comprehension. At this stage, students demonstrate their comprehending to new words by making connections between the sound, shape, and meaning within a word, as well as the connections between new words and previously learned words. Students can use their own language to explain a word. For example, a student may explain that 同学是在教室里跟我一起学习的人. Students can also provide a synonym and an antonym for the target word if applicable. They can put the new word into a certain category based on certain relationships of this new word with the existing words. For example, a student may put the word 同学 into a category with other words such as 学生 or 教师, as the learner might consider that they are people we meet in an educational institute. Another sign of comprehension is that students understand that a word may have multiple meanings in different contexts. Instruction should provide various activities to facilitate the development of cognitive skills on classification and on understanding how the word is used in different contexts.

第三阶段：理解阶段。在这一阶段，学生能通过新词内部音、形、义之间的联系以及新词与相关旧词之间的联系达到对新词的理解，具体表现在：（1）学生能用自己的语言解释新词。例如，学生对新词“同学”的解释可以是：同学是在教室里跟我一起学习的人。（2）学生能找出新词的同义词和反义词。（3）学生能根据新词与旧词之间的某种共同特征将新词归入相应的类别。例如，学生可能会把“同学”与“学生”“教师”等词归为一类，因为这些人都是在学校里可以遇见的。（4）理解的另一个表现是当新词出现在不同句子中时，学生能根据上下文语境确定该词的具体意义。在这一阶段，我们在教学上应该给学生提供多样化的活动，帮助他们提高对词进行分类的能力，以及辨别新词在不同语境中如何使用的能力。

Stage 4: Internalization. Once a new word is processed in the working memory, it needs to be transferred to the long-term memory to store in the mental lexicon so that it can be retrieved later when needed. Internalization is the process of storing the word in the learners' long-term memory. At this stage, the instructor should design classroom exercises that allow students to process the word in a meaningful way and in a cognitively deeper level. Meaningful processing means that learning is not forced or mechanical memorization. Rather, students are fully engaged in learning activities that are closely related to their daily lives and their interests. They enjoy the activities to a greater extent even though it may sometimes require considerable mental effort. Instructors should design and present comprehensive activities which require incorporating mental effort such as analysis, comparison, differentiation, and evaluation to help with internalization. The formats of such learning activities may include but are not limited to the types of communication-based, task-supported, problem-solving, or context-based activities.

第四阶段：内化阶段。新词一旦在工作记忆系统中完成加工，就会转入长时记忆系统中存储起来，成为心理词库的一部分，等待需要的时候被检索和提取。这个过程我们称之为“内化”。在这个阶段，练习是促进学生内化的关键。教师应该设计一些课堂练习，帮助学生对新词进行有意义的深度加工。有意义的加工意味着对新词的记忆不应是被动的或机械的，学生应该全身心地投入到与他们的日常生活和兴趣紧密相连的学习活动中去。尽管有时候这些活动会耗费他们相当多的脑力，但学生仍然对这些活动表现出极大的兴趣。教师在教学中应该多设计和进行一些综合性的教学实践活动，让学生综合运用分析、比较、区别、评估等思维方式促进其内化。这种类型的活动包括但不限于交际型、任务型、问题解决型或语境型综合练习活动。

Stage 5: Generation. With the intensive and extensive practice of word recognition and application in the previous stages, learners finally reach the stage of using the target words, either orally or in writing, in a creative way. That is, they can use the word in their own language and with linguistic ease. At this stage, learners may still have not fully mastered all syntactic and semantic aspects of a word, but they can use the word with confidence and accuracy in most linguistic situations. At this stage, in order to help students gain skills in using the target word, instruction should provide opportunities in which students can use the word frequently at a discourse level.

第五阶段：生成阶段。经过先前四个阶段对词进行的强化且大量的认读和应用训练，学习者最终到达了能在口头和书面上创造性地运用目的词的阶段。也就是说，他们已经能得心应手地运用目的词进行自我表达了。在这一阶段，学习者可能还没有完全掌握目的词的句法和语义知识，但在大多数语境中，他们已经能自信地、准确地使用目的词了。因此，这一阶段的教学重点是为学生提供更多的机会，让他们能经常在会话语境中使用目的词。

The key features of the above discussed cognitive model of five-stage word acquisition are summarized in Figure 3-1. The model provides us with an outline of the psychological process undergone when learning new words. Instruction, in general, should observe this process and teaching activities should be designed accordingly for beginning level learners. Otherwise, learning could be time-consuming and inefficient. For example, if comprehension is not achieved, internalization will be quite labored. In teaching reality, this cognitive processing order may not proceed precisely in a linear fashion. Each stage may interact with other stages. For example, at the perception stage, establishing a clear and vivid mental image of a word may directly relate to internalization of the word. If a word is not well internalized due to interference from the sound, shape, or meaning of a previously learned similar word, then we should provide another chance for learners to perceive the target word and make sure that the students have a clear perception of the difference in sound, shape, or meaning between the target word and the similar word learned previously. Therefore, instruction often does not proceed strictly in a linear manner, from stage 1 to 5; rather, we should allow for regression to earlier stages.

图3-1总结了上述五阶段词语习得认知模式的关键特征。这个模式为我们勾勒了词语习得的心理认知过程。一般来说，教学应该遵循这一过程，并设计相应的教学活动，尤其是在初级词汇课上。否则，教学就会事倍功半。例如，如果学生的认知水平还没有到达理解阶段就让学生对新词进行内化，那内化过程就会变得费时费力。在实际的教学中，词语习得的这五个阶段可能不是直线式推进的，每个阶段之间其实是相互影响的。例如，在感知阶段建立的目的词心理图像如果清晰且生动的话，会直接影响该词的内化。如果一个词因受先前已经学过的音似词、形似词或义似词的干扰而没有很好地被学习者内化，那么教师应该再给学生提供一次感知目的词的机会，直到学生对目的词和相似词在音、形、义上的区别有了清晰的感知。所以说，教学并不是严格地按照从第一阶段

到第五阶段的顺序直线式推进的，它允许阶段之间的交互和回归。

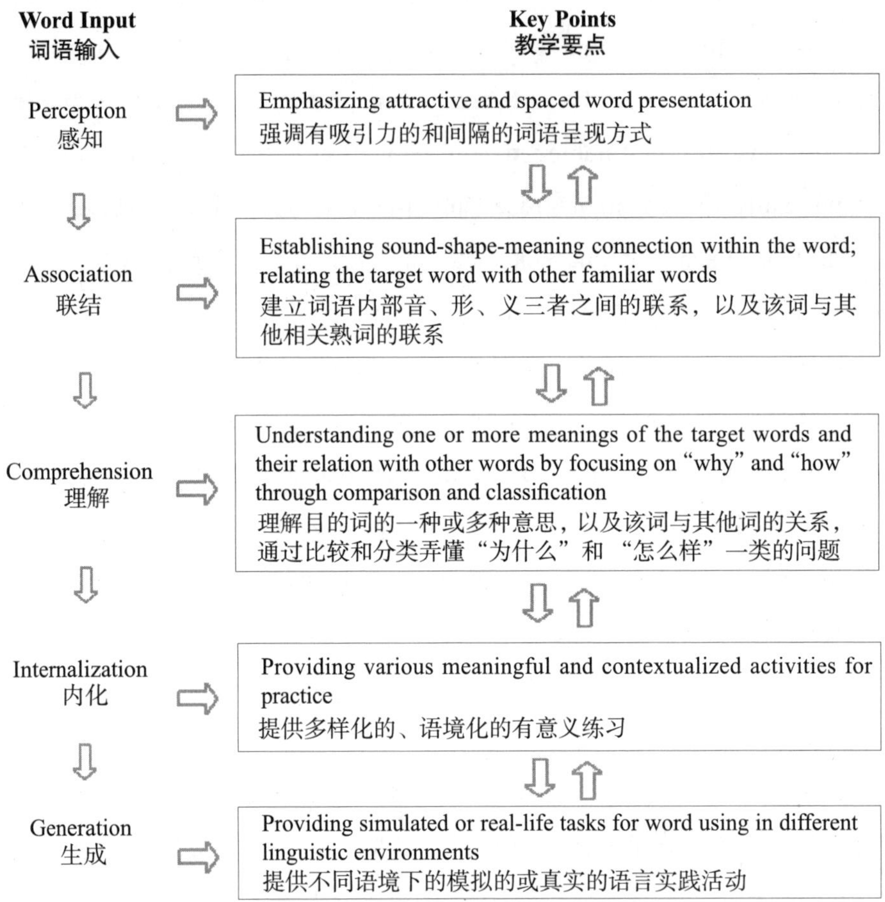

Figure 3-1　Cognitive Model of Five-stage Word Acquisition

图3–1　五阶段词语习得认知模式

3.1.2 Multilevel interactive-activation word identification model 多层次交互激活词语认读模式

One of the ultimate goals of word instruction is for learners to be able to recognize words automatically while reading. Naturally, we would like to know: after words are learned and stored in learners' long-term memory, how do learners identify the words when they encounter them in a reading text? Taft and Zhu (1997) proposed a multilevel interactive-activation model for word identification. This model holds that word recognition can happen at three different levels: word level, character level, and radical level. Take, for example, the word 睡觉, when it appears in 我昨天晚上很晚才睡觉，因为我要做作业. If the word 睡觉 is ready to be retrieved in a reader's mental lexicon, the whole word 睡觉 will be identified as the reader reads the sentence. However, if 睡觉 is temporarily not available for retrieval due to vague memory or because the reader may have confused this word with other words such as 瞌睡, 觉得, then the reader will look it as individual characters 睡 and 觉. Once the two characters are identified, the reader will try to put these together to figure out its meaning based on the meaning of the individual characters. During this process, it is possible that the individual character process may also help to activate the word 睡觉 because individual character access could serve as a retrieval cue for the word 睡觉. If the reader is not able to recall the individual character 睡 or 觉, then the reader will look at the radicals within the character and try to find clues to identify this character. For example, the radicals 目 and 垂 in the character may help to activate the meaning and sound of 睡, as 睡 is a phonetic-semantic compound in which 目 is a semantic radical and 垂 is a phonetic radical. However, 睡 is also an ideograph in which 垂 indicates a person sitting there with eyelids drooping down.

词语教学的终极目标之一是让学习者在阅读时达到词语认读自动化。我们自然想知道，当目的词存储到大脑的长时记忆系统中后，学习者在阅读文本中遇到该词时是怎样实现认读的。Taft 和 Zhu（1997）提出了一个多层次交互激活词语认读模式。这个模式认为，词语的认读可以在三种水平上进行——词水平、字水平和部件水平。以“睡觉”一词为例，如果句子“我昨天晚上很晚才睡觉，因为我要做作业”中的“睡觉”一词已经存储在读者的心理词库中，那么这个词是以整词的形式被提取和认读的。但是，如果读者记忆模糊或是把这个词与“瞌睡”“觉得”混淆在一起，在心理词库中一时找不到“睡觉”这个词，那么他就会将这个词辨认为“睡” 和 “觉”这两个字。一旦这两个字被辨认出来，读者会把这两个字合在一起并根据每个字的意思猜测“睡觉”的意思。在这一过程中，对单个字的辨认很可能会帮助读者想起“睡觉”这个词，因为“睡” 和 “觉”各自都可以成为“睡觉”的提取线索。如果读者辨认不出来“睡” 和 “觉”这两个字，那他会开始关注每个字中的部件，并尝试将部件作为线索来辨认汉字。例如，“睡”字中的部件“目”和“垂”可以帮助激活“睡”的字义和字音。因为“睡”是一个形声字，“目”是形旁，“垂”是声旁。当然，“睡”也是一个会意字，“垂”表示一个人坐在那儿，眼睑下垂，正在打盹儿。

The existence of radical level processing in word recognition was supported by an earlier study on adult character recognition, which revealed that the recognition process was affected by the number of perceptual components in the compound character. A character with fewer perceptual components was recognized more quickly. The author of the study concluded that stroke patterns (perceptual components) were the functional orthographic components in Chinese character recognition (Chen, Allport, & Marshall, 1996). Later studies also firmly supported the interactive-activation model for word identification. A study on lexical constituency model in reading Chinese (Perfetti, Liu, & Tan, 2005) concluded that because the radicals themselves are often standalone characters, they participate in both the word level and the “sublexical” level in word recognition: as a word at the higher level and as a potential cue to meaning or pronunciation at the sublexical level. The experimental studies on eye tracking during Chinese reading showed the existence of readers' parafoveal processing to radical-level semantic information extraction in reading compound characters (Yan et al., 2012). We must acknowledge the significance of the multilevel interactive-activation model for word identification for classroom instruction, because it, from a theoretical perspective, recognizes that radical knowledge plays an important role in character and word identification during reading.

Chen，Allport 和 Marshall（1996）早期进行的一项关于成人汉字认读的研究就证实了部件水平加工的存在。该研究表明了，汉字认读受合体字中知觉部件数量的影响，读者对知觉部件少的合体字认读更快。该研究认为，在汉字认读中，笔画模型（知觉部件）是功能性的缀字单位，之后的研究也得出了相似的结论。Perfetti、Liu 和 Tan（2005）的关于汉语语素的义项选择模式的研究表明，有些汉字部件本身可以独立成字，所以部件在汉字认读中参与两种水平的加工，一种是字水平的加工，另一种是部件水平的加工。部件水平的加工是为了给包含目的部件的字提供潜在的意义提示或发音线索。Yan 等人（2012）的眼动追踪实验研究表明，阅读合体字时，读者的眼球中央凹区域存在对部件的注视和语义信息提取。我们必须认识到，多层次交互激活词语认读模式对教学有着极为重要的意义，因为它在理论上证明了部件知识在字词认读中扮演着重要角色。

3.2 Psycholinguistic models on lexical access 词义提取的心理语言学模式

In this section, we will discuss psycholinguistic models on lexical access and the establishment of a lexical system. We will present two models. The first model is three-level interactive lexical access model which addresses the lower level processing during reading. The second model is CSL four-stage lexical development model which deals how CSL learners develop their vocabulary system.

接下来，我们将讨论阅读中词义提取的心理语言学模式和词汇系统的建立。我们主要介绍两种模式：第一种是三层次交互词义提取模式，该模式阐释了阅读过程中的低水平加工，即对字词的加工；第二种是汉语二语四阶段词汇系统发展模式，这一模式阐述了二语学习者是如何在大脑中建立汉语二语词汇系统的。

3.2.1 Three-level interactive lexical access model 三层次交互词义提取模式

Unlike alphabetic languages, in Chinese, the characters represent lexical morphemes—character boundaries rather than word boundaries are indicated by spaces. Therefore, processing Chinese words in a reading context includes at least three levels: character recognition, word segmentation, and lexical access (Shen, 2008).

与字母型语言不同，在汉语中，一个汉字基本上代表一个语素，但书写上字与字分开，而不是词与词分开。因此，在阅读过程中对词进行的加工至少分为三个层次：汉字辨认、断词和词义提取。（Shen，2008）

Character recognition is the activation of sound, shape, and meaning of individual characters in reading. As individual characters have multiple meanings, the exact meaning of a character in a reading text may not be determined at the initial stage. For example, when processing the sentence 我改天再去, the character 改 has meanings of *change*, *switch*, *transform*, *revise*, *alter*, etc. The reader may activate any of the multiple meanings of 改 during the character recognition process. When the second character 天 is recognized, the reader is able to choose a meaning for 改, as 改天 means "another day or an alternative day."

汉字辨认是指在阅读中激活汉字的音、形、义信息的过程。如果一个汉字有多个义项，那我们可能无法在汉字辨认的初始阶段就确定这个汉字在阅读文本中的确切意义。例如在加工句子"我改天再去"时，汉字"改"有"更改""转换""转化""修改""替换"等多个义项，读者在汉字辨认过程中有可能激活其中任何一个义项。只有当第二个字"天"被正确识读后，读者才能为"改"选择确切的义项，因为"改天"的意思是"另外一天或换一天"。

Word segmentation is to group relevant characters into lexical units and process them as words in ongoing reading. In the sentence 人人都说他是一个人才, deciding which is a word or not a word is not a straightforward task. We all know that 个人 (individual) is a word and 人才 (talented person) is also a word, but in this context, if we group 个人 together, it will lead to an inaccurate lexical access which results in inaccurate comprehension of the whole sentence.

断词是指在阅读中把相关的字组合在一起，并将之作为一个词进行加工的过程。例如，在"人人都说他是一个人才"这个句子中进行断词并不是一件简单的事，因为"个人"是一个词，"人才"也是一个词。但是在这个语境中，如果我们把"个人"组合在一起，那就会导致错误的词义提取，进而导致对句子的错误理解。

Lexical access refers to the process of gaining word meaning, syntactic properties, and pronunciation that best fit the context. The key for lexical access is to choose only a contextually relevant meaning for the word, to ensure successful comprehension of the reading text. Due to the linguistic factors that Chinese words consist of either one, two or more characters and individual characters have multiple meanings, readers in Chinese rely heavily on a more diffused, context-dependent strategy during reading for comprehension as opposed to a more focused word-dependent strategy often adopted by readers of alphabetic systems (Chen, 1992, 1999).

词义提取是指在阅读中获取适合上下文的词义、词的句法特征以及词的发音的过程。词义提取的关键是提取出那个与上下文语境相符的词义，只有这样才能确保阅读理解的准确性。汉语词可以由一个汉字构成，也可以由两个或两个以上的汉字构成，且有的汉字含有多个义项。正是因为汉语具有这样的语言学特点，所以与母语为字母型语言的读者采用的专注型词语依赖策略相对，汉语读者更倾向于采用分散的上下文依赖策略来确定词义。（Chen，1992，1999）

Now, let us further discuss how the three levels of cognitive processing, character recognition, word segmentation, and lexical access, interact with each other to complete lexical access during text reading. Let us first examine character recognition in a context. Studies (Mok, 2009; Shen & Li, 2012) reported that character recognition was faster when it was part of a word, no matter whether this word fits the meaning of the sentence, such as 人人in the sentence 人人都说他是一个人才. Recognition was slowest when the character was not part of a word or was grouped with other random characters such as in “人都” or “人他” situations. This evidence suggests that character recognition is the initial stage of lexical access, and the word context in which the character is embedded affects character recognition. As we mentioned earlier, the way in which characters are grouped to form a word is affected by the sentential context; therefore, initial word segmentation could be wrong. Readers will have to rely on the context information to confirm or disconfirm their decisions on word segmentation as they read. For example, in reading the sentence 人人都说他是一个人才, the reader may initially consider 人 as a word, but when the second and third characters are read, the reader will determine that 人人 should be a word. Under this type of circumstance, word decision is affected by the information obtained from the context. Word decision is based on the readers' comprehension of the individual character, but also on their initial comprehension of the context, although this comprehension is ongoing and not a final one. Thus, we can say that word segmentation is part of lexical access. A study on the segmentation of Chinese words during reading (Li, Rayner, & Cave, 2009) proposed a model of Chinese word segmentation. This model argued that Chinese word segmentation and word recognition are interactive processes involving top-down and bottom-up factors. The author proposed multiple levels for processing of words. The first level is a visual perception level that abstracts visual features from the stimulus. The second level is character recognition level, which recognizes characters using perceptual information from the first level and feedback information from the word recognition level. The third level is the word segmentation and recognition level, which receives information from both the character identification and the lexicon. This model shares many similarities with Shen's (2008) three-stage lexical access proposal. Based on existing studies, we present a three-level interactive lexical access model illustrated in Figure 3-2.

现在我们进一步探讨一下文本阅读中汉字辨认、断词、词义提取这三个层次的认知加工是如何相互作用完成词义提取的。我们先来讨论一下上下文中的汉字辨认。Mok（2009）以及 Shen 和 Li（2012）的研究表明，当目的字本身是词的一部分时，我们对该字的辨认速度较快，不管这个词是否适合句意，如“人人”在“人人都说他是一个人才”中；当目的字不是词的一部分，或者它跟其他字随机组合不成词时，我们对其辨认的速度最慢，如“人”随机组合成“人都”或“人他”时。这一证据表明，汉字辨认是词义提取的初级阶段，包含目的字的上下文语境会影响对该字的辨认。我们在前面提到过，汉字组合成词的方式取决于句子的语境，在没有理解句子的情况下，我们在初始阶段进行的断词可能是错误的，因此读者必须依赖语境信息来确认自己的断词决定是否正确。例如，在读句子“人人都说他是一个人才”时，读者最开始也许会把“人”看成一个词，但当读到第二个和第三个字时，读者便能确定“人人”应该是一个词。断词要受读者对上下文理解的影响：一方面，断词要基于读者对每个汉字的理解；另一方面，断词还要基于读者对上下文的初步理解，即使这种理解是不断变化的，不是最终的。因此我们可以说，断词也是词义提取的一部分。Li、Rayner 和 Cave（2009）在一篇关于汉语阅读断词研究的文章中提出了一个汉语断词模式。该模式认为，汉语断词和词语认读是一个“自上而下”与“自下而上”两种认知模式相结合的过程。研究者提出了多层次的词加工模式：第一层次是视觉感知，即提取出刺激物的视觉特征；第二层次是汉字辨认，即依靠从第一层次获得的感知信息和从第三层次断词和词语认读中获得的反馈信息辨认汉字；第三层次是断词和词语认读，第三层次的加工依赖于前两个层次的加工信息。这一研究与Shen（2008）提出的三层次加工说有很多相似之处。根据现有的研究成果，我们提出了三层次交互词义提取模式，具体请参看图3-2。

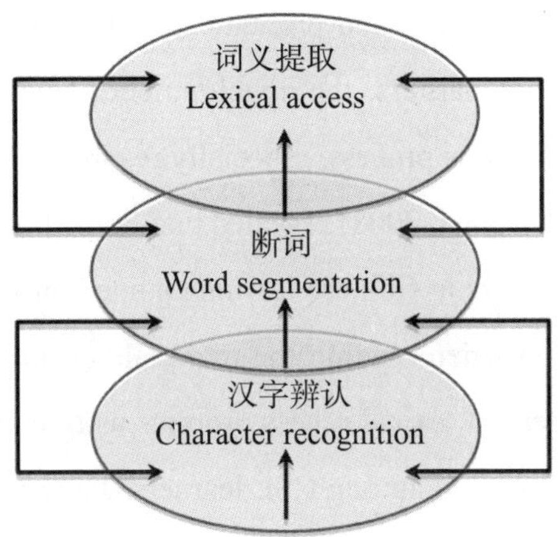

Figure 3-2 The Three-level Interactive Lexical Access Model

图 3-2 三层次交互词义提取模式

The model depicts the overlaps between the levels of character recognition and word segmentation and between the levels of word segmentation and lexical access. The pedagogical implication of this model is that word instruction should not stop at the place where students can identify words in isolation; rather, there is a continuum from recognizing individual characters to successful lexical access. Thus, context-based character instruction should be one of the important components of the entire word instruction.

从图3-2中我们可以看到，第一层次与第二层次有交叉重合，第二层次与第三层次也有交叉重合。这一模式对教学的启示是：词语教学不能满足于学生能正确地辨认汉字，教师还要认识到词语习得是一个从汉字辨认到词义提取的连续过程。因此，语境化汉字教学应该成为整个词语教学的重要组成部分。

3.2.2 CSL four-stage lexical development model 汉语二语四阶段词汇系统发展模式

We mentioned above that lexical access is the process of gaining word meaning, syntactic properties, and pronunciation that best fit the context. For English-speaking CSL learners, the development of word segmentation and lexical access skill is a slow process, especially regarding the aspect of semantic development. A study (Shen, 2008) revealed that English-speaking learners who completed 23 credit hours in Chinese learning gained only about 54% accuracy in word segmentation when reading the materials at their instructional level. This slow development of lexical access prompts us to take a closer look at the lexical development process among CSL learners. Jiang (2000) pointed out the two practical constraints on lexical development in L2 vocabulary instructional settings. One is the poverty of input in terms of both quantity and quality. For learners studying in a non-target language speaking environment, when a new word is introduced, the contextualized practice available is insufficient for learners to observe the changes of word meaning in various contextual situations. The other constraint is the presence of an established conceptual/semantic system that is closely associated with the L1 lexical system. That is, L2 learners rely on their L1 lexical system in learning new words in a second language, because the meanings of L2 words can be understood through their L1 translation. However, there is no perfect match for the meaning equivalence between L1 and L2. By pointing out the two constraints in lexical development, Jiang further proposed a three-stage L2 lexical development model. The first stage is the formal stage of lexical development. At this stage, the learner's attention is focused on the formal features of the word: its spelling and pronunciation, with little semantic, syntactic, or morphological information created or established within the lexical entry in the process. At this stage, the use of L2 words involves the activation of the links between L2 words and their L1 translations. The second stage is the L1 lemma mediation stage. In this stage, the use of L2 words is mediated by the lemmas of their L1 translations.

The last stage is the L2 integration stage. At this stage, a lexical entry in L2 will be very similar to a lexical entry in L1 in terms of both representation and processing. As the learners' experience in L2 increases, stronger associations are developed between L2 words and their L1 translations. The learners can simultaneously activate L2 word forms and their semantic and syntactic information of L1 equivalence. Jiang's model provided a general framework of lexical development for L2 as an alphabetic language. Inspired by Jiang's model, and based on CSL lexical accessing characteristics, we propose a four-stage Chinese L2 lexical development model: the L2-L1 direct mapping stage, L1 mediated generation stage, initial formation of the L2 lexical system stage, and full development of the L2 lexical system stage (please see Figure 3-3). We will discuss this model in detail below.

我们在前面提到过，词义提取是指在阅读中获取最适合上下文的词义、词的句法特征以及词的发音的过程。对于母语为英语的汉语二语学习者来说，断词和词义提取技能的提高是一个缓慢的过程，尤其是语义知识的增加。Shen（2008）的研究显示，母语为英语的大学汉语学习者修完23个汉语课程学分后，在阅读与他们的年级水平相当的材料时，断词的正确率只能达到54%左右。词义提取技能提高的缓慢性促使我们近距离地考察汉语二语学习者的词汇系统发展过程。Jiang（2000）指出，在二语词汇教学中存在两个制约学习者词汇系统发展的因素：一个是词汇输入在量和质上的不丰富。对于非目的语环境中的学习者来说，学习新词时，他们缺乏足够可以运用的语境化练习，也很少有机会观察到一个词在不同语境中的词义变化。另一个是已经建立的母语词汇系统的干扰。也就是说，学习者在学习二语中的新词时要依赖他们的母语词汇语义系统，即二语中新词的词义是通过母语的翻译获得的。但是这种翻译是不可靠的，因为母语与二语在词义上并不是完全对等的。指出了这两个制约因素之后，Jiang 进一步提出了一个三阶段二语词汇系统发展模式。第一阶段是形式阶段。在这一阶段，学习者将注意力基本集中在词的形式特征上，如拼写形式和发音，但对词的语义、句法和构词法特征则缺乏认识。在这一阶段，学习者对二语目的词的使用主要是通过激活目的词与母语翻译之间的联系而完成的。第二阶段是母语词目中介阶段（词目：词汇学中指列在西方词典中词条开头的词项）。在这一阶段，二语目的词的使用主要以母语词目为中介。最后一个阶段是二语词汇整合阶段。在这一阶段，二语词条在学习者头脑中的表征和加工形式达到了与母语相似的程度。随着学习者的二语词汇学习经验日趋丰富，母语词汇翻译系统与二语词汇系统之间建立了越来越紧密的联结。学习者在看到二语词时，可以同时激活对应的母语词的形式、语义和句法信息。Jiang 的模式为我们提供了字母型语言作为第二语言时的词汇系统发展总体框架。受到Jiang的模式的启发，同时又基于汉语二语词汇发展的特征，我们在这里提出一个四阶段汉语二语词汇系统发展模式。这四个阶段分别是：二语—母语直接对应阶段、母语为中介的生成阶段、汉语二语词汇系统形成的初级阶段以及汉语二语词汇系统完全发展阶段。具体请参看图3-3。下面我们将详细阐述这一模式。

Stage 1: L2-L1 direct mapping stage. At this stage, students learning Chinese target words heavily rely on L1 definitions and translations. They memorize word meanings based on L1 translations. Due to the very limited knowledge of the semantic aspect of target words, such as how many meanings a word may have, how and in which way a word can be connected with other words, the scope and restriction for using the word in context, etc., students hesitate to create sentences using newly learned target words and they feel more secure in memorizing sentences from the textbook and use these whenever it is possible, both inside and outside the classroom. At this stage, we may not observe many mistakes in students' word use.

第一阶段：二语—母语直接对应阶段。在这个阶段，学生学习汉语目的词主要依赖母语的解释与翻译。他们通过母语翻译来记忆汉语词的意思。学生由于对目的词的语义知识知之甚少，如不知道一个词有多少个义项，一个词与其他词是以什么样的方式联系在一起的，一个词在语境中的使用范围和限制是什么，等等，所以为了不犯错误，他们通常不会使用新学的目的词造句，而是选择背诵课文中的句子，并将之运用在课堂内外所有可以用的场合中。在这一阶段，我们可能很少发现学生在用词上的错误。

Stage 2: L1 mediated generation stage. As their Chinese vocabulary and syntactic knowledge increase, students gradually develop confidence to generate L2 sentences by using L2 target words. However, this generative process is still heavily mediated by L1. When they try to use the words in sentences, they will first work out a L1 sentence, then try to translate the L1 sentence into L2. Due to the drastic differences in semantics and grammar structure between L1 and L2, this L1 mediated, creative use of L2 words is often inaccurate. Due to limited communication opportunities in non-target speaking environments, L2 words are learned in the first stage mainly through association with L1 definitions or translations, rather than from the authentic linguistic context. Thus, we often observe various types of errors indicating that students are inappropriately applying learned orthographic, syntactic knowledge in word use. For example, a study (潘先军, 2002) reported that students try to use semantic radical knowledge to understand the meaning of 切 in the word 亲切. Because 切 has a semantic radical 刀, the students guessed that the word meaning for 亲切 is 自己砍 (one himself cuts). By analyzing this error, we can tell that the student was well aware of the role of the semantic radical in a compound character, but his semantic knowledge of the character 切 was still limited. A student may say that 我见面他, as a result of translation from the English sentence "I see him." because the learner is not aware of the grammatical restriction of the word 见面. In producing sentences, we can observe all kinds of mistakes due to inaccurate word use. A study on the development of semantic transfer in acquisition of L2 Chinese productive vocabulary (Shen, 2009) reported that English-speaking CSL learners who were beyond the intermediate level of Chinese study still heavily relied on their native language for productive vocabulary use. For example, a student would consider 这个词我学过，我认识是什么意思 as a correct sentence because 认识 can be translated into "to know" in English. Learners will not be able to correct these types of learning errors until they encounter a communication breakdown—in a situation where a native speaker or a more advanced learner points out the problem to the learner or they have opportunity to read correct expressions of using the target words in L2 reading texts.

第二阶段：母语为中介的生成阶段。随着学生汉语词汇知识和句法知识的增加，学生逐渐有了用汉语目的词进行造句的信心；但是在这个生成过程中，学生仍然十分依赖母语。当学生要用汉语目的词说一句话的时候，他们会先用母语说一下这句话，然后再把母语的句子翻译成汉语。但是，由于母语与汉语在语义和语法结构上有很大差异，学生生成的汉语句子通常会有错误。因为学生处于非目的语语言环境中，缺少与汉语母语者进行交流的机会，所以在第一阶段，他们主要是通过母语翻译来学习汉语词汇的，而不是从真实的目的语语境中习得的。我们经常会看到学生在用词上的各种错误，这些错误表明了学生在错误地运用学到的缀词知识和句法知识。例如，潘先军（2002）的研究发现，学生试图用表义部首知识理解汉字 "切"在"亲切"中的意思。因为"切"的表义部首是“刀”，学生就猜测“亲切”的意思是“自己砍”。从这个错误推断中我们可以看出，该生对表义部首在合体字中的作用已经有了很好的了解，但是对“切”的语义知识的了解仍然很有限。有的学生可能会说出“我见面他”这样的句子，这是因为学生直接把英文句子“I see him.”翻译成了中文，而没有意识到“见面”作为离合词的语法限制（即不可直接带宾语）。在学生生成的汉语句子中，我们可以看到许多错误都是由于用词不当。Shen（2009）针对汉语二语积极词汇习得中语义转换的发展进行了研究，研究结果显示，中级水平以上的母语为英语的汉语学习者在汉语积极词汇的运用中仍十分依赖他们的母语——英语。例如，学生会认为 “这个词我学过，我认识是什么意思”是一个正确的句子，因为“认识”的英文意思是“to know”。在这一阶段，学生是不会意识到这类错误的，除非他们在同汉语母语者或比他们更优秀的汉语学习者交流时对方指出了他们用词上的错误，或者他们在阅读中正好遇到了目的词的正确表达方式。

Stage 3: Initial formation of the L2 Chinese lexical system stage. As they continuously expand the breadth and depth of target vocabulary and increase their opportunities to use the target words in spoken and written communication, students gradually develop a L2 lexical system. During this stage, students rely less on their L1 for producing target language. They may not use L1 as mediation for the words that they feel quite confident to use, although they may still feel restricted in word using due to deliberately avoiding making mistakes. In general, they have a good sense of the differences in orthography, semantics, and syntax between L1 and L2. They understand the limitations of L1 mediation. As a result, they produce semantically and grammatically correct sentences, but obviously, their word use is not sophisticated and lacks variation.

We often observe these phenomena, where learners can present their ideas with considerable sophistication when using their native language, but when they switch to Chinese, we feel that they talk like elementary students.

第三阶段：汉语二语词汇系统形成的初级阶段。随着学生的汉语词汇知识在广度和深度上不断拓展，无论是在口头上还是在书面上，他们运用目的词的机会逐渐增多，他们的汉语二语词汇系统也在逐步形成。在这一阶段，学生在生成汉语句子时，对母语的依赖逐渐减少。对于有把握的词语，他们在使用时不再通过母语翻译，虽然为了避免犯错，他们在运用时还不是那么自如。总的来说，在这一阶段他们对母语与汉语在缀字（词）、语义、句法等方面的不同有了较好的认识，也认识到了母语翻译的局限性。他们能生成语义和语法都正确的汉语句子，但是很明显，他们的词语运用还不够熟练，生成的句子也缺少变化。我们会经常看到这些现象：学习者能用母语表达带有一定深度和复杂度的观点，但是当他们用汉语表达相同观点时，他们的表达水平就跟母语为汉语的小学生一样。

Stage 4: Full development of the L2 Chinese lexical system stage. At this stage, the learners no longer look like learners—they are skillful users of the target vocabulary and their language behavior is close to a Chinese native speaker. However, it is possible that most CSL learners are at the juncture of indefinitely approaching this stage, but never quite able to reach it if they do not have an opportunity to be immersed in a target language speaking environment for a prolonged period. Due to the complex nature of semantic aspects of the Chinese lexical system, it is not surprising that we may observe occasionally unconventional word usage for those CSL speakers who have studied and lived in China for three or more years.

Stage 4: Full development of the L2 Chinese lexical system stage
汉语二语词汇系统完全发展阶段

Features 特征

1. No L1 mediation is observed in word use 词语运用不再以母语为中介
2. Few error patterns are observed in word use 几乎没有规律性的用词错误
3. Chinese lexical system is well developed 汉语二语词汇系统已经完善

Stage 3: Initial formation of the L2 Chinese lexical system stage
汉语二语词汇系统形成的初级阶段

Features 特征

1. Fast growth of breadth and depth of target vocabulary 目的语词汇知识在深度和广度上快速增长
2. Chinese lexical system is formed, but lacks variation and sophistication 汉语二语词汇系统初步形成，但是比较简单，缺少变化
3. Use target words with confidence and seldom requires L1 mediation 能自信地运用目的语，很少借助母语翻译

Stage 2: L1 mediated generation stage
母语为中介的生成阶段

Features 特征

1. Start generalizing own sentences by using target words, but rely on L1 translation 开始用目的词造句，但是仍依赖母语翻译
2. Errors observed due to (1) lacking knowledge of incompatibility between L1 and L2 in syntax, semantics, and pragmatics; (2) over generalization 出现词语运用错误，原因有二：（1）缺乏母语和二语对应的句法、语义和语用等相关知识；（2）过度泛化

Stage 1: L2–L1 direct mapping stage
二语—母语直接对应阶段

Features 特征

1. Heavy reliance on L1 translation 十分依赖母语翻译
2. Rely on memorization of sentence patterns in word use 词语运用依靠对汉语句子的背诵
3. No obvious errors due to little generation in word use 因为很少生成汉语句子，所以很少有词语运用错误

L2 Chinese vocabulary input 汉语二语词汇输入

Figure 3-3 CSL Four-stage Lexical Development Model

图 3–3 汉语二语四阶段词汇系统发展模式

第四阶段：汉语二语词汇系统完全发展阶段。在这一阶段，学生的词语运用水平不再像个学习者，他们已经能够娴熟地使用汉语词汇，语言行为也与汉语母语者接近了。但是，大部分的汉语二语学习者如果没有在目的语环境中进行较长时间的沉浸式学习和生活的话，他们可能会一直处于不断接近这一阶段却永远到达不了这一阶段的过程中。由于汉语词汇语义系统的复杂性，我们不难发现，已经在中国生活和学习了三年甚至更长时间的二语学习者偶尔也会有用词不当的行为。

The proposed CSL four-stage lexical development model, although needs further validation and refinement, provides a general picture of learners' lexical development in vocabulary learning. Instructors must realize that vocabulary knowledge development is restricted by the psycholinguistic reality of the learners. Students' mistakes that we observe in the lexical development period reflect students' progress at each stage of lexical development. From this point of view, we welcome learning mistakes, because, by analyzing these mistakes, we can find which developmental stage the learner is currently at so that we can provide appropriate instructional intervention. The importance of instructional intervention is that it can facilitate the development. It can also arouse students' self-awareness of their problems during the development period.

虽然我们提出的汉语二语四阶段词汇系统发展模式仍需要进一步检验和完善，但它勾勒出了汉语二语学习者学习词汇时词汇系统发展的脉络。教师应该认识到，学习者词汇知识的增长是受制于其心理语言现实的。学生在二语词汇系统形成过程中出现的词语运用错误，也反映了其在词汇系统发展的不同阶段所取得的进步。从这个角度看，我们应该多关注学生学习过程中出现的错误，因为对这些错误的分析能让我们知道学生正处于词汇系统发展的哪个阶段，这样教师就可以进行适当的教学干预。教学干预的重要性在于，它不仅能促进各阶段的词汇系统发展，还能增强学生自己对用词错误的监控意识。

References 参考文献

潘先军. 2002. 形旁表意功能在留学生汉字学习中的负迁移及对策[J]. 汉字文化（3）：49-52.

Chen H-C. 1992. Reading comprehension in Chinese: implication from character reading times[M]. Chen H-C, Tzeng O J L. Language processing in Chinese. Amsterdam: Elsevier Science Publishers B.V. , 175-205.

Chen H-C. 1999. How do readers of Chinese process words during reading for comprehension[M]. Wang J, Inhoff A W, Chen H-C. Reading Chinese script: a cognitive analysis. Mahwah, NJ: Lawrence Erlbaum Associates, 257-287.

Chen Y P, Allport D A, Marshall J C. 1996. What are functional orthographic units in Chinese word recognition: the stroke or the stroke pattern? [J]. The quarterly journal of experimental psychology, 49A(4): 1024-1043.

Chung K K H. 2002. Effective use of Hanyu Pinyin and English translation as extra stimulus prompts on learning of Chinese characters[J]. Educational psychology, 22(2): 149-164.

Jiang N. 2000. Lexical representation and development in a second language[J]. Applied linguistics, 21(1): 47-77.

Li X, Rayner K. Cave K R. 2009. On the segmentation of Chinese words during reading[J]. Cognitive Psychology, 58(4): 525-552.

Mok L W. 2009. Word-superiority effect as a function of semantic transparency of Chinese bimorphemic compound words[J]. Language and cognitive processes, 24(7/8): 1039-1081.

Perfetti C A, Liu Y, Tan L-H. 2005. The lexical constituency model: some implications of research on Chinese for general theories of reading[J]. Psychological review, 112(1): 43-59.

Shen H H. 2008. An analysis of word decision strategies among learners of Chinese[J]. Foreign language annals, 41 (3): 501–524.

Shen H H. 2009.The development of semantic transfer in acquisition of L2 Chinese productive vocabulary[C]. Word Formation in Chinese, November. French Association for Chinese Teaching and Research, the University of Paris, Paris.

Shen W, Li X. 2012. The uniqueness of word superiority effect in Chinese reading[J]. Chinese science bulletin, 57(35): 3414–3420.

Taft M, Zhu X. 1997. Submorphemic processing in reading Chinese[J]. Journal of experimental psychology: learning, memory, and cognition, 23(3): 761–775.

Yan M, Zhou W, Shu H, et al.. 2012. Lexical and sublexical semantic preview benefits in Chinese reading[J]. Journal of experimental psychology: learning, memory, and cognition, 38(4): 1069–1075.

Chapter 4 第四章

Cognitive Theories and Chinese Character and Word Learning
认知理论与汉语字词学习

Cognitive science studies brain and brain function. From a cognitive perspective, the character and word learning process is a process whereby the brain processes information. How can we learn characters and words more efficiently and memorize them in a better way? The answer is that we should use cognitive information processing theories to guide our character and word instruction. In this chapter, we will discuss five cognitive theories that deal with information encoding, processing, and their relationship to character and word instruction, based on a previous study on this subject (沈禾玲, 2008). The five cognitive theories included in this chapter are: dual coding theory, cognitive load theory, level-of-processing theory, multisystem account theory, and competition theory.

认知科学研究大脑和大脑的功能。从认知角度看，字词学习的过程就是大脑加工信息的过程。我们怎样才能更有效地学习和记忆字词呢？答案是，我们应该用认知信息加工理论指导我们的汉语二语字词教学。在这一章，我们将以作者先前对这一课题的研究（沈禾玲，2008）为基础，讨论五种关于信息编码和加工的认知理论及其与字词教学的关系。

这五种认知理论分别是双编码理论、认知负荷理论、加工水平理论、多通道加工理论和竞争理论。

4.1 Dual coding theory 双编码理论

In Chapter 3, we discussed the cognitive model of five-stage word acquisition. The first stage of word acquisition is perception. After a word or a character is initially perceived by the learner and registered in the brain, the encoding process immediately follows. **Encoding** is the process by which information in one form is converted into another form, to be communicated using a set of methods or rules. For example, a written passage is coded with numbers and sent to another person by telegraph. Therefore, a code is a method to be used to transform a message into another form. From the character/word-learning viewpoint, encoding is a strategy or method used to process characters and words so that they can be easily comprehended and memorized by individuals.

在第三章，我们讨论了五阶段词语习得认知模式。这一模式的第一阶段是感知阶段。字词信息一旦被学习者感知到并注册到大脑中后，编码就立即开始了。**编码**是根据一定的方法或规则，将信息从一种形式转换成另一种形式的过程。例如，一段书面话语可以以数字的形式进行编码，然后通过电报传给另一个人。因此，“码”是转换信息形式所用的方法。从字词学习的角度看，编码就是运用某种策略或方法对字词进行加工，使它们容易被个体理解和记忆的过程。

Dual coding theory initially was proposed by Paivio (1969). The theory assumes that there are two cognitive subsystems in the brain, a nonverbal system specialized for dealing with nonlinguistic objects and events, and a verbal system specialized for dealing directly with language. The two systems function independently, but they are interconnected. Cognition involves the cooperative activity of the two systems (Paivio, 1986). The theory assumed three levels of meaning processing for incoming information: representational meaning, referential meaning, and associative meaning. (1) **Representational meaning** is obtained from either verbal or non-verbal representations of the information. In other words, the understanding of the new information is through verbal definition (logogen), or through imagery representation of the information (imagen). (2) **Referential meaning** is derived from the relationship between the verbal system and the nonverbal system. That is, understanding of new information occurs through the connection between the verbal definition and image of the new information. (3) **Associative meaning** is gained by activation of representations within the same verbal or nonverbal system (Paivio, 2007). A given task may require any or all of the three levels of processing in order to comprehend it. To give a concrete interpretation of the three levels of meaning processing, We use 同学 *classmate* as an example. If 同学 is presented as new information, representational meaning of it can be gained either through presenting a definition such as 同学是跟你一起学习的人 (a verbal representation) or by a picture of a person sitting in the same classroom with you (a nonverbal representation). The referential meaning is obtained by building a connection between the verbal description of 同学 and the picture of 同学, so that we know that both the verbal and imagery representations of 同学 are pointing to the same concept 同学. The associative meaning is accessed by understanding the connection of 同学 with other definitions or concepts within the verbal system, as well as within the nonverbal system. For example, 同学 is the person who sits in a classroom with you. It could be the person who studies with you in any time at any learning situation. It also could be a person who is not physically present, but who is in the same group with you via a distance learning setting. Within the imagery system, images of all types of 同学 in all types of learning situations could be activated as representations of 同学 in the learner's mind. Therefore, the concept 同学 is connected with many related situations such as classroom, school, teacher, or distance education, either in the verbal or nonverbal system.

双编码理论最早是由 Paivio（1969）提出来的，这一理论假设人的大脑中有两个认知子系统：一个是非语言系统，专门对非语言事物和事件进行加工；另一个是语言系统，专门对语言信息进行加工。这两个系统独立运行，但又相互联系。认知活动需要这两个系统互相合作。（Paivio，1986）双编码理论假设大脑对输入信息的意义加工分为三种水平：表征意义、参照意义和联想意义。（1）**表征意义**是大脑对语言或非语言信息的直接表征。换句话说，对新信息的理解是通过语言定义（概念）或意象展示（具象）获得的。（2）**参照意义**是通过建立语言系统和非语言系统之间的关系获得的。也就是说，对新信息的理解是通过语言定义所传递的信息与意象展示所传递的信息之间的联系获得的。（3）**联想意义**则是通过建立语言定义系统和意象系统内部表征信息之间的联系获得的。（Paivio，2007）对特定信息的理解可能需要一种水平的意义加工，也可能同时需要三种水平的意义加工。举个例子，如果"同学"是一个新词，其表征意义的获得可以通过给这个词下定义——"同学是跟你一起学习的人"（概念表征），也可以通过展示一张跟你坐在同一间教室的人的照片（具象表征）。参照意义是通过在大脑中让"同学"的概念表征与具象表征联系起来而获得的，这样我们就知道概念表征和具象表征指的是同一个信息——"同学"。联想意义是通过在语言定义系统和意象系统内部建立"同学"这个概念或具象与其他概念或具象的关系而获得的。例如，在语言定义系统中，"同学"可以是现在在教室里和你一起学习的人，可以是在任何时间段任何学习单位与你在一起学习的人，也可以是不跟你在一起但是与你在同一时间段通过远程教学一起学习的人。在意象系统中，各种学习形式中的“同学”意象被激活后都可以作为学习者对“同学”的表征具象。这样一来，“同学”这一概念在语言系统或非语言系统中都与其他许多事物发生着联系，如与教室、学校、教师、远程教学等之间的联系。

“Dural codes” refer to verbal code and imagery code. The two codes are used by individuals to process incoming information for comprehension. To give an example, giving a verbal definition for the concept “同学” is to use verbal code, while presenting a photo of “同学” is to use imagery code. Imagery code can be in different formats: visible format such as pictures and mental images, and invisible formats such as sound images, kinesthesia, tactile images, and emotional experiences. According to dual coding theory, any information can be encoded as verbal or imagery representation. If both verbal and imagery encoding methods are used, it will result in better learning and memorization than single coding (either verbal or imagery code). The reason is simple, as dual codes provide dual cues for recall. Thus, when newly learned information is recalled from the brain, if one code is lost, the brain still can use the other code to retrieve the information. That means when the word 同学 is presented, a learner can recognize this word by recalling the encoding cue, the verbal description of this word. If this cue is lost (forgotten), the learner can use an imagery cue, the picture of 同学, to retrieve the information needed for recognizing the word.

“双码”指的是把信息转化成个体所能够理解的语言码和意象码。例如，对“同学”下定义是语言码，一张同学的照片则是意象码。意象码可以是看得见的形式，如图片、心理图像；也可以是看不见的形式，如声觉、动觉、触觉以及情感体验。双编码理论认为，任何信息都可以用语言或意象两种形式表征。如果语言和意象两种表征形式同时运用，那么我们对信息的记忆就会优于只用一种表征形式的（只用语言码或只用意象码）。原因很简单，因为双编码为回忆提供了双重的提示线索。当新信息在大脑中被提取时，如果大脑暂时遗忘了其中一种编码，那么还可以用另一种编码提取信息。也就是说，当“同学”这个词呈现在学习者面前时，学习者可以通过回忆这个词的定义识别该词；如果暂时忘记了该词的定义，学习者还可以通过意象提示，如“同学”的照片，激活对该词的记忆，达到识别该词的目的。

Pedagogical implications 教学应用

Dual codes not only help with comprehension but also help with information retention and retrieval. Thus, by applying the dual coding theory to vocabulary instruction, we should use dual codes (both verbal and imagery codes) when introducing new words. This will allow students to dual-encode the new words.

双编码不仅有助于对信息的理解，而且还有助于对信息的保持和提取。将双编码理论应用在词汇教学中，意味着我们在向学生教授生词时就应该使用双编码（语言码与意象码），这样学生才能运用双编码对生词进行加工。

A study (Shen, 2010a) compared the learning effects of two instructional encoding methods in Chinese word instruction among English-speaking beginning college CSL students. One instructional method used verbal encoding only, and the other used verbal encoding plus imagery encoding.

Learning of both concrete words and abstract words was examined under these two encoding methods. When compared with the verbal encoding method, the verbal plus imagery encoding method did not show any superior effect in retention of the sound, shape, and meaning of concrete words, but a statistically significant difference was found for retention of the shape and meaning of abstract words. This confirms the effectiveness of dual encoding in Chinese word acquisition. The author explained the reason why we did not see a significant positive effect of dual encoding in learning concrete words. In teaching those concrete words, although the visual images were not presented to students in the control group, it was very possible that because of the concrete nature of these words, the students recalled mental images of these words that had previously been stored in their mental photo albums. During the instruction, when students saw these words, the relevant mental images were activated. To cite an example, when the word 起床 was introduced, an image of a person getting up from a bed could be evoked based on students' past experiences. For the abstract words, mental images were not readily retrieved from the students' mental photo album; therefore, the presence of visual images greatly facilitated encoding the words with imagery codes. The study reported that dual codes led to a better retention of the shape and meaning of the abstract words, but not the sound of the abstract words. Why? As mentioned earlier, Chinese lacks sound-to-spelling correspondence. In the study, the imagery coding method used imagery codes, but not acoustic ones; hence, there was no effect in retaining of the sound of words. By understanding this, in using dual codes for words instruction, especially for abstract words, we may consider three issues. One is that instruction should provide visual images such as pictures and visual actions to accompany the word, in addition to verbal explanations. Sometimes, presenting a single concrete picture for an abstract word may not be possible; thus, it would be helpful if diagrams (including figures and charts) are presented to help students comprehend the word. The second is that to help students learn the sound of words, instruction must place weight on using methods that enhance acoustic encoding or evoke acoustic images, together with other encoding methods. A study showed that when using electronic flashcards programmed with pronunciation of new words, it had a significant positive effect on memorization of the sound of new words (Zhu, Fung, & Wang, 2012). Thus, in addition to the practice of sounding out individual words, online or offline activities such as categorizing words according to the similarities and differences in initial sounds, final sounds, tones, or searching phonetic radicals in new words based on given sounds should be encouraged. These types of activities help students recognize patterns of pronunciation for words and allow students to be exposed to the sound of words and to practice them in a meaningful way. Another aspect is that instruction should not focus solely on new words at the representational meaning level; rather, it should lead to the associative level. Activities that help students to establish associations between the new words and learned words as well as other related items in both verbal and nonverbal systems should be followed after initial presentation of the new words.

Shen（2010a）比较了两种教学编码方式对母语为英语的成人汉语初级学习者词语学习的影响，一种是只用语言码进行教学，另一种是同时运用语言码和意象码进行教学，然后比较这两种编码方式在学习具体词与抽象词时的效果。在学习具体词时，两种编码方式在词的音、形、义的保持上没有统计上的显著差异；但是在抽象词的形和义的保持上，双编码教学的效果要明显优于语言码教学。这一结果证实了双编码教学在汉语词语教学中的有效性。在具体词的教学中，教师虽然只用语言码进行教学，没有向学生展示具体词的视觉图像，但由于具体词的具体性，学生大脑中很可能已经存储了关于这些词的心理图像。当学生看到这些词时，相应的心理图像就会被激活。这也是作者认为在具体词的教学中双编码教学未显示出显著效果的原因。例如，学生在学习“起床”这个词时，因为之前有过相关经验，所以过去存储的“一个人从床上起来”的心理图像会从大脑中激活。但是在学习抽象词时，学生大脑中并没有存储现成的心理图像，所以教学中展示的视觉图像会在很大程度上帮助学生对抽象词进行意象编码。但是，为什么双编码教学有助于对抽象词形和义的保持，而对音的保持却没有帮助呢？就像之前提到的，这是因为汉语本身缺乏音形之间的联系。该研究在用意象码进行教学的时候，只用了视觉意象，而没用听觉意象，所以我们看不到双编码教学对词中每个字音的保持效果。了解了这一点，我们在运用双编码进行词语教学时，尤其是在教授抽象词时，应该注意以下三点：第一，教学除了要用定义解释词语外，还应该提供关于词语的图像或视觉化动像等信息。有时候，我们很难为抽象词找到一张对应的图片，这时教师可以自己设计一些图表帮助学生理解。第二，为了帮助学生更好地学习词语的发音，教师应该运用其他编码方式设计一些能提高学生听觉编码能力和激活学生听觉意象的活动。Zhu、Fung 和 Wang（2012）的研究表明，在初级汉语课上运用有生词发音设置的电子词卡辅助教学在帮助学生记忆生词发音上有显著的效果。因此，除了让学生朗读生词之外，教师还可以运用线上与线下的多种教学活动引导学生关注生词的发音并进行有意义的练习，比如根据声母、韵母或声调的异同给生词分类，或根据所给的音节找出合体字的声旁。第三，在教授生词时，我们的教学活动不能只停留在表征意义加工水平上，还要引导学生达到联想意义加工水平。在完成表征意义的加工后，教师应该将教学重点放在帮助学生建立新词与相关旧词的联系，以及目的词与其他相关概念和意象的联系上。

4.2 Cognitive load theory 认知负荷理论

Cognitive load theory is an instructional theory initially proposed by Sweller (1988), which is based on Miller's limited capacity of short-term memory concept (Miller, 1956). One of revolutionary human memory models is the Atkinson-Shiffrin Model proposed by Atkinson and Shiffrin (1968). This model proposed a three-stage human memory system; that is, information is processed by a memory system through three stages. The first is a sensory register for storing incoming information for a few seconds. This information is then transferred to the second stage, short-term memory, for encoding. As information is encoded in the short-term memory, short-term memory also is referred to as working memory. At this stage, information can be held for about 30 seconds without repetition. Once the encoding is completed, the information will be passed to the third stage, long-term memory, where information can be stored forever if given enough rehearsal. Cognitive load refers to instructional load (or knowledge load) placed in the memory system. The cognitive load theory studies the cognitive load placed in the working memory. As the capacity of working memory is limited, overloading the working memory will negatively affect learning.

认知负荷理论作为一种教学认知理论最初是由Sweller（1988）提出的，它的基点是Miller（1956）的短时记忆容量有限理论。Atkinson和Shiffrin（1968）曾经提出过一个具有划时代意义的记忆模式——Atkinson-Shiffrin记忆模式。这个模式认为，信息在大脑记忆系统中要经过三个阶段的加工。第一阶段是瞬时记忆。这一阶段大脑能存储新输入的信息，但只能保持大概几秒钟。之后信息被转入第二阶段——短时记忆中进行编码，短时记忆也被称作“工作记忆”。在这一阶段，如果大脑不对信息进行重复编码的话，信息只能在大脑中保持30秒左右。一旦编码完成，信息就被转入第三阶段——长时记忆中。在这一阶段，如果我们能够对信息进行充分的复现，那么信息就可以永久地保存在大脑中。认知负荷，指的是附加在记忆系统之上的教学负荷（或知识负荷）。认知负荷理论主要研究工作记忆中的认知负荷，因为工作记忆的容量有限，认知超负荷会降低学习效率。

Three types of cognitive loads could affect efficiency of the working memory (Paas, Renkl, & Sweller, 2003). The first type is **intrinsic cognitive load**. This refers to the amount of learning materials for a specific class. Reducing the amount of learning materials will reduce the intrinsic cognitive load. In addition, compared with a poorly organized lesson, even if the amount of information is the same, a well-organized lesson with high element interactivity (elements of learning materials are interconnected) will reduce the intrinsic cognitive load. In order to eliminate intrinsic cognitive load without sacrificing information volume in a given lesson, the instructor should make an effort to reorganize the lesson to increase its level of internal interactivity. The second type of cognitive load is the **extraneous cognitive load**. This type of load is caused by inappropriate ways of presenting teaching materials to students. Put simply, the instructor's use of inappropriate teaching methods or procedures makes the materials more difficult to learn or causes unnecessary learning. The third type of cognitive load is **germane (effective) cognitive load**. In contrast to the extraneous cognitive load, the germane cognitive load represents the pedagogically sound and well-designed instructional methods or procedures used during instruction. This type of cognitive load enhances learning.

有三种认知负荷会影响工作记忆的效度。（Paas，Renkl，and Sweller，

2003）第一种是**内在认知负荷**。这种认知负荷是指具体一堂课中学习材料的量。减少学习材料的量就能减少学生的内在认知负荷。除此之外，在课文信息量相同的情况下，内容组织有序、内在互动性强的课文给学生带来的内在认知负荷要少于内容组织无序的课文带给学生的。为了在课文信息量保持不变的条件下减少学生的内在认知负荷，教师应该在课前对课文内容进行重组，增强课文内容的条理性和互动性。第二种是**外在认知负荷**。这种认知负荷是因为教师不恰当地组织教学而人为地增加了学习材料的难度，学生不得不花更多时间和精力去学习而造成的。第三种是**有效认知负荷**。与外在认知负荷相对，有效认知负荷表示教师在教学中采用了合理的教学方法和教学步骤。这种认知负荷能促进教学效果的提升。

Sweller (1994) pointed out that two critical learning mechanisms can be used to evaluate what is learned. One is schema acquisition and the other is the *automaticity* in the information process. A **schema** is a cognitive constructor organizing the elements of information according to an individual cognitive style. Human brain does not store information arbitrarily; rather, information is stored in an organized fashion. The knowledge stored in the brain is just like the books stored in a library, which are well organized so that they can be retrieved easily when needed. When a new book is acquired, the librarian will classify it into an existing category. If there is no existing category, then a new category will be created. The schema has the similar structure of categories in our memory. To give an example, when the new word 同学 is introduced, we could put it in our mental lexicon under a school category, based on meaning classification; we could also put it under a noun category based on classification of part of speech; or we could put in another specified category based on each individual preference. The key to schema acquisition is to establish connections between new knowledge and existing knowledge, so that new knowledge can be stored in an organized way.

Sweller（1994）指出，学习的有效性可以通过两个关键机制衡量：一个是图式习得机制，另一个是信息加工的自动化机制。**图式**是个体按照个人的认知风格组织信息的一种认知结构。人的大脑不是随机地、无组织地存储信息的，而是以一种高度组织化的方式存储信息。我们大脑中存储的知识就像图书馆里收藏的图书一样，它的排列是有序的，所以提取也很方便。当图书馆收到一本新书后，图书管理员就会把它归入已有的某个类别中；如果现有的分类不适合新书，那么图书管理员就会给新书新建一个类别。人脑中的图式也是根据相似的原理组织信息的。例如，学了新词 "同学" 后，我们可以根据意义之间的联系把它归到心理词库中的学校类别里，也可以根据词性把它归到名词类别里，或是根据个人的偏好把它归到其他的指定类别里。图式习得的关键是建立新知识与旧知识之间的联系，这样一来，新知识就可以有组织地被存储起来了。

Automaticity refers to processing of information automatically using learned knowledge without extra effort. After the word 同学 is learned, a learner is asked to read the sentence 生日晚会上，很多同学都来了，但是我的同桌没有来. How does the learner process the word 同学? One situation is the controlled process. The learner may search hard from the memory and try to recall the pronunciation and meaning of the word 同学. After several seconds of thinking, the learner recognizes the word and decodes its meaning. Another situation is automatic processing. The learner does not need to pay particular attention to the word 同学, he/she can effortlessly recognize this word. According to Sweller (1994), effective instruction leads students toward schema acquisition and automatic processing of knowledge. Any instructional activity that deviates from schema acquisition and automatic processing is considered extraneous cognitive load and should be reduced.

自动化是指在不需要额外努力的情况下，学习者就能用已经学过的知识对信息进行自动加工。例如，学完了“同学”一词后，学习者在阅读“生日晚会上，很多同学都来了，但是我的同桌没有来”这个句子时，是如何对“同学”这个词进行加工的呢？一种情况是控制型加工，即学习者要在大脑中努力地搜索这个词并回想它的音和义，经过几秒钟的思考后识别出这个词。另一种情况是自动加工，即学习者不需要对这个词多加关注就能毫不费力地将它识别出来。根据Sweller（1994）的研究，有效的教学能引导学生建立图式，最后达到对信息加工的自动化。任何不利于图式习得和加工自动化的教学活动都属于外在认知负荷，都应该尽量避免。

Pedagogical implications 教学应用

By applying the cognitive load theory to character/word instruction, classroom instruction should make efforts on the following aspects.

将认知负荷理论应用在字词教学上，我们在课堂教学中可以从以下几方面着手：

• Control the amount of vocabulary input to maintain a suitable intrinsic cognitive load

控制生词输入量，保持适当的内在认知负荷

Since the capacity of working memory is limited, students cannot process too many new words in a given time period. What amount of vocabulary is suitable for students in a single class period? There is no simple answer to this question as it depends on individual differences. However, the instructor can find out a baseline based on the vocabulary quiz performance. If the mean accuracy rate reaches 90% or more on a vocabulary test, this means the current vocabulary input amount is suitable for the students. If the accuracy rate either increases or declines, then the instructor should consider increasing or reducing the amount of weekly vocabulary learning. Another way is to have separate requirements for word recognition and production for beginning level learners. For instance, we can test students on all new words in the lesson for recognition, but only part of the new words for production. This approach is being adopted by more and more universities in the United States. As we discussed earlier that computer writing is quickly replacing handwriting, introducing computer writing and designing appropriate computer-supported character writing exercises will help reduce unnecessary intrinsic cognitive load in vocabulary learning.

工作记忆的容量是有限的，因此学生无法在给定的时间内加工太多的生词。那么，在一堂课上学生到底学多少个生词才是适量的呢？这个问题没有固定的答案，因为答案受学生之间个体差异的影响。但教师可以通过学生的生词测验成绩找到一个基本量：如果全班学生生词测验的平均正确率在90%以上，这说明当前的生词量是适当的；如果平均正确率比90%高或低，那么教师应该考虑增加或减少每周的生词学习总量。另一种办法是，在初级阶段对学习者的生词教学采取认读与默写分流的做法。例如，我们可以要求学生认读课文中所有的生词，但是只要求其写出其中的一部分即可。现在越来越多的美国大学开始采用这种教学方法。我们在前面提到过，电脑打字正在快速取代手写汉字。教师教会学生用电脑打字，并设计一些合适的电子的字词练习活动，可以减少学习者词汇学习过程中不必要的内在认知负荷。

• Minimize extraneous cognitive load 减少外在认知负荷

The cognitive load theory suggests that effective instructional materials (with high level of interactivity and cross reference between the components) will lead to effective learning because it will direct learners' cognitive resources toward activities that are relevant to learning rather than toward preliminaries to learning (Sweller, 1991). However, in some situations, the instructor may find that the lessons to be used in the class are poorly organized. Learners would have to put in great effort mentally to integrate the materials in order to comprehend the new words. To reduce the preliminary learning activities, the instructor should organize the learning materials into integrated formats so that they can be easily understood by learners. In a traditional classroom, the instructor introduces vocabulary according to the sequence that the vocabulary appears in the glossary and explains the words one by one. This type of method obviously increases extraneous cognitive load, as the new words are not well integrated, which may require memorization of new words in isolation. To minimize the extraneous cognitive load, we strongly suggest that the words be grouped based on meaningful categorization before presenting them to students. The instructor may review all the new words to be introduced and decide how to group them. For example, if a lesson is about "travel," the teacher could group the words according to the sequence of travel, such as prior to travel, during travel, and post-travel. When introducing the word group "Prior to travel," the instructor could introduce the words based on the theme "things we need to do prior to travel." Therefore, students could use this theme as a memory peg, to build interconnections among the words such as 地图, 旅行社, 航空公司, 订票, 售票员, 护照, 签证. There are many ways of integrating the new words for instruction—any creative way of integrating the new words for better comprehension from students should be encouraged. We will discuss this topic in detail in Chapter 6.

认知负荷理论告诉我们，有效的教学材料内部应该具有高度的互动性和参照性，这样的教学材料才能有助于学习，因为只有这样的教学材料才可以直接将学习者的认知资源引向与学习相关的活动而不是那些学习准备活动。（Sweller，1991）但是有时候教师会发现要教授的课文并不是那么有条理的，学生需要花费很大的精力做一些学习准备活动才能清楚教学材料之间的内在联系，才能理解新词。为了减少学生所做的这些学习准备活动，教师应该在课前对教学材料进行适当的处理，使之系统化，容易被学生理解。在传统课堂上，教师一般都是根据生词在生词表中的顺序一一讲解生词的。这种方式明显会增加学生的外在认知负荷，因为生词之间的排列缺少内部联系，学生只能按照生词表中的顺序孤立地记忆生词。为了减少学生的外在认知负荷，我们强烈建议教师在展示生词前，先将生词进行意义分类再分组呈现。教师可以先看一下要讲的生词有哪些，然后再考虑如何进行分类。例如，如果课文是关于“旅行”的，教师可以按旅行的顺序把生词分成三组：旅行前、旅行中和旅行后。在介绍“旅行前”这一组生词时，教师可以根据主题“旅行前要做的事”介绍生词。这样一来，学生就可以以这个主题为记忆支点建立“地图、旅行社、航空公司、订票、售票员、护照、签证”等词之间的内在联系。教学中有很多对生词进行分类的方法，如果学生自己想出来了一种有新意的、能帮助他们更好地理解和记忆生词的分类方法，我们应该给予鼓励。我们在第六章还会详细讨论如何在教学中对生词进行认知分组这一问题。

• Focus on establishing a schema 注重图式的建立

In designing word learning activities, efforts can be made on establishing a schema in learners' brain by paying attention to the following aspects:

(1) connecting the target word with a previously learned word by finding connections to sound, shape, and meaning; (2) connecting the target word with students' relevant life experiences; (3) connecting the target word with the other words in the same lesson; (4) sorting the newly learned words into different categories based on students' own classification rules; (5) presenting the target word in different linguistic contexts and then having students discuss how the target word is used in different linguistic situations; (6) providing real or simulated real-life situations for students to use target words for spoken and written communication.

在设计词语教学活动时，教师可以从以下几方面着手帮助学生在大脑中建立相关图式：（1）将目的词与先前学过的词联系起来，找出二者在音、形、义上的联系；（2）将目的词与学生个人的相关生活经历联系起来；（3）将目的词与同一篇课文中的其他词联系起来；（4）让学生根据自己的需要和特点对新词进行分类；（5）让目的词在不同语境中出现，引导学生探讨目的词在不同语境中的意思；（6）提供真实的或模拟的语言环境，让学生通过说和写的形式运用目的词。

• Strive for automaticity 力争自动化

Newly learned words will not be transferred to long-term memory for later automatic recognition without frequent review and substantial practice. Therefore, the instructor should provide sufficient activities to allow students to practice newly introduced words in the classroom. After a group of words are introduced, review activities should follow prior to introducing the next group of new words. Towards the end of class, comprehensive review activities should be provided to have students review all the words introduced in the class. To keep students highly motivated, the review activities should vary in their format and should progress from simple to comprehensive. Once a new lesson is completed, the teacher may purposefully design word learning activities for the next lesson which allows students to use words learned from the previous lesson when engaging in new learning activities.

如果没有进行频繁的复习和足够的练习，新学习的生词是无法转入长时记忆中以备需要时自动提取的，因此教师应该在课堂上安排足够多的活动，让学生充分练习新学习的生词。每一组生词学习完以后，教师要先安排复习活动，之后再学习下一组生词。临近下课，教师应该安排一些综合性的复习活动，让学生对该课的所有生词进行全面的复习。为了保持学生的积极性，复习活动的形式应该多样化，并体现出由简单到复杂的变化。新课学完后，教师还可以在下一课的教学中有意识地设计一些活动，让学生在新课的学习中能用到上一课学到的词语。

4.3 Level-of-processing theory 加工水平理论

Level-of-processing theory presents a memory model of how memory traces are passed through an information-process structure. Specifically, it is about how to process information in order to leave deep traces in the memory. Deep processing will enhance memorization and facilitate retrieval. This level-of-processing theory was initially proposed by Craik and Lockhart (1972). Rehearsal is well known to be the key that allows transfer of information from working memory to long-term memory. However, Craik and Lockhart hold that memory was enhanced more by depth of processing than by how long or how often the information was rehearsed. In other words, rehearsal is effective only when done in a deep and meaningful fashion. The theory suggests that memory occurs on a continuum from shallow to deep, with no limit on the layers of levels, but it is distinguishable in regard to shallow, intermediate, and deep levels (Craik & Lockhart, 1972).

加工水平理论是阐述信息加工过程中记忆痕迹是如何形成的这样一种记忆模式。具体地说，就是信息如何加工才能在记忆系统中留下比较深的痕迹。深加工才能提高信息的记忆效果，进而有利于信息的提取。加工水平理论最初是由Craik和Lockhart（1972）提出的。我们都知道，复现是把信息从工作记忆转入长时记忆的关键，但是Craik和Lockhart 认为，记忆的加深取决于信息的深度加工而不是复现的频度和时间长度。换句话说，有效的复现其实是对知识进行有深度、有意义的加工。这一理论认为，记忆是一个由浅到深的持续加工过程，我们虽然分不出到底有多少个层次，但是基本上能区分出三种水平的记忆加工，即浅度加工、中度加工和深度加工。（Craik and Lockhart，1972）

Shallow level processing involves analysis of physical and sensory characteristics. At this level, information is usually processed discretely and mainly by rote memorization. To give an example, for the word 政治, the learner may know its pronunciation zhèngzhì, but may not know the connection of the pronunciation with the components within the characters. The learner has memorized the definition of 政治 "social relations involving intrigue to gain authority or power," but really do not understand what this means. The intermediate level of memory relates to recognition and labeling. Learners can recognize the word 政治 when it appears as an independent item or in a context. They can tell that a government is 政治组织, but a school does not fit the definition. The deep level is the storage of meaning and networks of association. At this level, learners understand that both characters 政 and 治 are phonetic-semantic compounds and they understand the roles of phonetic and semantic radicals in those characters. They understand that 政治 can be combined with other words to express different meanings such as 讲政治,政治

学, 政治情况; they understand 政治 in a concrete way and can give examples about how 政治 can have many connections with their own daily life, how a school as a nonpolitical organization could be heavily involved with politics, and how 政治 could be very good for people, but also could destroy people. Although learners may have not gained a fully developed schema related to the word 政治, they can understand this word based on their existing experience.

浅度加工是指对信息的物质属性和感知特征进行分析。在这一水平上，信息加工的方式是零散的，以机械记忆为主。以“政治”一词为例，学习者知道它的发音是zhèngzhì，但是不知道这个发音与“政”“治”这两个汉字中的部件有什么关系；能背诵“政治”这个词的定义“与权威或权力有关的各种社会关系”，但是不知道这句话是什么意思。中度加工是指对信息进行识别和标记。例如，学习者能在不同语境中识别出“政治”这个词，能够理解政府是一个“政治组织”，但学校不是。深度加工是将信息所表达的意义及其网络联系存储在大脑中。在这一水平上，学习者知道“政”和“治”这两个字都是形声字，并且知道这两个字的声旁和形旁。他们知道“政治”可以和其他词结合表达不同的意思，如“讲政治、政治学、政治情况”。他们能以一种具体的方式理解这个词，能给出例子解释：“政治”是怎样存在于他们的日常生活的；学校作为一个非政治组织，是怎样卷入政治中的；“政治”如何能造福于民，如何能祸害于民。学习者大脑中还没有完全建立对“政治”这个词的图式，但是他们仍然可以基于自己已有的经验理解这个词。

From this discussion, we can tell that deeper processing involves meaningful processing. Meaningful processing arises when the target word is linked with learners' personal existing knowledge and experience. Target words "make sense" to learners. Meaningful processing is also an elaborate processing that makes the target information more distinctive and unique, thereby leaving a deeper impression on the learners' minds so that the information will not be easily forgotten.

从上述讨论中我们可以看出，深度加工是一种有意义加工。有意义加工是将目的词的学习与学习者个人已有的知识和经验结合起来的加工，它能让学习者感到目的词对他们来说是"有意义的"。有意义加工也是一种精细化加工，能让目的信息变得与众不同，从而在学习者大脑中留下深刻的印象，这样信息才不容易被遗忘。

Pedagogical implications 教学应用

By applying the level-of-processing theory to character and word instruction, we can adopt the following means to enhance the level of information processing.

将加工水平理论应用到字词教学中，我们可以采取下列措施提高信息加工水平。

• Explore etymological and orthographic information for new characters 让学生探索汉字的字源和缀字知识

The formation of Chinese characters is not random; rather, it is deeply rooted in Chinese culture. In Chapter 1, we mentioned the four methods of creating Chinese characters. By tracing down its etymological origin, students will find that each character is loaded with fascinating cultural content. Thus, let students gain etymological knowledge and analyze the orthographic structure of characters, and make students give a meaningful account of character formation are ways of helping with deeper processing. Shen's (2010b) study on radical knowledge development among beginning CFL learners reported a survey result on students' opinions of the most effective teaching methods in radical instruction. Students considered explanation of the etymology of the radicals (which also are root characters), their origins, and their orthographical development as one of the four most effective methods. Some teachers may be concerned that this will take up too much class time. However, giving an etymological account of characters not only facilitates deeper processing and stimulates students' learning interest, but also helps students find the orthographic patterns of character formation and semantic construction. By accumulating this type of knowledge, students can learn new characters by using learned orthographic knowledge. They will be more autonomous in character learning in the long run. Therefore, "sharpening the axe won't interfere with the cutting of firewood."

汉字不是随意形成的，它有着深厚的文化根基。在第一章，我们提到过汉字造字的四种方法。通过追溯汉字的起源，学生会发现每个汉字都承载着极富魅力的文化。这种对汉字字源和缀字知识进行探索的过程也是帮助学生进行深度加工的过程。Shen（2010b）做了一个关于初级汉语外语学习者部首知识发展的研究，其中的问卷调查结果显示，学生认为教师讲解部首（也是基本字）的起源以及其形体演变的过程是四种最有效的教学方法之一。有些教师可能会担心讲解汉字的字源知识会占用太多课堂时间，但是教师也应该看到，讲解汉字的字源知识不仅能促进学生对汉字的深度加工，还能激发其学习汉字的兴趣，帮助他们获得缀字知识。等积累的缀字知识达到一定的量，学生在学习新字词时就可以自觉运用这一知识去发现部首与合体字之间的关系。久而久之，学生就能在汉字学习中掌握更多的主动权。因此，学习汉字的字源和缀字知识是“磨刀不误砍柴工”。

• Increase the elaboration and effort level of encoding
增加编码的复杂度和困难度

As mentioned earlier, the level-of-processing theory suggests that more elaborate processing leads to a deeper processing because elaborate processing involves making information more meaningful by means of visual imagery, by relating new material to known information, and by arranging information into a meaningful structure (Craik & Tulving, 1975; Craik & Watkins, 1973). How can we increase the level of elaboration? One way is to provide more detailed, vivid description during word encoding. For example, when introducing the word 挑战 (*challenge*), the definition of 挑战 as a noun is "something that by its nature or character serves as a serious test" (*Random House Webster's College Dictionary*, 1991: 225). The instructor can present a picture showing a mountain climber hanging onto a cliff and trying to climb up to the peak of the mountain. The teacher can ask the students to talk about their feelings and thoughts about the topic "If I am the climber…", and then ask the students to discuss a 挑战 situation based on their own personal experiences or experiences of others they are familiar with. The instructor could ask students to summarize what kind of tasks or situations can be considered as 具有挑战性. This type of activity will make the encoding process more meaningful.

前面我们提到过，加工水平理论认为，精细化加工是一种有意义加工。它可以通过将信息形象化、将新信息与旧信息联系起来、将信息组成有意义的结构等方式深度加工信息。（Craik and Tulving，1975；Craik and Watkins，1973）那么我们怎么做才能在字词教学中提高信息加工的复杂度呢？一种方法是在字词编码时提供具体生动的描述。例如，在教授“挑战”一词时，我们知道作为名词，它的定义是“一种从性质和特点上能成为一种考验的事情”（*Random House Webster's College*

Dictionary，1991：225）。教师可以先出示一张图片，图片上是一名登山运动员正在奋力攀爬一个悬崖；然后让学生以“如果我是这名登山运动员，……”为话题说出他们的感受和想法；接着让学生说出自己生活中有过的相似经历或他们熟悉的人遇到过的相似经历；最后让学生总结一下什么样的任务或情况对他们来说是具有挑战性的。这样的字词教学活动会让学生对“挑战”这个词的编码加工变得更有意义。

Increased effort at the level of encoding processing is another way to create a long-lasting memory trace. One study in second language acquisition showed that learners who take more effort in processing materials have better memorization (Schneider et al., 2002). Laufer and Hulstijn (2001) proposed a task-induced involvement vocabulary instruction method, which is an excellent example of increasing the effort level of encoding. The involvement includes three components: need, search, and evaluation. *Need* is concerned with the need to achieve. *Search* is the attempt to find the meaning of a new L2 word or to find a L2 word to express an idea. *Evaluation* entails a comparison of a given word with other words, a specific meaning of this word with other meanings the word represents, or combining the word with other words in order to assess whether a word does or does not fit its context (Laufer & Hulstijn, 2001).

增加编码的困难度是另一种加深记忆痕迹的方法。Schneider 等人（2002）进行的一项二语词汇习得研究显示，学生在新词加工上花费的精力越多，记忆的效果就越好。Laufer 和 Hulstijn（2001）提出了一个任务导入型词汇教学方法，这个方法能很好地增加编码的困难度。任务导入型词汇教学方法包含三个要素：需要、寻找和评价。“需要”是指学生对新词的学习是出于解决问题的需要；“寻找”是指学生积极在大脑中搜寻有关的词语来表达自己的想法或观点；“评价”是指将给定的词与其他词进行比较，或者将这个词的某个具体义项与其他义项进行比较，或者将这个词与其他词组合起来，以此评估这个词是否符合上下文语境。（Laufer and Hulstijn，2001）

Based on this idea, we propose a four-component method for task-based vocabulary instruction. The four components are need, search, discrimination, and evaluation. *Need* refers to students' need to learn new words to complete a task or to solve a problem. They are intrigued to learn. *Search* means that students search for the new words that they need to solve the problem. They actively find the sound and meaning to match the shape of the new words. *Discrimination* refers to finding the differences and similarities among related words and finding out the unique features of each new word under learning. *Evaluation* is assessment of the learning result and finding out whether students have learned the new words needed for task completion or problem solving. Below is an example to illustrate the use of this method in teaching Chinese words.

受任务导入型词汇教学方法的启发，我们在这里提出一个四要素任务型词汇教学方法。这四要素分别是需要、寻找、甄别和评价。“需要”是指学生学习新词是出于完成任务或解决问题的需要。受解决问题这一愿望的驱使，学生有了学习新词的需要。“寻找”是指学生在大脑中搜寻解决问题所需要的新词等。“甄别”是对相关新词之间的相同点和不同点进行鉴别，找出每个新词独有的特征。“评价”是指学生对自己的学习成果进行评价，主要看自己是否运用新学习的生词解决了问题或完成了任务。下面我们用一个具体的例子展示这一教学方法。

Teaching Example 2 Four-component method for task-based vocabulary instruction

教学示例 2 四要素任务型词汇教学方法

Content: Making a Plan for Camping at a National Park

学习内容：制定一个去国家公园野营的计划

Sheet 1

The words to be learned 本课要学的生词

月、日、几点、集合、大峡谷、优胜美地①、火车、灰狗②、黄石公园、汽车、校车、飞机、睡袋、船、手电筒、蜡烛、避蚊油、帐篷、爬、火柴、钓鱼 、篝火晚会、出发、飞盘、看书、划船、野餐、星期、湖

Need 需要

To make students feel that they are motivated in learning new words as they have a need to learn the new words to solve problems.

让学生对本课要学习的生词产生兴趣。为了解决问题，他们需要学习新词。

Step 1: Warm up. The instructor asks students to talk about whether they like camping and to share their camping experiences with the others.

第一步：热身。教师可以问学生是否喜欢野营，还可以让学生把他们的野营经历跟班上其他同学分享。

① 优胜美地，是 Yosemite 的中译名。Yosemite 是美国加利福尼亚州 Yosemite National Park 的简称。

② 灰狗，是美国著名的长途汽车公司 Grayhound 的中译名。

Step 2: Propose a task. Assume that the class is going to go camping at a national park next week. The students' task for this class is to make a camping plan.

第二步：发布任务。假设下星期全班要去一个国家公园野营，学生这节课的任务是制定一个野营计划。

Students all agree to the proposal and feel that they want to learn the new words for making a camping plan.

学生都同意这一提议，他们想学习有关的生词来制定这个野营计划。

Search 寻找

A task sheet (see below) is presented to the students. The instructor asks the students to form small groups to make a camping plan based on the questions provided in the task sheet. In this step, students need to find appropriate words and study them to complete the task.

教师将野营计划的任务清单（见下）展示给学生，要求学生以小组为单位根据任务清单上的问题制定野营计划。学生需要从生词表中找出相应的词来完成这个任务。

Sheet 2

野营计划（Camping plan）

- 什么时候去
- 去哪里（只选一个）
- 怎么去
- 带什么
- 做什么

Step 3: Students are required to sort out all the words from the word list into categories based on the questions listed in Sheet 2. Below is an example of a completed word sorting sheet.

第三步：学生需要将生词表上的词按任务清单上的问题进行分组。下面是一个样例。

Sample Sheet

野营计划（Camping plan）

- 什么时候去（星期 月 日 出发 几点 集合）
- 去哪里（大峡谷 优胜美地 黄石公园）
- 怎么去（火车 灰狗 汽车 校车 飞机 船）
- 带什么（睡袋 手电筒 蜡烛 避蚊油 帐篷 火柴）
- 做什么（爬 钓鱼 篝火晚会 飞盘 看书 划船 野餐 湖）

Step 4: Students learn the words and make a plan. In addition, they can add their own words for answering the questions and add more questions to the list.

第四步：学生学习生词，并制定野营计划。此外，他们也可以根据表达需要增加些新词或新问题。

Step 5: Each group shares their plan with the whole class and provides justification for their choice for each question (e.g., why choose to go to Yosemite or Grand Canyon).

第五步：每组向全班展示自己制定的野营计划并说明理由（例如，为什么选择去优胜美地或大峡谷）。

Discrimination 甄别

Guide students to understand the semantic differences of related words and how they are used in different contexts.

教师引导学生理解相关词语在语义上的不同及在不同语境中的用法。

Step 1: The instructor presents a group of words and asks students to point out the differences in these words and to give examples using them.

第一步：教师展示下面这一组词，让学生说出其不同点并举例说明怎么运用这些词。

比较：（1）野营　野炊　野餐　　（2）野趣　野味　野生

Step 2: The instructor asks students to group into pairs and to pick a word from the list and search previously learned meaning-related words from their mental lexicon to form a question. Students can follow examples presented by the instructor (such as "比较：湖，海，河").

第二步：学生两人一组，先从生词表中选一个词，然后再从已有的心理词库中找出与该词有意义联系的其他词。学生可以按照教师提供的例子进行这一活动，如"比较：湖，海，河"。

Step 3: Exchange the completed answers with another group and work on the answers for the questions which are not listed on the task sheet, but raised by other groups.

第三步：各组之间交换上述问题的答案，并回答那些没有列在任务清单上但由其他组提出来的问题。

Step 4: Each group presents its camping plan to the whole class in an oral presentation.

第四步：各组向全班口头汇报他们的野营计划。

Evaluation 评价

To evaluate whether students have learned the new words from Sheet 1 and to what degree they have learned the new words.

检查学生是否已经学会了生词表中的词，评估他们对每个词的掌握程度。

Step 1: One group chooses two questions from Sheet 2 to ask other groups. The other groups must answer questions both orally and in writing using the newly learned words. Groups take turns to work on this task until all groups have had a chance to ask and answer questions.

第一步：其中一组学生从任务清单中任选两个问题请其他组回答，回答问题的那组必须用刚学习的生词以口头和书面两种形式回答问题。各组轮流问答。

Step 2: Each group presents their written plan via a document camera to the whole class. The class members read the written plan and critique the accuracy of word use. Students are encouraged to find and correct mistakes made in the written responses of the other groups.

第二步：每组通过投影仪向全班展示他们的书面计划，其他学生可以评点其在语境中的用词准确度。教师应鼓励学生相互找错误并改正错误。

(Teaching Example 2 is contributed by Helen H. Shen, The University of Iowa)

• Encourage students' self-elaboration
鼓励学生进行自发性的复杂编码

Creating encoding uniqueness is another way to enhance a memory trace. A study (Kuo & Hooper, 2004) compared different methods of mnemonics used among high school CSL learners learning Chinese words. One of these was student-self-generated encoding. In this condition, students were encouraged to create their own memory aids by drawing a picture, writing a sentence, or inventing a story associated with characters. The result showed that the student-self-generated mnemonics group performed best in follow-up vocabulary testing. Another study (Shen, 2004) compared three encoding conditions in learning Chinese words among English-speaking intermediate college CSL learners. Condition 1 was self-generated elaboration in which students created a method for memorizing the sound, shape, and meaning of the words. Condition 2 was instructor-guided elaboration in which the instructor explained the etymology of the words, if applicable, analyzed the radicals, and gave examples of word use in a context. Condition 3 was rote memorization in which students simply repeated the sound, shape, and meaning of the words without elaboration. Both student-self-generated elaboration and instructor-guided elaboration significantly improved word retention, although instructor-guided elaboration was superior to student-self-generated elaboration. These studies provided evidence that in word instruction, in addition to instructor-guided elaboration, teachers should encourage students to make self-reference elaboration, because this type of elaboration directly relates to the student's own experiences and their own learning styles, which enhances memorization.

创建独特的编码方式也是一种加深记忆痕迹的方法。Kuo和Hooper（2004）比较了将汉语作为第二语言学习的高中生运用不同记忆方法学习新词的效果。其中一种记忆方法是让学生进行自发的复杂编码，也就是鼓励学生运用自己的方式对新词进行编码，如为新词画图、造句或创作一个故事。研究结果表明，鼓励学生进行自发的复杂编码的实验组在之后的词语测验中，成绩要优于其他对照组。Shen（2004）比较了母语为英语的成人中级二语学习者的三种编码方式在词语学习上的效果：方式一是学生自发的复杂编码，即学生自己创造一种方法记忆新词的音、形、义；方式二是教师指导下的复杂编码，即教师介绍词源知识、分析词中汉字的部首以及举例说明新词在语境中的用法；方式三是简单编码，即机械地记忆新词，不断重复新词的音、形、义，不进行复杂编码。结果表明，学生自发的复杂编码和教师指导下的复杂编码都能显著提高学生的词语记忆效果，但后者的词语学习效果最好。这些研究证明，在词语教学中，教师除了指导学生进行复杂编码外，还应该鼓励学生进行自发的复杂编码。因为这种编码方式能将新词与学生已有的生活和学习经验直接联系起来，并且符合学生独特的学习风格，这些都能帮助学生加深记忆痕迹。

4.4 Multisystem account theory 多通道加工理论

The multisystem refers to the human sensory system that uses multimodality to perceive events and objects. This sensory system includes visual, aural, tactual, taste sensation, feeling, and motor senses. The multi-system account theory proposed by Engelkamp (2001) is predicated on dual coding theory, but it provides a detailed account of the role of the nonverbal system in language learning based on a series of empirical studies. Tulving (1972) proposed two types of memory systems: episodic memory and semantic memory. Episodic memory receives and stores information about temporally dated episodes or events, and the temporal-spatial relations among these events. Therefore, it is stored as an autobiographical form in the memory system. Semantic memory, on the other hand, is a system for storing information in schema form and uses language or other verbal symbols. It does not register perceptible properties or inputs, but instead registers cognitive referents of input signals (Tulving, 1972). For example, if a person is talking about his friend, he may describe his friend with words like "friendly, helpful," and "likes to play basketball" from his semantic memory. However, this person may also recall an image of his friend's smile when they first met, how his friend accompanied him to find the materials he needed in the library, or a scene of his friend playing basketball on one occasion from episodic memory. The semantic and episodic memory systems can operate independently, but they are also interdependent as they support and complement each other to provide full recall of events.

多通道加工理论中的“多通道”指的是我们的感知系统是运用多条感知通道感知事件和事物的。感知系统包括视觉、听觉、触觉、味觉、感觉和动觉。多通道加工理论是由Engelkamp（2001）提出的，它以双编码理论为基础。该理论在一系列实证性研究的基础上对非语言系统在语言学习中的作用做了进一步的阐述。在早期，Tulving（1972）提出了两种记忆系统：情节记忆和语义记忆。情节记忆是对事件或经历的时间性记忆，或是对事件的时空关系的记忆，因此它常以一种照相式的形式把事件存储在记忆系统中。语义记忆，是用语言或其他语言符号把信息加工成图式存储在记忆系统中。语义记忆系统记录的不是输入信号的可感知特征，而是对输入信号的一种认知结果。（Tulving，1972）例如，当一个人提到他的朋友时，他会从自己的语义记忆系统中提取出“友好、会帮助人、喜欢打篮球”等词或短语进行描述。但同时，这个人也会回忆起他与朋友第一次见面时朋友笑的样子，朋友是怎样陪他在图书馆里找他所需要的资料的，以及朋友某一次打球时的情景，这些都是由情节记忆系统提供的。情节记忆系统和语义记忆系统既相互独立又相互依赖，它们相互补充共同提供对事物的完整记忆。

Engelkamp (2001) holds that the episodic memory consists of subsystems based on the human multiple sensory modalities such as the motor system and the tactual system. Each system encodes information based on its unique sensory channel. Therefore, if we use multiple modalities instead of a single modality to encode information, when we recall the information, each modality will contribute a unique cue to the recall of this information. The multisystem account theory pays special attention to the role of enactment in the encoding process. In a series of experimental studies, Engelkamp (2001) confirmed that enacted learning contributes to information retention.

Engelkamp（2001）认为，情节记忆是由人体多条感知通道组成的多个子系统构成的，如动觉系统和触觉系统。每个子系统根据它对事物的独特感知通道对信息进行编码，因此如果我们运用多条感知通道而不是单一感知通道对信息进行编码，我们在提取该信息的时候，每一条感知通道都会提供一条独特的提示线索帮助我们快速、准确地提取信息。多通道加工理论尤其重视感知型加工在编码中的作用。经过一系列实证性研究，Engelkamp（2001）证实了感知型学习有助于对信息的保持。

The multisystem account theory suggests that we should take advantage of learners' episodic memory in word learning to achieve a maximum effect of retention and recall. Because it provides additional memory cues for the same object, and it reduces the interference from other information as the multiple cues will support each other and strengthen the memory. It also helps with comprehension as the concept is supported by concrete evidence. More importantly, it also increases learning interest by involving enacted activities.

多通道加工理论启示我们，教师在词语教学中应该充分利用学习者的情节记忆，最大化地提高记忆效果。因为情节记忆为同一信息提供了额外的提示线索，多条提示线索之间互相支持和印证能强化学习者的记忆效果，减少其他信息带来的干扰。情节记忆也有助于学习者对新词的理解，因为它为抽象的概念提供了具体的语言事实。更重要的是，情节记忆中的感知型活动能更好地激发学生对词语学习的兴趣。

Pedagogical implications 教学应用

Based on the multisystem account theory, we should take the following methods into consideration during character and word instruction.

根据多通道加工理论，我们在字词教学中可以考虑采用以下教学活动：

• Drawing 画画

Ask students to provide illustrations based on etymological knowledge for difficult characters. This method is especially effective in the beginning level class because it helps students understand the pictograph-origin of Chinese characters. The illustration can be a concrete or symbolic sketch of a character. We can also ask students to draw the pictograph of the characters. Afterwards, we can ask students to guess the target characters based on each other's illustrations. As individual students have their own unique way of processing a character, personal drawing is an excellent way of letting students express their uniqueness in character encoding. In using this method, the instructor would need to set a time limit because some students may spend too much time on the quality of their sketches. We should let students understand that the main purpose of sketching the characters is to comprehend and memorize the characters, rather than to compete how well they can sketch.

教师可以让学生根据汉字的字源知识为汉字画画，尤其是针对复杂的汉字。这一方法在初级阶段的教学中尤其有效，因为它能帮助学生了解汉字的象形本源。学生为汉字作的画可以是具体的，也可以是象征性的、符号式的速写。教师也可以让学生直接画出汉字的象形字。画完之后，教师可以让学生根据彼此所画的汉字画猜测对应的汉字。因为每个学生都有自己独特感知汉字的方式，所以汉字画其实是一个极好的让学生展示自己独特汉字编码方式的途径。使用这一方法时，教师应该规定好活动的时长，以免学生把太多时间花费在提高画作的质量上。我们应该让学生明白，画汉字画的主要目的不是比谁画得好，而是要通过这种方式增强学生对汉字的理解和记忆。

- **Acting out 动作演示**

Acting out the word is another way of using episodic memory. It not only means using body action to act out the action words, but also means using all sensory modalities to sense the words. For example, when introducing the word 唱歌, we can have a student actually sing a song for a minute. When introducing the word 汽油, we can ask students to describe their feeling when they smell 汽油.

用动作把词语表演出来是另一个运用情节记忆学习词语的方法。表演不仅仅意味着用动作把动作词语演示出来，还意味着用全部的感知通道感知词语。例如：教授“唱歌”一词时，我们可以真的让学生唱一分钟的歌；教授“汽油”一词时，我们可以让学生描述一下闻到汽油时的感觉。

- **Role-play 角色扮演**

Students can take roles to perform a word in contexts such as 我喝醉了 and 我很快乐. We can also ask students to make semantic connections between words by making a short dialog or a skit; or to group the related words based on a theme such as “a birthday party” or “dining in a restaurant.”

学生可以选定角色，并将新词在语境中表演出来，例如表演“我喝醉了”和“我很快乐”。教师可以让学生通过编对话或小品的形式建立新词之间的语义联系，或者用一个主题把相关的新词串联起来，如“生日聚会”或“在餐馆吃饭”，然后分角色表演。

Here, we must point out that the use of enacted instruction methods is time-consuming, so instructors must consider the necessity of using this type of methods and not overuse them. Another thing the instructor should know is that episodic memory supplements semantic memory but does not replace semantic memory. The ultimate goal of word instruction is to help students store the information in the semantic memory in a schema format. Therefore, when using the enacted methods, we should always connect them with semantic encoding and make sure students understand the word conceptually with the support from the episodic details.

需要指出的是，感知型教学活动是很耗费时间的，教师应该充分考虑和评估是否有使用这类活动的必要，不要滥用。还需要注意的是，情节记忆只是对语义记忆的补充，并不能代替语义记忆。词语学习的最终目标是帮助学生将信息以图式的方式存储在语义记忆系统中。因此，在运用感知型教学活动时，我们应该把它与语义编码结合起来，确保学生能在情节编码的帮助下理解和掌握词义。

4.5 Competition theory 竞争理论

The competition theory proposed by MacWhinney (1987; 2001) is a language acquisition theory, but is fully rooted in the retrieval-induced forgetting theory of cognitive science. The retrieval-induced forgetting theory, a classic theory initiated by McGeoch (1932; 1942), holds that forgetting is caused by two types of interferences: proactive interferences in which the previously learned events interfere with the memory of later-learned events, and retroactive interference in which the subsequently learned events interfere with the memory of previously learned events. These two types of interferences are caused by the competition among memory traces. Further studies revealed that the competition for memory traces could be caused by: (1) the memories associated with a common cue compete for access to conscious recall when that cue is presented; (2) the cued recall of an item will decrease as a function of increasing in the strength of its competitor's association with this cue; (3) the act of retrieval is a learning event in the sense that it enhances subsequent recall of the retrieved item (Anderson et al., 1994). The repeated retrievals of a given item will strengthen that item, causing loss of retrieval access to other related items.

作为语言习得理论，竞争理论是由MacWhinney（1987，2001）提出的，但这一理论是以认知科学的提取—导入遗忘理论为基础的。提取—导入遗忘理论是经典的遗忘理论，最初由McGeoch（1932，1942）提出。该理论认为，遗忘是由两种干扰造成的——前摄干扰和后摄干扰。前摄干扰是先前学习的材料干扰了对后来学习材料的记忆，后摄干扰是后来学习的材料干扰了对先前学习材料的记忆。这两种干扰的产生是记忆痕迹之间相互竞争的结果。Anderson等人（1994）的进一步研究表明，记忆痕迹之间的竞争可能是由下列原因造成的：（1）当目标提示线索进入意识水平时，与它相关的其他提示线索也被激活，并同时进入意识水平与其竞争；（2）如果与目标提示线索相关的非目标提示线索激活强度增强，那目标提示线索的激活强度就会减弱；（3）对目标信息进行提取本身就是一个复习活动，它能使后续的对同一目标信息的再提取变得更容易。也就是说，重复提取某种信息会强化对该信息的提取并弱化对其他相关信息的提取。

Based on the retrieval-induced forgetting theory, the competition theory assumes that the connection of lexical items in mental lexicon can vary in their degree of activation when they are retrieved. During lexical processing, items are in competition with one another in terms of connection in phonology, orthography, and semantics. In each of these competition, the item that wins out is the one with the greatest activation. An item must dominate over its competitors for a sufficiently stronger and longer period to emerge as the winner. The theory proposed four factors that can raise or lower the activation of an item: cue support effect, completeness of match effect, dominant effect, and previous activation effect (MacWhinney, 1987). We will explain these four factors in detail while connecting them to vocabulary learning in Chinese.

基于提取—导入遗忘理论的观点，竞争理论假设心理词库中词与词之间的联结强度会随着提取频率的变化而变化。在提取目的词的过程中，与目的词在语音、构词、语义等方面有联系的词会参与竞争，在竞争中获胜的词就会首先被激活。一个词只有在提示线索强度上和提取时间上都比其他词占优势才能在竞争中取胜。竞争理论认为，有四个因素会影响一个词的激活度，它们分别是线索支持效应、线索吻合度、主导效应和先前激活效应。（MacWhinney，1987）下面我们将从汉语词汇学习的角度对这四个因素做详细阐述。

Cue support effect: The cue support effect refers to the connection between recall cues and the item to be retrieved. If a cue is strongly activated, it will have a strong connection to the item. For example, when the target word to be recognized is 打雷, if learners have strong recall cues such as a vivid image of lightning, and acoustic memory of thunderous sound, then 打雷 will be successfully recognized and it will not be recognized as 打擂.

线索支持效应指的是提示线索与被提示词之间的联结强度。如果提示线索的激活度很高，那么它与被激活的词之间的联结强度也高。假设被提取的目的词是“打雷”，如果学习者拥有激活度很高的提示线索，如关于闪电的清晰影像和关于雷声的听觉意象，那么目的词“打雷”就会被提取，而不会被提取为另一个形近音似词“打擂”。

Completeness of match effect: The cues for a certain item have a complete match with the target item. If the cues do not provide as good an overall match of the targeted item as an alternative item does, the alternative item may be retrieved. When seeing the word 打雷, if the learner has no ambiguousness about its pronunciation (dǎléi), and its meaning (*to thunder*), the recognition of 打雷 would be more successful than in the situation where the learner is not sure whether 雷 should be pronounced as léi or lèi, or if 雷means *thunder* or *lightning*.

线索吻合度是指提示线索与目的词相吻合的程度。如果提示线索与目的词吻合度不高，那么最终被提取的可能会是另一个相似词。当看到“打雷”这个词时，如果学习者对它的发音dǎléi和意义“云层放电时发出巨大响声”不存在认识上的模糊性，那么“打雷”被提取的可能性就大；反之，如果学习者不清楚“雷”的发音是léi还是lèi，“雷”的意思是“巨大的声音”还是“闪电”，那么“打雷”被提取的可能性就小。

Dominant effect: The decision to go with one competitor over another is based on the extent to which that competitor dominates over the other competitors. If the target word to be recognized is 形势, other similar sounding words such as 形式 may be activated from the memory during recognition. However, during the competition of these items, if the learner has better recall cues for 形式 than 形势, then 形式 will be put in the dominant position. Once it is in the dominant position, the item starts to have a dominant effect on processing. Even though it is wrong, the learner tends to believe that the dominant competitor is the correct word. As a result, the wrong item 形式

rather than 形势 will be retrieved.

主导效应是指学习者最终决定提取哪个词是由词的主导地位决定的。假设我们要提取的目的词是“形势”，那么其他同音词如“形式”在提取过程中也会在大脑中被激活，并参与竞争。在竞争过程中，如果学习者大脑中“形式”的提示线索强度强于“形势”的话，“形式”一词就会处于主导地位。一旦占据主导地位，该词就将发挥主导效应。虽然它不是目的词，但是受主导效应的影响，学习者倾向于相信这个词是目的词，从而导致提取出现错误。

Previous activation effect: If a similar item was previously activated, it will receive further activation in processing a similar target item. For example, now that the words 电灯, 电话, 电线 have been introduced and the learner knows that the three items are all related to 电, if 电灯 is frequently retrieved previously, then when 电线 is presented to the learner, the learner may read it as 电灯. The reason is that 电灯 has been activated previously and it becomes a stronger competitor in the completion of retrieval.

先前激活效应是指如果与目的词相似的词先前被激活过，那么在提取目的词时，它会被再度激活。例如，学生学习“电灯、电话、电线”这三个词时，知道这些词都与“电”有关。如果“电灯”是之前经常被提取的词，那当“电线”一词呈现在学生面前时，学生很可能会把它读成“电灯”。因为这个词先前被提取了多次，在相似词中成了一个较强的竞争者。

A study that analyzed English-speaking advanced CSL learners on lexical errors in reading Chinese text reported that students make three types of errors

(陈绂, 1996). These error types are excellent samples to explain the retrieval failure due to the four types of effects mentioned above. The errors are caused by the failure during competition between the target item and other sounds, shapes, and meanings of similar items. According to the author, one type of error is the retrieval of a word of a similar shape instead of the target word. For example, students read 动员 as 功员, 迈步 as 边步. The second type of error is retrieval of a word of similar meaning, such as students read 出售 as 出货, 阅览 as 读览, 不应 as 不该. The third type occurs when the target word is mixed with a familiar synonymous word or meaning-related word such as when 参与 is read as 参加, 农业 as 农村, and 外汇 as 外币.

陈绂（1996）针对母语为英语的高级汉语二语学习者的用词错误进行了一项研究，其结果显示，学生在阅读汉语文本时常犯三种错误：第一种是提取字形相近的词，如把“动员”读成“功员”，把“迈步”读成“边步”；第二种是提取意义相关的词，如把“出售”读成“出货”，把“阅览”读成 “读览”，把“不应”读成“不该”；第三种是把目的词与熟悉的近义词或意义相关的词相混，如把“参与”读成“参加”，把“农业”读成 “农村”，把“外汇”读成“外币”。这些错误恰恰是上述四个因素导致的，都是目的词在提取时与音近、形近或义近词竞争失败所致。

Pedagogical implications 教学应用

With an understanding of competition theory in vocabulary instruction, we should consider students' errors in character recognition and lexical access as part of the normal learning process in lexical knowledge development. However, the retrieval-induced errors could be reduced if instruction can incorporate the following measures.

如果理解了词汇教学中的竞争理论，我们就应该知道，学生会在汉字认读和词义提取中犯错是学生词汇知识发展过程中的正常现象。虽然如此，但如果教师在教学中能运用以下方法的话，那因提取而诱发的字词错误就会大大减少。

• Utilize multiple codes for encoding 采用多种编码方式

The cue support effect hints that once a word is introduced, if the brain stores strong cues that associated with the target word, the recognition of the target word will be easier and faster. Therefore, our instruction should endeavor to provide multiple codes such as verbal, imagery, and enacted codes for encoding. This multiple coding would create multiple cues for recall. To cite an example, when introducing the word 困难, the verbal encoding method could explain the etymological formation of the characters 困 and 难, how each character contributes to the word meaning 困难, and how the word is used in context. The imagery approach for 困难 could be photos of encountering some difficulties, or recalling difficult situations that students have encountered in the past. The enacted encoding of 困难 could be to ask students to hold their breath as long as they can and then express what kind of feeling they have (if they encounter breathing difficulty). These multiple encoding methods will leave a deeper memory trace for better retrieval. If one cue is lost in the memory, additional cues can still be used for recall.

线索支持效应告诉我们，当学生学习一个词语时，如果他们大脑中储存了与目的词有很强关联的提示线索的话，那么再认就会变得快速而容易。因此，我们在教学中应该努力为学生提供目的词的多种编码方式，比如语言码、意象码、动作码。多种编码可以为目的词的提取提供多条提示线索。例如，当我们向学生讲解“困难”一词时，我们可以运用语言码进行教学，向学生介绍“困”和“难”这两个字是怎么形成的，每个字的意思跟“困难”这个词的意思有什么联系，以及“困难”一词在语境中是怎么使用的；我们也可以运用意象码进行教学，向学生展示遇见各种困难时的图片，或者请学生回忆生活中遇到困难时的场景；我们还可以运用动作码进行教学，让学生试着屏住呼吸感知呼吸的困难等。多种编码会在学生大脑中留下比较深的记忆痕迹，这样，如果一条线索丢失了，学生还可以利用其他线索进行提取。

• Pay attention to comparison and contrast 运用比较和对比

On many occasions, the retrieval failure is not because the word is lost from our memory, but because there is interference by similar items. The target item often fails to be retrieved because a similar item is in a stronger position in competition. As a result, that similar item is retrieved. By understanding this point, our instruction should use comparison and contrast methods. In order to build schemata for word learning, we need to relate the new target word to old words with similar sound, shape, and meaning so that the new item can be integrated into a schematic system. However, at the same time, we also need to direct students' attention to the differences in those similar items to eliminate confusions introduced by the sound, shape, and meaning similarities. In comparing the similarities and differences between the target word and learned similar words, we must not only compare the target word with related Chinese words, but also compare the semantic scope of the target Chinese word with its L1 equivalent. For example, the word 灿烂 can be translated into English as “brilliant.” In Chinese, 灿烂 can be used to modify a person's smile, such as 灿烂的笑容, but in English, it is not conventional to say “brilliant smile.” In English, we can say “he is brilliant,” but we do not say 他很灿烂, because in Chinese, 灿烂 does not have the meaning of “extremely smart,” but it can be used to indicate “outstanding” in all aspects, such as 灿烂的一生. This kind of comparison can help reduce the confusion or interference from L1 on L2 word study.

在很多情况下，目的词之所以提取失败并不是因为我们遗忘了这个词，而是因为其他相似词的干扰。当相似词在与目的词的竞争中处于优势地位时，最终被提取的就是相似词而非目的词。理解了这一点，我们在教学中就要多采用比较和对比的方法。为了在大脑中建立目的词的图式，我们需要在新词与它的音似词、形似词和义似词之间建立联系，这样新词就可以融入已有的图式系统中去。但同时我们也要引导学生注意相似词之间的不同点，消除因音、形、义上的相似而带来的困惑。在比较目的词与已学相似词之间的异同时，我们不仅要与汉语中的相似词进行比较，还要注意比较目的词与学生的母语对应词在语义范围上的差异。例如，汉语词“灿烂”可以翻译成英语“brilliant”。在汉语中，“灿烂”可以用来形容人的笑容，如“灿烂的笑容”；但是在英语中，我们一般不说“brilliant smile”。在英语中，我们可以说“he is brilliant”（他极其聪明）；但在汉语中，我们却不可以说“他很灿烂”，因为“灿烂”在汉语中没有“极其聪明”的意思，但“灿烂”可以形容一个人在各方面都很出色，如“灿烂的一生”。这种比较会帮助学生减少由母语负迁移带来的困惑和干扰，使学生对目的词的语义范围和感情色彩有更为清楚的了解。

• Schedule systematic review 安排系统的复习

Previous activation effect implies that frequent retrieval of old words having sound, shape, or meaning connections with the target word will affect the retrieval of the target word. Therefore, increased opportunity of practicing and using newly introduced words is critical for reducing the interference from frequently retrieved old words. For planning a review, we should take advantage of two cognitive effects: spacing effect and variation effect (Jahnke

& Nowaczyk, 1998).

先前激活效应告诉我们，频繁提取先前学过的与目的词在音、形、义上有联系的词会干扰对目的词的提取。要减少这种干扰，创造更多的机会让学生对新词进行复习和运用就变得很重要。在制定复习计划时，教师应该充分利用两种认知效应：间隔效应和变化效应。（Jahnke and Nowaczyk，1998）

The spacing effect refers to arranging a review in a spaced or distributed fashion. Consider that we review 30 words in a 30-minute class. We should not ask students to repeatedly read one word for one minute and then move to the next word. A much better way is to read words 1-30 and then start over again with a different order. Spaced practice is much more effective than massive practice. The reason is simple. When a word initially appears, the brain will process it as a new stimulus that requires attention and effort for processing. If the word is repeated massively in a single time slot, the learner will treat each subsequent repetition as a rest opportunity and use no effort and pay less attention to the target item because the target item has already been recognized (Dempster, 1987). The variation effect means that during the review process, the instruction should use different methods to review the same set of words, to make each review unique for the purpose of drawing learners' attention. Below is an example of variation in methods for learning the same set of words.

间隔效应是指复习活动应该是间歇性的或分散性的，而不是集中性的。假设要在30分钟的课上复习30个词，我们不应该让学生在一分钟内重复复习同一个词，下一分钟再复习另一个词。比较好的方法是：先让学生把这30个词从头到尾读一遍，然后把顺序打乱后再从头到尾读一遍。间隔复习比集中复习有效得多，理由很简单：当一个词第一次出现时，我们的大脑会把它当作一个新刺激，并且集中注意力对它进行加工；如果一个词在同一个时间段内多次重复出现，因为该词在第一次出现时已被认读，所以当这个词复现时，我们的大脑不仅不会对其进行再加工，反而会趁机休息。（Dempster, 1987）变化效应是指在复习时，教师应该使用不同的方法复习同一组词。这样做是为了让每一次复习都变得与众不同，这样才能吸引学生的注意力。下面我们具体看一下如何使用不同的方法学习同一组词。

Teaching Example 3 Variation in methods for learning the same set of words

教学示例 3 用不同的方法学习同一组词

Method 1: Picture–word match. Ask students to determine the corresponding words by looking at the pictures.

方法 1：图—词匹配 。学生看图并找出对应的词。

Method 2: Pick three cards and test your classmates. Ask each student to choose three cards from the same group of vocabulary cards and then walk around the classroom to ask a classmate to choose one of the cards to read and explain its meaning. Repeat the activity until three classmates are tested.

方法2：选三张词卡考考你的同学。每名学生先从同一组生词卡中抽选三张，然后在教室里走动，选一名同学让其从中选出一张，并对词卡上的词进行认读和语义解释。请挑选三名同学重复以上活动。

Method 3: Find the words from the sentences. The teacher either speaks or presents the target words in a written sentence and has the students point out which words in the sentence are the target words.

方法3：从句子中找目的词。教师说出或书面展示出含有目的词的句子，让学生指出哪些词是目的词。

Method 4: Draw a word net. The teacher asks students to create a few categories and then to sort the target words into the established categories according to their meaning connections within each category. For example, a category of eating food will allow students to classify any food and eating related words into that category.

方法 4：构建词语网络图。教师先让学生创建几个类别，然后让学生根据目的词与已建类别之间的意义联系将目的词归入相应的类别。例如，如果其中一个类别是“吃食”，那么学生就可以把食物以及与吃有关的词归入这一类。

Method 5: Tell a story using the target words. Students can create a story based on the theme provided, by using relevant target words.

方法 5：用目的词讲故事。学生可以根据给定的主题，使用相关的目的词编一个故事。

Method 6: Information gap. Divide the target words into two groups and write them on sheets A and B. Have the students work in pairs. Student A holds sheet A and student B holds sheet B. Student A can ask student B to guess a word from sheets A based on information he/she provides to Student B. For example, Student A asks student B “一个星期里，什么时候不用上班?” Student B will guess the word 周末.

方法 6：信息差。教师首先将目的词分成两组，分别写在生词单A和B上。学生两人一组，学生A持生词单A，学生B持生词单B。学生A从生词单A中选择一个词进行描述，学生B根据学生A所提供的信息猜出目的词。例如，学生A问学生B：“一个星期里，什么时候不用上班？”学生B就可以猜出那个词是“周末”。

(Teaching Example 3 is contributed by Helen H. Shen, The University of Iowa)

References 参考文献

陈绂. 1996. 谈对欧美留学生的字词教学[J]. 语言教学与研究（4）.

沈禾玲. 2008. 认知理论及其在汉语作为二语的字词教学中的应用[J]. 中国文字研究（1）: 149-158.

Anderson M C, Bjork R A, Bjork E L.1994. Remembering can cause forgetting: retrieval dynamics in long-term memory[J]. Journal of experimental psychology: learning, memory, and cognition, 20(5): 1063-1087.

Atkinson R C, Shiffrin R M. 1968. Human memory: a proposed system and its control processes[M]. Spence K W, Spence J T. The psychology of learning and motivation: advances in research and theory. New York: Academic Press, 89-195.

Chandler P, Sweller J. 1991. Cognitive load theory and the format of instruction[J]. Cognition and instruction, 8(4): 293-332.

Craik F I M, Lockhart R S. 1972. Level of processing: a framework for memory research[J]. Journal of verbal learning and verbal behavior, 11: 671-684.

Craik F I M, Tulving E. 1975. Depth of processing and the retention of words in episodic memory[J]. Journal of experimental psychology: general, 104(3): 268-294.

Craik F I M, Watkins M J. 1973. The role of rehearsal in short-term memory[J]. Journal of verbal learning and verbal behavior, 12(6): 599-607.

Dempster F N. 1987. Effects of variable encoding and spaced presentations on vocabulary learning[J]. Educational psychology, 79(2): 162-170.

Engelkamp J. 2001. Action memory: a system-oriented approach[M]. Zimmer H D, Cohen R L, Guynn M J, et al.. Memory for action: a distinct form of episodic memory. New York: Oxford University Press, 49-96.

Engelkamp J, Jahn P. 2003. Lexical, conceptual and motor information in memory for action phrases: a multi-system account[J]. Acta psychologica, 113: 147-165.

Jahnke J C, Nowaczyk R H. 1998. Cognition[M]. Upper Saddle River, NJ: Prentice Hall Inc.

Jocoby L L, Craik F I M. 1979. Effects of elaboration of processing at encoding and retrieval: trace distinctiveness and recovery of initial context[M]. Cermak L S, Craik F I M. Levels of processing in human memory. Hillsdale, New York: Lawrence Erlbaum

Associates.

Kuo M-L A, Hooper S. 2004. The effects of visual and verbal coding mnemonics on learning Chinese characters in computer-based instruction[J]. Educational technology research and development, 52(3): 23–34.

Laufer B, Hulstijn J. 2001. Incidental vocabulary acquisition in a second language: the construct of task-induced involvement[J]. Applied linguistics, 22(1): 1–26.

MacWhinney B. 1987. The competition model[M]. Macwhinney B, Bates E. Mechanisms of language acquisition. Hillsdale, NJ: Lawrence Erlbaum Associates, 249–308.

MacWhinney B. 2001. The competition model: the input, the context, and the brain[M]. Robinson P. Cognition and second language instruction. Cambridge, UK: Cambridge University Press, 69–90.

McGeoch J A. 1932. Forgetting and the law of disuse[J]. Psychological review, 39: 352–370.

McGeoch J A. 1942. The psychology of human learning[M]. New York: Longmans, Green and Co.

Miller G A. 1956. The magical number seven, plus or minus two: some limits on our capacity for processing information[J]. Psychological review, 63: 81–97.

Paas F, Renkl A, Sweller J. 2003. Cognitive load theory and instructional design: recent developments[J]. Educational psychologist, 38(1): 1–4.

Paivio A. 1969. Mental imagery in associative learning and memory[J]. Psychological review, 76: 241–263.

Paivio A. 1986. Mental representations: a dual coding approach[M]. New York: Oxford University Press.

Paivio A. 2007. Mind and its evolution: a dual coding theoretical approach[M]. Mahwah, NJ: Lawrence Erlbaum Associates.

Schneider V I, Healy A F, Bourne, Jr L E. 2002. What is learned under difficult conditions is hard to forget: contextual interference effects in foreign vocabulary acquisition, retention, and transfer[J]. Journal of memory and language, 46: 419–440.

Shen H H. 2004. Level of cognitive processing: effects on character learning among non-native learners of Chinese as a foreign language[J]. Language and education, 18(2): 167–182.

Shen H H. 2010a. Imagery and verbal coding approaches in Chinese vocabulary instruction[J]. Language teaching research, 14(4): 485–499.

Shen H H. 2010b. Analysis of radical knowledge development among beginning CFL learners[M]. Everson M E, Shen H H. Research among learners of Chinese as a foreign language. Honolulu, HI: University of Hawaii, National Foreign Language Resource Center, 45–65.

Sweller J. 1988. Cognitive load during problem solving: effects on learning[J]. Cognitive science, 12: 257–285.

Sweller J. 1991. Cognitive load theory and the format of instruction[J]. Cognition and instruction, 8(4): 293–332.

Sweller J. 1994. Cognitive load theory, learning difficulty, and instructional design[J]. Learning and instruction, 4(4): 295–312.

Tulving E. 1972. Episodic and semantic memory[M]. Tulving E, Donaldson W. Organization of memory. New York: Academic Press, 381–403.

Zhu Y, Fung A S L, Wang H. 2012. Memorization effects of pronunciation and stroke order animation in digital flashcards[J]. CALICO Journal, 29(3): 563–577.

Chapter 5 第五章

Chinese Character and Word Learning Strategies and Training
汉语字词学习策略及其训练

5.1 Chinese character and word learning strategies: concept and scope 汉语字词学习策略：定义和范围

In the *Modern Chinese Word Dictionary*《现代汉语词典》(2016:132), 策略 is defined as guiding principles for action and format of combat. In English, "strategy" comes from the ancient Greek term "strategia," meaning generalship or the art of war (Oxford, 1990:7). Therefore, "strategy" is related to the ways and means of winning a battle or combat. By extending this definition to classroom learning, learning strategies are actions, methods, or mental processes that learners employ during learning to acquire knowledge. Chinese character and word learning strategies are part of the learning strategies that learners utilize for learning characters and words.

在《现代汉语词典》（2016：132）中，"策略"的定义是"根据形势发展而制定的行动方针和斗争方式"。在英语中，"strategy"一词源于古希腊语的"strategia"，本义为斗争方式或战争的艺术。（Oxford，1990：7）因此，"策略"是为了在斗争中取胜而使用的方式和方法。我们把这一定义引申到课堂学习中，那么学习策略就是学习者为获取知识而采取的行动、方法或思维方式。汉语字词学习策略是学习策略的一部分，是学习者学习汉字和汉语词时所采用的方法。

Character and word learning strategies are created and utilized by learners. Although each strategy is different, strategy-induced learning shares some common features. First, it is goal-directed learning. Learners create or adopt certain strategies for solving a certain character/word-learning problem. For example, to memorize the word 兴奋 (*excited*) a student created a story in which a farmer sees a big field, so he is very excited (Wei, 2010). Second, it is self-regulated learning. Learners themselves decide which strategy to use, how to use it, and when to use it for learning words. Third, it is individualized learning. Due to the differences in cognitive styles and learning behaviors, each learner may have a set of preferred learning strategies. One strategy that is effective for one learner may not work for another learner. Here is a story from the author:

> *Asking students to make and use vocabulary cards to learn words is a common strategy, so I asked students to make vocabulary cards themselves and brought them to the class for vocabulary learning activities. However, a student once told me that he made these cards just to fulfill the class requirement, but never used them after the class because it worked better for him to read words from the list than to flip vocabulary cards for memorizing words.*

Some learners prefer listening to music when learning characters and words, and others do not. Therefore, we can recommend learners to use certain character and word learning strategies, but cannot force them to accept certain strategies if they do not feel comfortable in doing so.

字词学习策略是由学习者创造并使用的。虽然每种策略不尽相同，但策略导向型学习却有其共性。首先，这是一种以目标为导向的学习，学习者创造或采用某种策略是为了解决某个具体的字词学习问题。例如，为了记住“兴奋”这个词，有个学生编了一个情景故事——一个农民看见一片很大的田地，所以他很兴奋。（Wei，2010）其次，这是一种自律性学习。学习者自己决定用什么策略、怎么用以及什么时候用。最后，这是一种个性化学习。每个学习者的认知风格和学习行为各不相同，他们各有自己偏爱的学习策略。一种策略对这个学习者有效，并不意味对另一个学习者也有效。下面是作者遇到的一个例子：

> 用词卡学习生词是学生常用的一种学习策略，所以我要求学生自己制作词卡并将之带到课堂上参加各种以词卡为道具的学习活动。但是，有一次一个学生对我说，他做词卡只是为了完成我布置的课堂任务，课下他从来不用词卡学生词，因为对他来说，读生词表中的生词比翻转词卡更容易记住生词。

有些学习者喜欢边听音乐边学习字词，有些则不喜欢。因此，我们可以向学习者推荐那些已被实践证明有效的字词学习策略，但是如果他们觉得某种策略不适合自己的话，我们也不能强迫他们接受。

Learning strategies have been studied for decades, but we still lack adequate criteria to establish a standard taxonomy. Nonetheless, scholars tend to agree to classify the learning strategies into four general categories: cognitive strategies, metacognitve strategies, social strategies, and affective strategies (Takač, 2008). **Cognitive strategies** are direct learning strategies relating to purposeful mental action or activity of processing learning materials such as encoding, comprehension, memorization, and application. **Metacognitive strategies** are strategies that do not directly involve knowledge processing, but they facilitate execution of cognitive strategies such as setting up goals, planning learning steps, and evaluating learning results. Three types of knowledge are required for creation of metacognitive strategies: personal knowledge, task knowledge, and strategic knowledge (Wenden, 1998). Personal knowledge is how the learners understand themselves as a learner, such as knowledge of personal language proficiency, learning habits, interests, behavior, and motivation. Task knowledge is learners' knowledge about the purpose of a task and how it will serve their language learning needs. For example, learners know how many words they should learn in a lesson, how many of the words they should be able to read and write, and whether they are required to use the newly learned words in new contexts. Strategic knowledge refers to knowledge of available strategies that learners can use and how to use them to reach the goal based on the learner's personal learning habits and style. **Social strategies** are the strategies related to the way that individual learners learn through cooperation or interaction with others, such as interacting with teachers, classmates, friends, and native speakers. **Affective strategies** are the strategies used by learners to motivate themselves to learn, to eliminate distractions caused by emotional fluctuations, and to control their feelings when they are in a bad mood.

对学习策略的研究虽然已经进行数十年了，但我们仍没有制定出一个标准的策略分类框架。然而，学者们基本上倾向于把学习策略分成四大类：认知策略、元认知策略、社交策略和情感策略。（Takač，2008）**认知策略**是直接学习策略，指的是大脑通过有目的的心理行为或活动直接对学习材料进行认知加工的策略。例如，编码、理解、记忆和应用。**元**

认知策略是间接学习策略，虽然没有直接参与对学习材料的认知加工，但是它能促进认知策略的运用。例如，制定学习目标、规划学习步骤、评价学习结果。元认知策略的运用需要具备三种知识：个体知识、任务知识和策略知识。（Wenden，1998）个体知识是学习者对自己作为一个学习者的了解，如对自己的二语水平、学习习惯、学习兴趣、学习行为和学习动机的了解。任务知识是学习者对任务目标及其是如何满足他们的学习需要的了解。例如，在一篇课文里，学习者知道有多少个生词需要学习，这些生词中有哪些词需要认读、哪些词需要默写，以及他们是否需要学会在新语境中运用这些生词。策略知识是学习者在充分了解自己的学习习惯和学习风格的基础上，知道他们可以运用哪些策略以及如何运用这些策略达到学习目标。**社交策略**是学习者如何通过与别人的合作和互动学习字词的策略，如与教师、同学、朋友和汉语母语者如何互动。**情感策略**是学习者鼓励自己学习、消除情感波动带来的学习干扰以及控制不佳情绪时采用的策略。

Since character and word learning strategies are part of learning strategies, in general, the above discussed four types of strategies can be applied to character and word learning. However, character and word learning is different from other learning tasks such as grammar, reading, and writing; therefore, individuals may adopt specific strategies that more precisely fit character and word learning. For example, a social strategy might be to have a native language partner as a conversation partner to improve oral proficiency. Asking the language partner to point out the errors in word use or pronunciation during communication is a strategy for improving word knowledge.

字词学习策略是学习策略的一部分，上述提到的四类学习策略的分类也适用于字词学习策略。但是，字词学习与语法、阅读、写作等其他学习是不同的，学习者自己可能会采用一些更加适合于字词学习的精准化策略。例如在社交策略上，为了提高口语水平，学习者可以选择与汉语母语者结成语伴；为了增加词语知识，学习者可以请语伴在交流中指出他在用词或词语发音上的错误。

5.2 Studies on Chinese character and word learning strategies 汉语二语字词学习策略的研究

The first empirical study on character learning strategy in a classroom environment among CFL learners was conducted by McGinnis (1995). In total, 29 participants were asked to self-report about their character-learning strategies during a five-week summer immersion program. Rote repetition was the most frequently used strategy and the next was creation of idiosyncratic stories about the characters. Another study by Ke (1998) investigated English-speaking beginning college CFL students' perceptions on the relative effectiveness of various types of character learning strategies. The 223 students participating in the study were asked whether they agreed or disagreed with the 11 statements predesigned by the author. The majority of the participants agreed that learning character components (semantic and phonetic radicals) was more effective than learning stroke order or creating their own stories about what characters look like to them. A small-scale study by 曾金金 (2000) investigated character learning strategies among German-speaking college CFL learners from beginning to advanced levels. This study also adopted a self-report data collection method. According to the author, learners reported 15 types of learning strategies that they used in their character learning. The most common ones were: repeatedly writing the characters, using vocabulary cards, and using radical knowledge.

第一个针对汉字学习策略进行实证性研究的学者是McGinnis（1995），他调查了29名母语为英语的汉语二语学习者在课堂教学环境中使用的汉字学习策略。在他的研究中，29名参与者对他们在为期五周的暑期沉浸式汉语学习中所用的汉字学习策略进行了汇报。该研究发现，机械性重复是学习者最常使用的学习策略，其次是学习者自己编造一个关于汉字的小故事。Ke（1998）调查了母语为英语的成人初级汉语学习者对不同汉字学习策略相对有效性的看法，参与此项研究的223名学生需要对研究者提前设定好的11项有关学习策略的陈述进行认同或不认同的判断。结果表明，大部分参与者认为学习汉字部件（声旁和形旁）比学习笔顺或给汉字编小故事更有效。曾金金（2000）调查了母语为德语的初级到高级的成人汉语学习者的汉字学习策略。这一研究也是让学习者对自己所用的汉字学习策略进行汇报，然后收集和分析报告数据。根据曾金金的统计，学习者一共提到了15种汉学学习策略，其中最常用的学习策略有重复抄写汉字、使用字卡学习汉字，以及利用部首知识学习汉字。

A more comprehensive study on character learning strategies of non-native beginning college CSL learners was conducted by 江新 and 赵果 (2001). 138 students with different foreign language backgrounds who were studying in a target language speaking environment participated in the study. The results showed that 36 learning strategies were commonly used by the students. Of the 36 commonly used strategies, 31 were cognitive strategies and 5 were metacognitive strategies. A factor analysis revealed that the 31 cognitive strategies could be grouped into 6 groups: group 1, stroke strategies—studying stroke order and writing characters according to the correct order; group 2, sound-meaning strategies—paying attention to the sound and meaning of the characters; group 3, shape strategies—paying attention to the physical shape of the characters and repeatedly writing them; group 4, inductive strategies—revealing the similarity of characters in sound and shape by analyzing the phonetic and semantic radical within; group 5, reviewing strategies—reviewing the learned characters; group 6, application strategies—using learned characters in reading and writing. For metacognitive strategies, two groups of strategies were identified. Group 1 was monitoring, finding and analyzing the errors made by students themselves during the learning process. Group 2 was planning, making a plan for character learning based on goals. In a subsequent study (赵果 & 江新, 2002), the researchers further investigated the correlation between the six identified groups of cognitive strategies and character learning performance. The application strategies had positive correlations with the character production performance. The shape strategies had negative correlation with the recognition of meanings of characters.

江新和赵果（2001）针对母语非汉语的大学初级汉语二语学习者的汉字学习策略进行了一项综合性研究，138名母语背景各不相同但均在目的语环境中学习的学生参与了该研究。研究结果表明，学生常用36种学习策略。在这36种常用学习策略中，31种是认知策略，5种是元认知策略。通过因素分析，研究者又将31种认知策略细分为6组：第一组是笔画策略，即学生学习汉字的笔顺并按照笔顺书写汉字；第二组是音义策略，即学生注重对汉字音义的学习；第三组是字形策略，即学生注重对汉字间架结构的学习并重复抄写汉字；第四组是归纳策略，即学生通过分析汉字的声旁和形旁，对形近字、同音字进行归纳；第五组是复习策略，即学生对学过的汉字进行复习；第六组是应用策略，即学生运用新学的汉字进行写作和阅读。研究者还把元认知策略分为两组：一组是监控，即学生对自己在汉字学习中所犯的错误进行监控并分析；另一组是计划，即学生根据学习目标制定学习计划。赵果和江新（2002）在稍后的一项研究中进一步对这6组认知策略与汉字学习效果之间的相关性进行了调查。结果表明，应用策略与汉字书写成绩之间存在显著的正相关，字形策略与汉字意义识别之间存在显著的负相关。

Another comprehensive study on character learning strategies conducted in a non-native language learning environment (Shen, 2005) involved 95 English-speaking college CFL learners from beginning, intermediate, and advanced levels. The study adopted a three-step data collection procedure that used three questionnaires. A statistical procedure of factor analysis was used to classify the identified strategies into groups based on underlying commonalities of factors. The study identified 30 commonly used character-learning strategies. Among these, 24 were cognitive strategies, five were metacognitive strategies, and one was a social strategy, as presented in Table 5-1.

Shen（2005）在非目的语学习环境中进行了另一项综合性研究，该研究的参与者是95名母语为英语的大学初级到高级的汉语学习者。该研究先采用三个调查问卷分三步收集数据，然后用因素分析法对识别出来的学习策略按照其内在的共同特征进行分组。这一研究归纳出了30种常用的汉字学习策略，其中24种为认知策略，5种为元认知策略，1种为社交策略，具体请参见表5-1。

Table 5-1 30 Commonly Used Character Learning Strategies

表 5-1 30种常用的汉字学习策略

Strategy Item 策略条目	Category 分类
1. Repeat the sound when the character is first introduced 汉字第一次出现时重复朗读	C
2. Pay attention to the tone and associate it with Pinyin 注意声调及其与拼音的联系	C
3. Preview the new words before class 课前预习生词	M

（续表）

Strategy Item 策略条目	Category 分类
4. Write the character down when it is first introduced 汉字第一次出现时把它写下来	C
5. Find an equivalent word from the native language 从母语中找到对应词	C
6. Preview the new words the night before class 学习生词的头天晚上预习生词	M
7. Review newly learned words by writing them many times 通过反复书写复习刚学过的生词	C
8. Visualize the character 在大脑中描绘汉字的字形	C
9. Pay attention to how the character is used in context 关注汉字在句中的使用	C
10. Check reference sources for a character's meaning 在相关资料中查询汉字的意思	C
11. Review words by going over notes and example sentences 通过重温课堂笔记和例句复习生词	C
12. Determine if one character in a new compound word has been learned before 确定复合词中的汉字以前是否学过	C
13. Quiz oneself 自我测验	M
14. Look at strokes and associate the character with a similar character already learned 注意汉字的笔画，并把这个字与已学过的相似字联系起来	C
15. Say the character and visualize it 说出汉字并在大脑中形成视觉意象	C
16. Listen carefully when the new character is first introduced 汉字第一次出现时仔细听它的发音	C
17. Recognize radicals which have been learned before 识别汉字中已学过的部首	C
18. Pay attention to stroke order 注意汉字的笔顺	C
19. Determine how new words are used in conversation 明确生词在对话中是如何运用的	C

（续表）

Strategy Item 策略条目	Category 分类
20. Use the new words orally in a sentence 在口语中运用生词	C
21. Read the new words out loud and associate its sound with the meaning and shape 大声地读生词，并把生词的音与其形和义联系起来	C
22. Say the character when writing it 书写汉字的同时读出汉字的音	C
23. Find out the meaning of the radical in the character 查明汉字中的部首所表示的意义	C
24. Find the connection between the new character and previously learned radicals in terms of sound, meaning, and shape 找出新字与新字所包含的已学部首在音、形、义上的联系	C
25. Ask others how they use a certain character in sentences 询问其他人，看他们在句中是如何运用某个汉字的	S
26. Review newly learned words before class and quizzes, and on weekends 在课前、测验前和周末复习新学的生词	M
27. Memorize the sound first, then the meaning and shape 先记字音，再记字义和字形	C
28. Associate the sound of a character with its meaning and shape 建立字音与字义、字形之间的联系	C
29. Do homework first before memorizing the new characters 在记忆新字前先完成作业	M
30. Listen to conversation by native speakers 听汉语母语者之间的对话	C

Note: C=Cognitive strategies, M=Metacognitive strategies, S=Social strategies.
注：C=认知策略，M=元认知策略，S=社交策略。

A factor analysis revealed that these 30 commonly used strategies could be classified into eight groups based on their commonalities. Among the eight groups, groups 1–7 were cognitive strategies: group 1, cognitive strategies relating to learning characters by using orthographic knowledge, such as paying attention to graphic structures, making connections with previously learned similar characters, visualizing the graphic structure of the character, and making use of phonetic and semantic information in components; group 2, cognitive strategies dealing with learning new characters/words by understanding their meanings in different written and spoken contexts; group 3, cognitive strategies relating to learning behaviors of effectively memorizing and retaining newly learned characters such as making mental linkages among the sound, shape, and meaning of a character and relating the new word to its context in both oral and written methods; group 4, cognitive strategies relating to receiving new character information at the initial stage from the instructor, such as listening carefully to the pronunciation and tone, observing stroke order carefully and trying to write the new character down when it was first introduced; group 5, cognitive strategies of memorization that emphasize the use of the sound of the character as a cue for making connections to the meaning and shape; group 6, cognitive strategies related to seeking reference for understanding the new characters, such as relating new characters to the first language and asking how they are used in context; group 7, cognitive strategies using an aural approach to improve retention of new characters that had already been introduced, such as listening to native speakers and saying the word to oneself; group 8, metacognitive strategies such as structured review before and after class. The study revealed that learners considered group 1 orthographic knowledge-based learning strategies and group 8 structured review were most helpful in preparing for their character/word quizzes.

通过因素分析，研究者将这30种常用的汉字学习策略根据其内在的共同特征分成了8组。其中，1-7组是认知策略：第一组是运用缀字知识学习汉字的策略，如关注字形的间架结构、与先前学过的相似字建立联系、形成对汉字整体字形的视觉意象、利用声旁和形旁学习；第二组是通过不同的口语和书面语语境理解字词意义的策略；第三组是关于有效记忆汉字与保持记忆效果的策略，如在大脑中建立汉字音、形、义三者之间的联系，以口头或书面的方式将生词放在句子中记忆；第四组是关于初始阶段如何从教师那里获取汉字信息的策略，如仔细听汉字的发音与声调、仔细观察汉字书写时的笔顺，以及当汉字第一次出现时把它写下来；第五组是关于如何将字音作为记忆支点并把它与字形和字义联系起来记忆汉字的策略；第六组是关于如何通过查找其他资料理解汉字的策略，如把新字与学习者的第一语言联系起来、弄清楚如何用新字造句；第七组是关于如何通过听的方式加强汉字记忆效果的策略，如仔细听汉语母语者的发音、把包含某字的生词大声说出来给自己听；第八组是元认知策略，如有计划地进行课前预习和课后复习。研究表明，在这8组学习策略中，学习者认为第一组——以缀字知识为基础的学习策略和第八组——有计划地进行课前预习和课后复习的学习策略对准备字词测验最有效。

A later study (Sung & Wu, 2011) adopted Shen's (2005) strategy questionnaire, involved 108 first-year CFL learners in the US, examined not only the learners' character learning strategies but also the influence of factors such as gender (male vs. female), home background (heritage learners vs. non-heritage learners), and previous language learning experiences on learners' choosing and using strategies. The factor analysis result showed that learners used six types of strategies: (1) practicing words in a natural language environment; (2) establishing association between new and old words; (3) paying attention to the structure of characters such as strokes and radicals; (4) using mechanical techniques for memorization; (5) grouping words; (6) paying attention to the pronunciation. The study also showed that gender and home background brought the differences in using mechanical techniques.

For example, female heritage learners used type 4 strategy more frequently than the male heritage learners. Gender, home background, and previous language learning experiences together also affected the use of type 3 strategy. The male heritage learners who had not studied any other foreign language used this strategy most frequently compared with all other groups. While the female heritage learners who had not studied any other foreign language used the same type of strategy least often. A related study (Grenfell & Harris, 2015) investigated 11- to 15-year-old female students in a UK school. The factor analysis revealed that female students use three types of strategies: (1) focus on the whole character by using it in contextual situations, (2) focus on strokes by paying attention to the character stroke components, (3) focus on prior knowledge by relating character learning to existing experience and world knowledge.

Sung 和 Wu（2011）在稍后进行的一项研究中也采用了Shen（2005）研究中使用的学习策略调查问卷，她们不仅调查了美国108名母语为英语的初级汉语学习者汉字学习策略的使用情况，还调查了性别、家庭背景（华裔与非华裔）及外语学习经历对学习者学习策略的选择和使用的影响。因素分析的结果显示，学习者主要使用6种学习策略：（1）在自然语言环境中练习使用词语；（2）建立新旧词语之间的联系；（3）关注汉字本身的结构，如笔画、部首；（4）对汉字进行机械性记忆；（5）对词语进行分组；（6）注重汉字的发音。研究结果还显示，性别和家庭背景是造成学习者在第四种学习策略的使用上产生差异的主要因素。具体来说，华裔女性学习者在第四种学习策略的运用上比华裔男性学习者更频繁。性别、家庭背景和外语学习经历这三种因素共同影响了第三种学习策略的使用。从未学过任何外语的华裔男性学习者在第三种学习策略的运用上比其他组更频繁，而从未学过其他外语的华裔女性学习者则较少运用第三种学习策略。Grenfell 和 Harris（2015）进行的一项相关研究调查了英国一所中学里11～15岁女生的汉字学习策略使用情况，因素分析结果表明，女生主要使用三类学习策略：（1）从汉字整体入手，在句子或语境中练习使用汉字；（2）从笔画入手，关注汉字笔画的间架结构；（3）从学生已有的知识入手，将新字的学习与已有的生活经验和背景知识联系起来。

By adopting Shen's strategy questionnaire (Shen, 2005), Sung (2014) further investigated college beginning American learners of Chinese on commonly used character learning strategies and their relationship with character/word tests. The results showed that phonological-knowledge-related strategies were effective in aiding phonological comprehension of Chinese characters (understanding the character meaning by hearing it). Strategies that helped the participants acquire graphic features of characters were effective in enhancing students' performance in graphic comprehension, graphic production, and phonological production in the test.

Sung（2014）采用Shen（2005）研究中使用的学习策略调查问卷又进一步调查了美国大学初级汉语学习者常用的汉字学习策略与字词测验成绩之间的关系。结果表明，与语音知识有关的学习策略能帮助学生记住汉字的音（听到音后能知其义），与字形记忆有关的学习策略能帮助学生在测验中正确识别汉字的音、形和义。

In the information age, strategies that learners use for character learning in a paperless environment becomes an important topic of our research. One study (Qian, Owen, & Bax, 2018) adopted Shen's (2005) strategy questionnaire with some modification investigated mobile-assisted Chinese character learning strategies among adult distance learners. The participants were 22 UK-based beginner-level distance learners. By using data collection methods of online survey, learning diary, and email interviews, the results showed, in addition to commonly used strategies reported in Shen's study (2005), learners used five more new strategies: (1) use an online dictionary to find out how the character is used in context; (2) use a Pinyin input method to choose/identify characters; (3) focus on the phonetic component of a character; (4) pronounce the character oneself, and then listen to the model pronunciation (from the computer); (5) preview all the new characters in each lesson (from the computer) before going into a particular one.

在信息化时代，学习者在无纸化语言环境中使用什么样的策略学习汉字已经成为一个重要的研究课题。Qian、Owen 和 Bax（2018）采用 Shen（2005）研究中使用的学习策略调查问卷，经略加修改后调查了英国22名初级远程汉语学习者运用电子移动设备学习汉字的策略使用情况。研究者采用在线调查、学习日记、电子邮件采访等方式收集相关数据，数据分析结果显示，学习者除了运用Shen（2005）研究中提出的常用学习策略之外，还使用了5种新策略：（1）利用在线词典查找目的字在句中使用的具体方式；（2）用拼音输入法找出目的字；（3）关注电子材料中显示的汉字声旁；（4）看到电子材料中显示的汉字后，自己先根据拼音读出来，然后再与课件中提供的标准发音对照；（5）先预习新课中的所有生字，然后再逐一学习。

One study (Wang, Spencer, & Xing, 2009) investigated the effects of metacognitive beliefs and strategies on character learning performance. In that study, the metacognitive beliefs refer to learners' beliefs of their own learning and their positive expectations for their learning performance and value of success. Data on 45 English-speaking beginning college Chinese learners' metacognitive beliefs, metacognitive strategies, and their character learning performance were analyzed. A positive correlation was found among the three; that is, learners who were confident about their ability to learn the language and understood their responsibility in planning their learning did well in their character tests.

Wang、Spencer 和 Xing（2009）调查了元认知态度取向与元认知策略对汉字学习效果的影响。元认知态度取向是指学习者对自己学习能力的信心和对自己学习效果和成功价值的积极期望。该研究分析了45名母语为英语的大学汉语学习者的元认知态度取向、元认知策略与汉字学习效果之间的关系。结果表明，三者之间呈正相关。也就是说，那些对自己学习能力比较自信并知道如何规划自己学习的学习者，他们的汉字测验成绩也相对较好。

The above studies show that CSL learners used a wide variety of cognitive strategies in their character and word learning, but they paid less attention to the use of metacognitive strategies, social strategies, and affective strategies. The learning reality is that metacognitive strategies sometimes play important roles in character and word learning. Here is a story from the author of the book:

A student came to my office and told me that he wanted to drop the Chinese class because he had a busy schedule and could not find a time to work on Chinese characters every day. I asked him to show me his daily schedule book. I went over his schedule and pointed out to him that there were a few time slots that he could use for character learning each day. After this meeting, the student decided not to drop the class, as he was convinced that he actually had time to study characters on a daily basis.

This story shows us that some students do poorly in character and word learning not because they have problems in using cognitive strategies, but because they lack metacognitive strategies and do not know how to monitor their own learning.

以上研究表明，汉语二语学习者在字词学习中会使用各种各样的认知策略，但是对元认知策略、社交策略和情感策略的使用却不多。事实上，元认知策略有时候对字词学习起着十分重要的作用。请看下面这个例子：

> 有个学生到我办公室来，告诉我他不想继续选修中文课了，因为他每天的学习日程都很紧，根本没有时间学习汉字。我让他把学习日程表拿出来给我看看。看完他的日程表后，我给他指出来他每天其实是可以找出几个时间段学习汉字的。这一次谈话过后，那个学生决定继续选修中文课，因为他相信，他每天是可以抽出时间学习汉字的。

这个例子告诉我们，有些学生的字词学习效果不理想不是因为他们不会使用认知策略，而是因为他们很少使用元认知策略，不知道如何监控自己的学习行为。

In summary, character and word learning strategy research is still an evolving field. Although the number of existing studies on CSL character learning strategies is limited, these studies have convinced us that learners use a wide range of learning strategies in their character learning and that good learning strategies play a positive role in character acquisition.

综上所述，目前对汉语二语字词学习策略的研究仍然处在一个不断发展的阶段。虽然已有的关于汉字学习策略的研究数量还不是很多，但这些研究已经证明了学习者在汉字学习中运用了很多学习策略，而且好的学习策略在汉字习得中确实发挥着重要的作用。

5.3 Identifying and training on character and word learning strategies 识别和训练字词学习策略

In the previous section, we concluded that character learning strategies have a positive effect on character learning. Therefore, pedagogically, it is necessary for classroom instructors to help students identify character learning strategies as well as provide strategy training so that students can learn good character learning strategies. A study (柳燕梅, 2009) on the necessity, teachability, and effectiveness of strategy training for Chinese character learning among Chinese L2 learners conducted at Beijing Language and Culture University has concluded that: (1) participants considered that strategy training was necessary in helping with their learning characters; (2) learners who participated in the strategy training courses showed that they use more strategies in their daily character learning than the control group, which means that the training increased learners' conscious awareness of using strategies; and (3) learners in the experimental group purposefully used a number of strategies, which significantly reduced the extent of character writing time during the memorization process compared with the control group. This study provided a positive note that strategy training is beneficial to learners. In this section, we will discuss how to identify useful character and word learning strategies that students are using and how to organize an effective strategy training workshop.

在上一节中我们得出了结论，汉字学习策略确实对汉字学习起着积极作用。因此，从教学上看，教师是有必要在课堂教学中帮助学生识别不同的汉字学习策略并提供相应的策略训练，这样学生才能学到好的、适合自己的汉字学习策略。柳燕梅（2009）针对策略训练的必要性、可教性和有效性在北京语言大学的汉语二语学习者中展开了研究，结果发现：（1）参与者都认为策略训练能帮助他们学习汉字，是有必要的；（2）参加了策略训练的学习者在日常汉字学习中比没参加的运用了更多的策略，这说明训练能增强学习者的策略使用意识；（3）跟对照组相比，参加了策略训练的实验组学习者能有目的地使用一系列策略记忆汉字，大大减少了反复抄写汉字的次数。这一研究有力地证明了，策略训练能促进学习者的汉字学习。下面我们将讨论如何帮助学生识别有用的字词学习策略以及如何有效地组织学习策略训练。

5.3.1 Identifying effective character and word learning strategies used by your students 识别学生运用的有效字词学习策略

Experienced instructors often collect good character and word leaning strategies from their students. They may wish to introduce those strategies to new students. However, learning is personal and individual. Strategies that fit previous students may not entirely fit the current students. Therefore, it is the best that instructors identify what strategies their current students are using prior to introducing any other strategies to the students, because students' self-developed strategies may fit their own cognitive style and learning habit better. It is necessary that, every year, instructors help students to identify their character and word learning strategies and determine which are effective. Instructors may adopt the following methods to help students identify effective character and word learning strategies:

有经验的教师常常会收集学生使用的有效字词学习策略，并希望将这些字词学习策略介绍给其他学生。但是，学习是一种个性化的个体行为，那些适用于之前学生的学习策略不一定也完全适用于现在的学生。教师最好在向学生介绍其他学习策略之前先帮助他们识别出他们正在使用的学习策略是什么，因为学生自己琢磨出来的学习策略可能更适合他们自己的认知风格和学习习惯。教师有必要每年都帮助学生总结一下他们正在使用的字词学习策略，并协助他们确定哪些学习策略是有效的。教师可以采取以下措施帮助学生识别有效的字词学习策略：

Classroom observation. During the class, the instructor should give students opportunities to demonstrate how they use strategies in learning new words. The instructor can give each student a few new words and ask them to do a self-study. The instructor can then walk around and observe how the students learn those new words, such as how they learn the sound, shape, and meaning of each word. Afterwards, the instructor could ask each student to report their learning results or give a mini-quiz to evaluate their learning results. This will help students determine the effectiveness of the strategies they used for learning new words.

课堂观察。在课堂上，教师应该给学生提供机会让他们展示自己的学习策略。教师可以先给每个学生分配几个生词让他们自学。在这期间，教师可以在教室里来回走动，观察学生使用的学习方法，如他们是怎么学习每个生词的音、形、义的。之后，教师可以让学生汇报一下他们的学习结果，或者进行一个小测验评估其学习效果。这样做可以帮助学生判断他们所用的学习策略是否有效。

Student self-reporting. The instructor asks students to think introspectively about what kind of strategies they use in character and word learning based on the established categories. For example, the instructor can first give the students the definition of cognitive, metacognitive, social, and affective strategies, and then ask students to name the strategies they use and to classify them into the four categories. Students then can share their learning strategies with each other.

学生自我汇报。教师先给学生介绍一下前面提到的四种学习策略，然后请学生自我反思一下，他们在平时的字词学习中所用的学习策略属于哪种。例如，教师先告诉学生什么是认知策略、元认知策略、社交策略和情感策略，然后让学生说说他们用的是什么策略，属于哪个类别。学生之间可以就他们各自所使用的学习策略相互交流。

Questionnaire. On some occasions, some students may not be aware of the strategies they are using for character learning. The instructor can provide a list of strategies observed in the classroom or self-reported by previous and current students. Based on collected strategies, the instructor can develop a structured questionnaire that asks the students to rate the frequency of using each strategy listed in the questionnaire on a five-point Likert scale. Completion of the survey would provide students with an idea of the kind of strategies they are using. The Likert scale was invented by the American psychologist Rensis Likert. The five-point scale for the current example would be a scale with 5 choices from 1–5 as follows: 1. Never or almost never true of me; 2. Generally not true of me; 3. Somewhat true of me; 4. Generally true of me; 5. Always or almost always true of me. Students would be asked to mark only one statement from the five based on their true feelings for using each of the strategies listed in the questionnaire. For example, if the strategy item is "Pay attention to the tone and associate it with Pinyin" (Shen, 2005), and the student feels that he/she seldom uses that strategy, then, the number "1" should be marked. Once students have marked their choices for all strategy items in the questionnaire, then they can sort out the strategy use from the list, based on the number from high to low. A high number indicates a more frequently used strategy. After identifying the strategies that students are using in their character learning, the next step is to ask students to evaluate which strategies they think are most helpful for memorizing the sound, shape, and meaning of characters as well as their character/word tests by rating in a five-point Likert scale again. After students have finished evaluating the strategies, they should be asked to sort out the strategies from more useful to least useful based on their own ratings. After that, students should have a good picture about their strategy use.

调查表。有时候，学生自己可能都没有意识到他们是在用什么策略学习汉字。这时，教师可以设计一个调查表，在表上列出自己在课上观察到的或其他学生汇报过的学习策略，然后让学生通过五分点的李克特量表对这些学习策略的使用频率进行判定。完成判定后，学生就能发现哪些策略是他们正在使用的。李克特量表是由美国心理学家Rensis Likert发明的。五分点是指由1到5的五项选择："1"代表"从来都不是真实的"，"2"代表"基本上不是真实的"，"3"代表"有时候是真实的"，"4"代表"基本上是真实的"，"5"代表"总是真实的"。教师让学生根据自己的真实情况对所列的每项学习策略按这五个等级进行判定。例如，调查表上列出的一项学习策略是"注意声调及其与拼音的联系"（Shen，2005），如果填表的学生认为他/她几乎不用这项策略，那么他/她应当勾选"1. 从来都不是真实的"。选完后，学生可以根据每项学习策略后自己所选的数字按照从大到小的顺序重新排列所有的学习策略。数字大的是学生自己常用的策略，数字小的则是不常用的策略。接下来，教师可以让学生评估一下哪些策略对他们的汉字学习和字词测验最有帮助。学生同样可以使用五分点的李克特量表来甄别哪些策略对自己来说是最有效的，然后按照有效性从大到小的顺序重新排列所有的学习策略。通过这些活动，学生将会对自己的策略使用情况有一个清晰的认识。

5.3.2 Training on character and word learning strategies 字词学习策略的训练

Strategy training includes two aspects of preparation: one is to compile a strategy taxonomy and the other is to make a training plan to outline the training procedures. We will discuss these two in detail below.

组织策略训练需要做两方面的准备：一是编制一个学习策略分类表，确定要介绍哪些策略；二是制定一个策略训练计划，概述训练的步骤。下面我们将详细探讨这两方面。

• Compiling a strategy taxonomy 编制学习策略分类表

Helping students to identify their effective character and word learning strategies can direct students' attention to how they learn and encourage them to discover and create learning strategies that fit their own learning styles. However, discovering and creating an effective learning strategy by the students themselves alone would take a long time, as students are not able to judge the effectiveness of a strategy until it has been used many times. If instructors have identified good strategies that have been proved effective from learning practice, then introduce these strategies to students and train them for using the strategies, so that students will be able to use many more strategies in their learning. Training on character and word learning strategy is a fast way to have students gain good quality learning strategies in a short period of time. Prior to strategy training, the instructor would need to compile a strategy taxonomy which includes the four types of strategies already discussed. When compiling the taxonomy, for choosing cognitive strategies, teachers may pay attention to the following aspects:

帮助学生识别有效的字词学习策略能让学生更关注他们是怎么学习字词的，同时也能鼓励他们探索和创造适合自己学习风格的学习策略。但是，让学生自己探索和创造有效的学习策略不是一朝一夕就能做到的，因为学生只有在某个策略使用了多次之后才能判断这个策略是否真正有效。如果教师已经从学习实践中识别出了一些已被证明有效的学习策略，把这些策略介绍给学生，并训练他们使用这些策略，那么学生就可以在字词学习中运用更多的学习策略。学习策略训练可以让学生在短时间内就获得较好的学习策略，但是在训练之前，教师首先要编制一个包含四种学习策略的分类表。在制表时，对于认知策略的选择，教师应该考虑如下因素：

Strategies helping to conceptualize. These are strategies used to understand the sound, shape, and meaning of the target word through analysis of components within the target word, analysis of morphological structure of the words, and comparison of the word with other similar words to establish a clear concept of the target words. An example would be understanding that the character 瓷 is a phonetic-semantic compound by identifying the phonetic radical 次, the semantic radical 瓦, and two perceptual components in the phonetic component—冫 and 欠. If a word is a disyllabic word, such as 打击, after analyzing the individual characters 打 and 击, students would learn the strategies to figure out the morphological structure of this word. They should know that this is a coordinate word as 打 and 击 both are verbs and the semantic importance of each word is equal. Students should know the meaning of the word 打击 as a whole, and how it differs from 打架, not only by judging the word meanings but also by judging the word structures. Here, 打击 is coordinate structure but 打架 is verb-object structure.

能帮助概念化的策略。能帮助概念化的策略是指通过分析目的词所包含的汉字的部件、目的词的构词方式并对比目的词与相似词的异同了解目的词的音、形、义，最终在大脑中形成对目的词的清晰认识的一类策略。例如，在学习“瓷”这个字时，学生能理解“瓷”是一个形声字，声旁是“次”，形旁是“瓦”，而且声旁“次”由两个知觉部件构成——“冫”和“欠”。如果要学的词是个双音节词，例如“打击”，学生在分析完“打”和“击”这两个字以后，还应该学习该词的构词方式。也就是说，他们应该知道“打击”是一个联合词，“打”和“击”都是动词，每个字的语义在这个词中是同等重要的。学生不仅要知道“打击”和“打架”在语义上的不同，还应该知道他们在构词方式上的不同。从构词方式看，“打击”是联合结构，而“打架”是动宾结构。

Strategies helping to establish association. This includes two types of strategies. One is creating mental linkages among the sound, shape, and meaning within the word, such as reading out loud the word, visualizing its shape, using a finger to write it in the air several times, and attaching a meaning to the sound and shape. The second type of strategy is to associate one word with another word. Strategies of this type can include using a story or dialog to integrate a series of target words, or associating either sound or meaning to the first language to find a memory peg, such as using the English word “bar” which has a similar sound with the character 吧, and the English meaning of “bar” as a “counter for selling wine or drinks” which is directly related to 酒吧. So the connection between “bar” and 酒吧 helps memorize 酒吧. Grouping words based on themes is another way of making association between words, such as using “hospital” as a theme to group the words 医生, 病人, 心脏病, 吃药, and 打针 together.

能帮助建立联结的策略。这类策略又可以分为两小类：一类是能帮助建立词语内部音、形、义之间联结的，如大声朗读词语，在大脑中描绘该词的词形并形成视觉图像，用手指反复书写词语，把词义与其音、形联系起来，等等。另一类是能帮助建立目的词与其他词之间联结的，如用一个故事或对话把一系列目的词串起来，通过将目的词的音、义与对应的第一语言中的词联系起来形成记忆支点。例如，英语中的“bar”与汉语中的“吧”音似，“bar”的其中一个意思是卖酒或饮料的柜台，如果让学生在“bar”与“酒吧”之间建立起联结，那么记住“酒吧”就很容易了。另一种建立联结的方法是将词根据主题进行分组。例如，我们可以将“医院”作为主题，在“医生、病人、心脏病、吃药、打针”等词之间建立起联结。

Strategies helping to make connection. This means to connect the words with personal life experiences or previously learned words, and to find synonyms and antonyms for the target words. For example, for the word 酒吧, students can ask themselves whether they have seen or have been to a 酒吧 in their own country. What experience have they gained about 酒吧? If they have never been to a 酒吧, do they know any person, either a friend or a family member, who has been to a 酒吧? They can also make some connections between this word with the previously learned word 九, which has the same pronunciation, and other previously learned words, 酒瓶, 酒杯, and 喝酒, which can be seen in 酒吧. If the target word is 思念, students can connect this word with a learned synonymous word 想念 to help remember the meaning of the word.

能帮助建立关系的策略。这类策略是将目的词与个人生活经历、以前学过的词联系起来，找出目的词的近（同）义词和反义词。仍以“酒吧”

为例，学生可以问下自己有没有在自己国家见过酒吧或去过酒吧。关于酒吧，他们有什么样的经历？如果他们从来没有去过酒吧，那他们所认识的人，朋友或家人有没有去过酒吧？学生还可以将“酒吧”中的“酒”字与以前学过的同音字如“九”联系起来帮助记忆字音；也可以将“酒吧”与以前学过的“酒瓶、酒杯、喝酒”等词联系起来，这些词所表示的事物或行为都是在酒吧中能经常看到的。如果目的词是“思念”，学生可以将这个词与学过的同义词“想念”联系起来，从而记住“思念”的意思。

Strategies of using imagination. This type of strategy helps to create mental images of the words. For example, when the word 英雄 is introduced, students can visualize a hero or heroic behavior, which is stored in their mind. When they learn the phrase 山雨欲来风满楼, students can create a mental picture of this scene.

运用想象力的策略。这类策略能帮助学生形成目的词的心理图像。例如：学习“英雄”这个词时，学生可以在大脑中回想某个英雄人物的形象或某种英雄行为；学习 “山雨欲来风满楼”时，学生可以在大脑中想象这一视觉景象。

Strategies of using animation. This type of strategy involves using physical action, such as acting out a word with a gesture or an action, including drawing.

运用动作的策略。这类策略主要是运用体态动作，如用某种姿势或某个动作把词表演出来，也包括用画画的方式将词表现出来。

Strategies for application. This type of strategy involves using the target characters/words either in a simulated or authentic language situation to complete communication tasks.

应用字词的策略。这类策略主要是指在模拟的或真实的语境中运用所学字词完成交际任务。

For metacognitive strategies to be included in the training, the instructor can consider the following aspects:

关于策略训练中的元认知策略，教师可以考虑以下方面：

Time planning. This refers to strategies used for planning where, when, and how to study characters and words. This type of strategy involves working out a weekly or monthly written plan, and putting the plan in a noticeable or easy-to-find place as a reminder, as well as finding and using all possible discrete times, such as 5 or 10 minutes, to study characters and words.

时间规划。时间规划指的是计划在什么地方、什么时候、如何学习字词的一类策略。这类策略包括：制定每周或每月的书面学习计划，并将计划贴在醒目的或容易看到的地方时刻提醒自己；找出并尽可能地利用所有的碎片时间学习字词，5分钟或10分钟都可以。

Enforcing a schedule. Once students have their schedules worked out, if the plan is not enforced, the learning will not happen. Strategies such as staying with the plan on a daily basis, changing the plan if it does not work, or asking others (roommates or friends) to give a reminder can help make sure that the scheduled time is used for character and word study.

执行计划。学习计划制定了以后如果不执行，那么学习就无法进行。督促自己执行计划的策略有：每天按计划行事；如果计划不切实际，那就赶紧改变计划；请别人（室友或朋友）提醒自己。这些都能督促学生按计划进行字词学习。

Monitoring strategy use. This refers to determining what strategies the learner is using and in what way the learner uses it, and whether a certain strategy is helpful. For example, if a student gets a good or bad character/word test result, the student may wish to reflect on what kind of learning strategies are useful for preparing for this type of tests.

使用监控策略。监控策略是指让学习者自己确定应该用什么策略、如何使用以及策略对自己是否有用。例如，如果学生在字词测验中的成绩很好或很不好，那他/她可能会反思一下什么样的学习策略对准备字词测验是有用的。

Since social strategies are related to learning characters and words by communicating with others, this could include pair or group work in the classroom and language practice with others outside of class. The training may focus on strategies of finding opportunities for socialization and strategies of how to communicate with others with limited target words and how to work cooperatively with others. We have observed that some students are quite outgoing and they often drop into the instructor's office to practice oral Chinese and use newly learned words. Some students are reluctant to practice the target language with others, even inside the classroom. Therefore, we should encourage students to use strategies to find opportunities such as living with a roommate who speaks Chinese, or living with a Chinese family, finding a language partner on campus, making friends with a native speaker, pairing with classmates after class to work on Chinese, signing up for electronic communication such as online chatting, blogging, and email exchanges for the purpose of learning and using characters and words.

社交策略是通过与他人交流学习字词的策略，既包括课堂上的两人或多人小组活动，也包括课外与其他人一起进行的语言实践活动。社交策略的训练重点应放在如何寻找机会与他人交流、如何利用有限的目的词展开交流，以及如何与他人合作完成交流上。通过观察我们发现，有些学生非常外向，经常到教师办公室来运用新学的词语跟教师练习口语；有些学生则不太愿意与别人交流，即使在课堂上也是如此。我们应该鼓励学生多找机会与人交流，如找一个说汉语的人做室友，住到中国家庭里去，在学校里找一个语伴，与汉语母语者交朋友，课后与同学结对练习汉语，通过网上聊天、博客、电子邮件等电子通信手段学习和运用字词。

Affective strategies are related to building students' confidence, increasing their self-motivation, and controlling anxiety and frustration during learning. Young college students, especially in the beginning level classes, are just starting their college life, which is very different from high school life. They need to learn to be more independent and self-regulated. Sometimes, they have difficulties in controlling their own emotions in adverse situations such as feeling that they are falling behind in the class due to a personal, health, or family matter. The training on affective strategies may focus on two aspects. One is how to solve a problem on one's own. For example, how to handle the situation when doing poorly in an exam, how to handle feelings of falling behind in the class, having difficulty in using words or understanding a conversation partner's wording, and how to reduce anxiety by thinking and doing something positive. The other aspect is how to find a place to talk about the problem. For example, talk to teachers, classmates, parents, and friends to seek advice.

情感策略是帮助学生在学习过程中树立信心、进行自我激励以及控制焦虑和绝望情绪的策略。年轻的大学生，尤其是新生，刚开始他们的大学生活，由于大学生活与高中生活截然不同，他们更需要学会独立生活和自我约束。有时候他们在逆境中无法控制自己的情绪，如当他们因个人私事、身体状况或家庭情况的影响而成绩落后时。情感策略的训练重点包括两个方面：一是如何依靠自己解决困难，如怎么面对考试没考好的情况，怎么调节成绩落后时自己的消极情绪，怎么处理与对方交流时自己找不到合适的词进行表达或听不懂对方措辞时的尴尬，怎么通过想一些或做一些积极的事缓解学习的焦虑感，等等。二是如何找到一个合适的场合或对象讨论自己面临的问题。例如，学生可以向老师、同学、父母以及朋友咨询解决问题的办法，寻求他们的帮助。

• Steps for strategy training 策略训练的步骤

Once the strategy taxonomy is compiled and the instructor knows what strategies the students should learn, the next step is to run training workshops that can include the following steps:

编制好了策略分类表，教师也就知道了学生应该学习哪些字词学习策略，那下一步就是怎么进行学习策略的训练。下面的步骤仅供参考：

Planning. The instructor needs to work out a schedule for training, such as time, duration, and number of strategies to learn for each training session. The instructor should also make sure that each session introduces only a number of strategies and will not overload students.

计划。教师需要制定一个训练计划，这个计划应该包括训练开始的时间、训练的时长、训练的阶段以及每个阶段要学习的策略的数量。教师在制定计划时还应该确保每个阶段只进行几种策略的训练，不要让学生超负荷学习。

Demonstrating. After each strategy is introduced, if possible, the instructor should demonstrate how to use it in different learning situations to reach a certain goal. Some cognitive strategies are not visible, so the instructor needs to use think-aloud methods to demonstrate strategies. For example, when learning the character 春, the instructor would demonstrate that memorization of this character can be done by thinking about three persons embracing the sun in the springtime.

示范。介绍完每个策略之后，如果条件允许的话，教师应该给学生示范下如何在不同的学习情况下使用该策略达到特定的学习目标。有些认知策略是内隐的，不容易观察到，这时教师可以用边想边说的方法展示这些策略。例如，学习汉字“春”时，教师可以通过边想过说“三个人在春天里拥抱着太阳”的方式示范记忆这个汉字的方法。

Practicing. For maximum outcome of strategy training, the training should not be just a matter of introducing strategies to students, but also a matter of making sure that students actually will use the strategy in their own learning. Thus, enough time should be allocated to have students practice using the strategy on site. The practice could be individual or in a small group. During strategy practice, students may have a creative way of using a certain strategy or have created a new strategy for learning a word.

练习。为了使策略训练的效果最大化，我们的训练不能只停留在向学生介绍策略，还要确保学生能将学到的策略付诸实践。因此，教师在介绍完一种策略后要留出足够的时间让学生当场练习如何运用这一策略。练习可以是个人形式的，也可以是小组形式的。在练习期间，学生有可能以一种创新的方式运用某种策略，甚至会创造出一种新的学习策略。

Feedback. Once students gain confidence in and feel comfortable about using newly learned strategies, the instructor may ask students to report, either in oral or in written form, on their experience learning and using strategies, such as which strategies are easy to learn and to use, which strategies do not work for them, and what problems they encountered while using the newly learned strategies. The instructor can then make some adjustments in strategy training, based on the students' feedback.

反馈。等学生有了足够的信心能得心应手地运用所学策略后，教师就可以让学生以口头或书面的形式汇报一下他们学习和使用这些策略的经验和体会，如哪些策略容易学和用，哪些策略对他们不适用，在学习和运用过程中遇到了哪些困难。这样，教师就可以根据学生的反馈对策略训练计划进行适当的调整。

Evaluating. It is possible that some students do not see effects of strategy use because certain strategies may not fit their cognitive style. It is also possible that students may not use a strategy appropriately. Therefore, the instructor should ask students to do self-evaluation of strategy use after a certain period of practice. The evaluation can be qualitative, provided by verbal comments, or quantitative, provided by rating the strategies on a scale. This will give students an idea regarding how well the newly learned strategies work.

评估。有些策略对某些学生并不起作用，这很有可能是因为这些策略不适合他们的认知风格，也有可能是因为学生没有恰当地运用这些策略。因此，教师可以在学生运用某策略一段时间后，让学生就策略的运用情况进行自我评估。评估可以是定性的，如进行口头评论；也可以是定量的，如让学生用量表对策略进行评定。评估结果能让学生确定新学习的策略的可行性与有效性。

Sharing. The instructor should provide opportunities to let students share their ways of using strategies. Sometimes one strategy works well for one student, but not for another student. The problem is not the strategy itself, but inappropriate use of the strategy. For example, some students may report that radicals are not useful in helping to learn compound characters. These students probably do not know that radical strategy helps only for semantic transparent compound words, not for opaque words. Therefore, they should not apply this strategy to every character.

分享。教师应该给学生提供机会让他们交流一下他们是如何运用策略学习字词的。有时候，一种策略对某个学生有效，但对另一个学生却无效。问题可能不在于策略本身，而在于学生对策略的不当使用。例如，有些学生认为部首知识对学习合体字并没有用，这些学生可能不知道，部首知识对学习那些形义透明度高的合体字有用而对那些形义模糊的合体字不起什么作用。因此，学生不应该运用部首分析的策略学习每一个汉字。

During the training, the instructor should bear in mind that character and word learning strategies could be idiosyncratic. It is important that we respect individual differences and do not force students to use strategies that they do not feel comfortable to learn or to use.

在训练期间，教师应牢记，字词学习策略可以是非常个性化的。我们要尊重个体之间存在的差异，不能强迫学生学习和运用那些他们觉得不适合自己的学习策略。

The effectiveness of character and word learning strategy training is also affected by a number of factors (Chamot & Rubin, 1994). One is students' language proficiency level. Usually high proficiency students use more strategies and also learn more quickly. The second is the difficulty level of the language tasks. For example, strategies used for recognition of characters/words may be easier to learn than strategies used to produce target characters/words in written form. Another factor is the difference in language modality. Mastering a word means hearing a word by understanding its meaning, speaking the word by using one's own language, reading and understanding the meaning of the word in different contexts, and writing the word by using one's own language. In general, reading and listening as receptive activities are easier than speaking and writing. In addition, motivation is also a factor affecting strategy training. Students who are highly motivated and who have positive learning attitudes toward strategy learning may learn better than students who are not interested in strategy learning or who do not believe that strategies are helpful in their learning.

策略训练的有效性受多种因素的制约。（Chamot and Rubin，1994）一是学生的目的语水平。一般来说，目的语水平比较高的学生使用的学习策略比较多，而且对新策略的接受也会更快一些。二是语言学习任务的难度。例如，字词认读策略可能比字词默写策略更容易掌握。三是语言表现形式的差异。掌握一个词，意味着听到这个词时能知其义，能用这个词口头表达自己的想法，当这个词在不同文本中出现时能知其音、会其义，能用这个词书面表达自己的看法。一般来说，读和听作为接受性语言活动要比说和写这种产出性语言活动容易。除此之外，学习动机也是影响策略训练有效性的一个因素。学习动机比较强和对策略学习抱有积极态度的学生要比那些抱有消极态度或怀疑态度的学生学得好。

As mentioned earlier, strategy learning is individualized. A strategy that works well for one group of students may not work for another group of students due to their cognitive differences. Therefore, it is best that we do not set up strategy training as a required course. It may work better to make it an elective course or a workshop. Participation in this type of training is not mandatory.

正如我们前面所提到的，策略学习是一种个体化的学习活动。由于学生的认知差异，有的策略对一些学生适用但对另一些学生可能就不适用。因此，我们最好不要将策略训练课设为必修课，以选修课或研讨会的形式开展策略训练可能更有效。学生参与训练应该是自愿的，而不是强制性的。

References 参考文献

江新，赵果. 2001. 初级阶段外国留学生汉字学习策略的调查研究[M]. 语言教学与研究（4）：10-16.

柳燕梅. 2009. 汉字策略训练的必要性、可教性和有效性的试验研究[J]. 世界汉语教学（4）：280-288.

曾金金. 2000. 德国学生学习汉字的情况及其学习策略[J]. 语言研究：国际汉语教学学术研讨会论文集：327-331.

赵果，江新. 2002. 什么样的汉字学习策略最有效?[J]. 语言文字应用（2）：79-85.

中国社会科学院语言研究所词典编辑室. 2016. 现代汉语词典(第7版)[M]. 北京：商务印书馆.

Chamot A U, Rubin J. 1994. Comments on Janie Rees-Miller's " a critical appraisal of learner training: theoretical bases and teaching implications" [J]. TESOL quarterly, 28(4): 771−776.

Grenfell M, Harris V. 2015. Memorisation strategies and the adolescent learner of Mandarin Chinese as a foreign language[J]. Linguistics and education, 31: 1−13.

Ke C. 1998. Effects of strategies on the learning of Chinese characters among foreign language studies[J]. Journal of the Chinese language teachers association, 33(2): 93−112.

Manzo U C, Manzo A V. 2008. Teaching vocabulary-learning strategies: word consciousness, word connection, and word prediction[M]. Farstrup A E, Samules S J. What research has to say about vocabulary instruction. Newark, DE: International Reading Association, 80−105.

McGinnis S. 1995. Students' goals and approaches[M]. Chu M. Mapping the course of the Chinese language field: Chinese language teachers association monograph series. Kalamazoo, MI: Chinese Language Teachers Association, 3:151−168.

Oxford R L. 1990. Language learning strategies: what every teacher should know[M]. Boston, MA: Heinle & Heinle Publishers.

Qian K, Owen N, Bax S. 2018. Researching mobile-assisted Chinese-character learning strategies among adult distance learners[J]. Innovation in language learning and teaching, 12(1): 56−71.

Schmitt N. 1997. Vocabulary learning strategies[M]. Schmitt N, McCarthy M. Vocabulary: description, acquisition and pedagogy. Cambridge, UK: Cambridge University Press, 199−227.

Shen H H. 2005. An investigation of Chinese-character learning strategies among non-native speakers of Chinese[J]. System, 33(1): 49−68.

Sung K-Y. 2014. Novice learners' Chinese-character learning strategies and performance[J]. Electronic journal of foreign language teaching, 11 (1): 38−51.

Sung K-Y, Wu H-P. 2011. Factors influencing the learning of Chinese characters[J].

International journal of bilingual education and bilingualism, 14: 683−700.

Takač V P. 2008. Vocabulary learning strategies and foreign language acquisition[M]. Tonawanda, NY: Multilingual Matters, LTD.

Wang J, Spencer K, Xing M. 2009. Metacognitive beliefs and strategies in learning Chinese as a foreign language[J]. System, 37: 46−56

Wei J-C. 2010. An investigation on methods and techniques in beginning Chinese vocabulary Instruction[D]. Unpublished MA thesis, The University of Iowa.

Wenden A L. 1998. Metacognitive knowledge and language learning[J]. Applied Linguistics, 19 (4): 515−537.

Chapter 6 第六章

Models for CSL Character and Word Instruction 汉语二语字词教学模式

In the previous chapters, we discussed how the unique orthographic features of Chinese language pose challenges to CSL learners in character and word learning, how learners' first language causes negative transfer to Chinese character and word acquisition, how learners cognitively process Chinese words, how instruction should apply cognitive theories to maximize instructional effect in character and word instruction, and how we identify and train effective character and word learning strategies. In this chapter, we present two models for CSL character and word instruction based on the discussions from the previous chapters. The first one is the three-dimensional character and word instruction model for Chinese as a second language, which is a general model to be applied to character and word instruction at all levels of college Chinese classrooms. The second one is a beginning level character and word instruction model for active learning, which particularly focuses on beginning level vocabulary instruction.

在前面的章节中，我们讨论了汉语独特的缀字特征是如何给汉语二语学习者的汉字学习带来挑战的，学习者的第一语言是如何给汉语字词习得造成负迁移的，学习者是如何对词语进行认知加工的，字词教学是如何应用认知理论最大限度地提高教学效果的，以及我们应该如何识别和训练字词学习策略。基于前面章节对这些问题的讨论，在这一章我们提出了两个汉语二语字词教学模式：第一个是三维度汉语二语字词教学模式，第二个是促进主动学习的初级汉语字词教学模式。前者是大学汉语课堂字词教学中普遍使用的一种模式，后者只适用于初级汉语字词教学。

6.1 Three-dimensional character and word instruction model for Chinese as a second language 三维度汉语二语字词教学模式

The model consists of three dimensions: fostering meaningful character and word learning from a cognitive processing perspective; promoting skill automatization from a linguistic perspective; and adopting a three-tiered instructional approach from a pedagogical perspective. Copious teaching examples are provided to illustrate the three-tiered instructional approach.

这个模式由三个维度构成：第一个维度是从认知加工的角度促进有意义的字词学习，第二个维度是从语言学的角度促进技能的自动化，第三个维度是从教学的角度采用三层次的教学途径。后面我们将提供丰富的教学示例具体说明三层次的教学途径。

6.1.1 Fostering meaningful character and word learning 促进有意义的字词学习

• Definition for meaningful learning 有意义学习的定义

Meaningful learning, initially proposed by Ausubel (1963), is the opposite of rote learning. Rote learning refers to memorizing learning materials without full understanding and the new information being learned is not integrated into the learners' existing knowledge system. In a meaningful learning condition, in contrast, the learning materials are fully comprehended by the learners and they know how to incorporate the newly learned materials into their existing knowledge system. Ausubel (1977) explained two conditions that must be met for meaningful learning to happen. One is that learners need to relate the new learning task nonarbitrarily and substantively to what they already know and the other is that the learning task must be potentially meaningful to the learners. In other words, it relates to the learners' structure of knowledge on a nonarbitrary basis. Meaningful learning can be receptive as long as the learning materials are subsumable and learners actively relate the materials to their own cognitive structure (Ausubel, 1962). In Chapter 4, we introduced the concept, schema, which is a cognitive construct developed by learners to organize knowledge in a meaningful way within their brains. Meaningful learning is a type of learning that facilitates schema acquisition. Based on this discussion, we define that the meaningful character and word learning as a learning that makes connections between the newly learned characters/words and an existing cognitive schema, refines and expands the existing schemata, or constructs new schemata.

有意义学习最初是由Ausubel（1963）提出的，它与机械性学习正好相对。机械性学习是指学习者对学习材料的记忆没有建立在完全理解的基础上，新的知识也没有融入学习者已有的知识体系中。与此相反，有意义学习是指学习材料完全被学习者所理解，并且学习者知道如何把新学习的材料融入自己已有的知识体系中。Ausubel（1977）详细说明了有意义学习发生的两个必要条件：一个是学习者必须在新材料与已有知识之间建立一种特定的、实质的联系，另一个是学习材料对学习者来说必须有潜在的意义。也就是说，学习材料与学习者已有的知识结构之间是有机联系的。只要学习材料是可被包容的，而且学习者能积极地将学习材料融入他们的认知结构中去，有意义学习就容易被学习者所接受。（Ausubel，1962）在第四章，我们介绍了“图式”这个概念，它是学习者为了在大脑中把新材料有意义地组织起来而建立的一种认知结构。因此，有意义学习能促进图式的习得。基于上述讨论，我们把有意义的字词学习定义为：学习者把新学的字词有机地融合到自己已有的认知图式中，并提炼和发展已有图式或建立新图式的一种学习。

• Stages of meaningful character and word learning
有意义字词学习的阶段

Since the initial proposal of meaningful learning by Ausubel (1963), this topic has been substantially investigated, including the application of this theory in character and word learning. Stahl (1983) proposed that meaningful vocabulary learning occurs when learners acquire both definitional word knowledge and contextual word knowledge. According to Stahl (1985), definitional knowledge is defined as knowledge of the relationships between a word and other known words. Contextual knowledge is defined as knowledge of a core concept and how that concept is realized in different contexts. Shuell (1990) held that meaningful cognitive learning is an active, constructive, and cumulative process in which learning is characterized by both qualitative and quantitative changes. Shuell (1990) further proposed that learning goes through initial, intermediate, and terminal phases. In the initial stage, the learner memorizes facts and uses a preexisting schema to interpret the isolated pieces of data. The information acquired during this phase is concrete rather than abstract and is bound to the specific context in which it occurs. In the intermediate phase, the learner begins to see similarities and relationships among these conceptually isolated pieces of information. New schemata that provide the learner with more conceptual structures are formed, but do not allow the learner to function on a fully autonomous basis. In the terminal phase, the knowledge structures and schemata formed become better integrated and function more autonomously. The characteristic of this phase is performance rather than learning. Knowledge has been transformed into skills. Predicated on this general framework, we propose a three-stage meaningful character and word learning framework for CSL. The three stages consist of comprehension, internalization, and integration. The key point of meaningful character and word learning is that students are actively and constructively involved in all stages of learning. The characteristics of meaningful learning in each of the three stages are illustrated below.

自从 Ausubel（1963）提出有意义学习理论以来，学者们对这一理论进行了大量的研究和验证，其中也包括把这一理论应用到字词学习中。Stahl（1983）认为，有意义的词汇学习只有当学习者习得了词的定义知识和上下文知识后才会发生。根据Stahl（1985）的观点，定义知识是指一个词与其他已知词之间关系的知识，上下文知识是指词的核心概念知识以及这一概念在不同上下文中的体现。Shuell（1990）认为，有意义的认知学习是一个积极的、富有建设性的、积累的过程，而且在这一过程中，学习会发生量和质上的变化。Shuell（1990）又进一步提出，有意义的认知学习需要经过初级、中级和高级三个阶段。在初级阶段，学习者记忆语言事实并用大脑中已有的图式理解个别信息。在这一阶段，学习者获得的信息是与具体情境相关联的，还没有上升到抽象水平。在中级阶段，学习者开始意识到个别信息之间的相似性和关联性并逐渐形成展示这种关系的新图式，但是还不能自动运用这些新图式。在高级阶段，学习者的客观知识结构与所形成的主观图式之间建立起了很好的联系，学习者能运用图式自动获取新知识。这一阶段的特点是知识已经被转化为技能，学习者可以自如地运用所学到的知识。以这一框架为基础，我们提出了一个三阶段的汉语二语有意义字词学习框架。这三个阶段分别为理解阶段、内化阶段和整合阶段。有意义字词学习的关键是让学生积极地、富有建设性地投入每个阶段的字词学习中。下面我们具体说明一下有意义学习每个阶段的学习特征。

Stage 1: Comprehension. In this stage, learners learn the definition of new words and try to make sense of the new words through various drills. Take the word 意思 as an example. Learning is characterized by a number of observations: (1) being able to analyze the orthographic structure of individual characters such as that 意 and 思 both have a heart radical; 意 has three perceptual units, and 思 has two perceptual units. (2) being able to recognize the word when it is seen. (3) being able to reproduce the word after hearing it. (4) being able to understand core meanings of the word (see the list in Chinese below). (5) being able to produce a sentence using the word according to provided model sentences illustrated in the parentheses below:

第一阶段：理解。在这一阶段，学习者学习新词的定义，并通过各种形式的操练理解新词的意思。以“意思”一词为例，这一阶段能观察到的学习者学习特征有：（1）能够分析每个汉字的结构，如能分析出“意”和“思”都含有部首“心”，知道“意”由三个知觉部件构成，“思”由两个知觉部件构成；（2）看到这个词时能认出来；（3）听到这个词后能写出来；（4）能理解这个词的核心意义（见下面所列）；（5）能模仿范例（见下面括号内的句子）进行造句。

意思：

① 可以指语言文字代表的“内容”。（“信任”的意思就是相信你。）

② 可以代表“意见”或“愿望”。（我的意思是我暑假去一趟中国。）

③ 可以代表“心意”。（这双鞋你就收下吧，这是我的一点小意思。）

④可以指一种趋向。（看起来，他没有要跟我和好的意思。）

⑤可以指一种情趣。（玩电子游戏真是太有意思了。）

However, meaningful learning will not take place if the instructor just asks students to look up new words in the dictionary or glossary and use each word in a sentence (Thelen, 1986), and if students are not actively and constructively motivated to explore new words. At this stage, instructors should try to boost the enthusiasm of learning and motivate students to explore the words by themselves and make new word learning a personal experience. Activities such as showing pictures to students and asking them to find corresponding words for the pictures, grouping students into pairs to ask each other questions based on the target words; asking students to pick a few of their favorite words to learn by themselves and then to teach the words to other students, or asking students to categorize new words based on their own classification rules and then to explain to the class how they categorized the new words, are all helpful in stimulating students' learning interests.

但是，如果教师只是让学生在词典或生词表中查找词的解释，然后让学生用词造句，有意义学习就不会发生；（Thelen，1986）如果学生并没有积极地、富有建设性地去探索新词的知识，有意义学习也不会发生。因此，在这一阶段，教师应该努力激发学生的学习热情，鼓励学生自己去探索与新词相关的知识，使新词学习成为学生的个人体验。教师可以开展一些教学活动激发学生的学习兴趣，例如：向学生展示图片并让学生根据图片找出相应的词；两人一组互相就目的词提问；让学生选出他们最喜欢的词先自学，然后再教给其他学生；让学生根据自己的分类原则对新词进行分类，然后向全班学生解释如此分类的原因。

Stage 2: Internalization. After initial comprehension, the learners try to memorize the words by finding connections between the newly learned words with other existing words in their mental lexicon. The learning at this stage is characterized by changes in the existing schema. The changes include expanding the existing schema due to incorporation of new knowledge, and forming new schemata caused by inconsistencies between new knowledge and existing knowledge. For example, the learner gradually realizes that in addition to the core meanings, the word 意思 possesses other different meanings (see the list of sentences in the Chinese section):

第二阶段：内化。经过第一阶段的理解，学习者在这一阶段试图通过寻找新词与已储存在心理词库中的其他词之间的联系记忆新词。这一阶段的学习特征表现在已有图式的改变上。这种改变包括已有图式的扩展（由于融入了新知）和新图式的形成（由于已有图式与新知之间的矛盾）。例如，学习者逐渐意识到“意思”一词除了核心意义之外，还有其他解释，如在以下句子中的意义：

① 不好意思，我先走了。
② 这两个年轻人整天形影不离，好像有点儿意思。
③ 你这个人真有意思，连这么点面子也不给。
④ 你这个人真有意思，连周末都不休息，真是个工作狂。

Therefore, the learner may conclude that the meaning of 意思 in a particular sentence depends on the particular context. For example, the word meaning of 意思 in Sentence ① “不好意思，我先走了” is to express a light apology; in Sentence ② “这两个年轻人整天形影不离，好像有点意思” it is to indicate two people have developed special feelings toward each other; in it is Sentence ③ “你这个人真有意思，连这么点面子也不给” it is to express the speaker’s unsatisfactory feeling toward the person referenced in the sentence; in Sentence ④ “你这个人真有意思，连周末都不休息，真是个工作狂” it is to express the speaker’s respectful feeling toward the person referenced in the sentence.

因此，学习者可能会得出结论：“意思”这个词在不同句子中的确切意思取决于上下文。例如，“意思”在句①“不好意思，我先走了”中表示说话人的微微歉意，在句②“这两个年轻人整天形影不离，好像有点儿意思”中表示说话人感觉这两个人可能相爱了，在句③“你这个人真有意思，连这么点面子也不给”中表示说话人的一种不满情绪，在句④“你这个人真有意思，连周末都不休息，真是个工作狂”中隐含着说话人对所提及对象的敬业精神的赞赏。

The learner also understands that 意思 has certain degree of overlap with words such as 内容, 意见, 愿望, 心意, 趋向, and 情趣, but they are not equal and cannot be substituted for each other in many contexts (see the Chinese sentences illustrated below):

学习者还明白了“意思”与“内容、意见、愿望、心意、趋向、情趣”等词在意义上有一定程度的交叉，但不等同，他们在许多语境中是不能互相替代的，如下面所列的：

① 这篇文章的内容与形式不太一致。（“内容”不能用“意思”替代）

② 这件事你做得不对，我对你有意见。（“意见”不能用“意思”替代）

③ 您的心意我领了，但是您的钱我不能收下。（“心意”不能

用 “意思”替代）

At this stage, different forms of practicing the target words in different linguistic contexts are critical to aid internalization. To make practice meaningful, the exercises should be thoughtfully designed. The content should invoke the students' interests; it can be related to students' existing world knowledge and real-life situations. The content should also be challenging, but within the students' reach under instructors' guidance. The content should cover a wide range of linguistic contexts in which students understand how the words are used in different contexts. The format of exercises should vary to attract students' attention. At this stage, instruction should give more weight to task-based and problem-solving exercises over discrete non-contextual drills.

在这一阶段，教师在不同语境中用不同的形式练习目的词对促进学生的内化至关重要。为了使练习变得有意义，教师在设计练习时应该考虑以下方面：练习的内容应能激发学生的学习兴趣，与学生已有的背景知识和实际生活相联系；练习的内容应具有挑战性，但应在学生的能力范围之内，学生能够在教师的指导下完成练习；练习的内容应该包含各种语境，确保学生能懂得新词在各种语境中的运用；练习的形式应该多种多样，能吸引学生的注意力。这一阶段教学活动的重心应该放在任务型或问题解决型的练习上，而不再是非语境化的单项操练上。

Stage 3: Integration. Toward the end of this stage, the newly learned target words are assimilated and integrated into the learners' knowledge system and they can use the target words with ease to create their own sentences and express ideas either in speaking or writing. The characteristics of learning at this stage indicate that the learner can use the target words in their daily life communication on topics that are congruent with their proficiency level; the learner is able to judge the appropriateness of using the word in a context from syntactic and pragmatic perspectives. The newly restructured schemata are relatively stable, and function appropriately until a discrepancy occurs at the time when a new linguistic situation cannot be explained by the existing schemata relating to the assimilated target words. At this stage, the instruction is focused on learner' application of target words in their daily life communication. Word learning tasks for this stage can include the following activities: interviewing with native speakers or other Chinese-speaking friends to get information, expressing opinions on certain topics, watching TV programs, listening to radio broadcasts on selected topics, writing journals or other theme-based short essays, and reading selected online or offline materials to get information; and classroom presentations to report their interview or reading results. In designing these activities, the instructor should bear in mind that the focus of these activities is on word application. Thus, the instructor should purposefully highlight words to be used in those activities. This will be helpful to increase students' conscious level of using words.

第三阶段：整合。到整合阶段的后期，新学习的词语已经融入学习者已有的知识体系中，学习者能够得心应手地运用新词造句，并通过口头或书面形式表达自己的观点。这一阶段的学习特征表现在：学习者在日常生活交流中能运用新学到的词语解决那些与他们汉语水平相当的问题，能够从句法和语用的角度判断语境中的用词合适与否。那些新近重构的图式也保持着相对的稳定并正常发挥着作用，除非遇到一个无法用现有的包含目的词的图式解释的新语境。在这一阶段，教学应该侧重于让学习者在日常生活中运用所学到的目的词。这一阶段的词语学习任务可以包括以下活动：通过采访汉语母语者或其他说汉语的朋友获取新信息，针对某个话题发表自己的看法，有选择地看电视、听广播，写日记或其他主题的小短文，阅读经过筛选的在线的或线下的阅读材料获取新信息，然后通过课堂汇报的形式展示他们的采访或阅读成果。在设计这些活动时，教师应该明确的是，开展这些活动是为了促进学生对新词的应用，所以教师应该强调哪些词应该在活动中运用，增强学生的词语运用意识。

• Factors affecting meaningful learning
影响有意义学习的因素

The progress of meaningful character and word learning from stage 1 to 3 is a developmental continuum of learners' character and word knowledge from receptive to productive status. It is a change of exercise formats from controlled drill practice to uncontrolled task completion and purposeful application. During this process, several factors affect the effectiveness of meaningful learning. These factors include cognitive, cultural, linguistic, and communication factors.

有意义字词学习的三个发展阶段反映了学习者的字词知识从接受型发展到产出型是一个持续的过程，与此同时，练习的形式也从控制型的单项操练发展为开放型的任务完成和有目的的应用。在这个过程中，有意义学习的效果会受一些因素的影响，这些因素包括认知因素、文化因素、语言学因素和交际因素。

Cognitive factors. In Chapter 4, we introduced the cognitive load theory. This theory states that the working memory of the human brain is limited and can process only a certain amount of information within a limited time period. In vocabulary instruction, we cannot introduce excessive numbers of new words in a single time slot as students can process only a limited amount of words introduced no matter how meaningful the encoding process might be. Cognitive load is determined by a couple of factors. One is students' target language proficiency level. Beginning level students may take a much longer time to learn a new word than advanced students, as they have not established a well-structured Chinese word encoding and processing system in their brains. The other is students' linguistic background. Students who previously have learned other foreign languages may have accumulated more experience regarding how to learn L2 words than those who have never been exposed to a foreign language.

认知因素。在第四章我们介绍了认知负荷理论，这一理论认为人类大脑的工作记忆容量有限，在有限的时间内只能加工一定量的信息。因此，在词汇教学中，无论编码过程多么有意义，我们都不能在一个时间段内向学生介绍过多的新词。认知负荷由两个因素决定：一个是学生的目的语水平。学会同一个新词，初级水平的学生花费的时间往往要比高级水平的学生多得多，因为他们大脑中还没有完全建立汉语词的编码和加工机制。另一个是学生的语言学习背景。以前学过其他外语的学生比没学过外语的学生多积累了一些第二语言词汇学习的经验。

Cultural factors. During character/word learning, barriers may be created if a certain cultural knowledge which is required is not explicitly and adequately explained for accurate comprehension of the meaning of a target word by the student (Meyer, 2000). Some words are common which are easy for students to understand, such as 面包, 水果. Some are unique and observed only in certain cultural settings, as depicted in stories from the author of this book:

文化因素。在字词学习过程中，如果为理解目的词所需要的文化知识没有被讲清楚、讲透彻，那就会造成学生的字词理解障碍。（Meyer，2000）有些词很常见，学生很容易理解，如“面包、水果”；但有些词就比较特殊，只出现在特定的文化背景中。下面是文化因素影响字词理解的几个例子：

When I introduced the character 米, I told students that 米饭 was a main dish on the dining table in China. Southern Chinese eat a lot of cooked plain rice. Students were puzzled. When I asked them how they prepared the rice for a meal, they told me that they seldom ate rice; rice was always considered a side dish. They never ate plain rice. They often added milk to rice. This cultural barrier could often be observed in class. For example, some abstract words such as 孝道 and 妇道 may be understood by students by their literal meaning, but the students have greater difficulty in comprehending the implied and inferred meanings due to a lack of relevant knowledge of Chinese culture.

当我向学生介绍汉字“米”时，我对学生说，在中国，“米饭”是主食，中国的南方人吃很多白米饭。学生感到很困惑。当我问他们在他们的餐桌上米饭是做成什么样的时，他们告诉我，他们很少吃米饭，米饭是副食不是主食。他们从来都不吃白米饭，经常把牛奶放在米饭里。在课堂上，这种文化上的差异随处可见。例如，有些抽象词，像“孝道”“妇道”之类的，学生能理解字面意思，但是由于缺乏相关的文化知识，他们很难理解其中的深层含义。

These stories tell us that it is not easy for students to integrate the meaning of the target words into their existing schema due to the differences introduced by a new culture.

这些例子告诉我们，由于学生对某种文化不了解，要把目的词融入他们已有的图式中其实并不容易。

Linguistic factors. If certain linguistic knowledge (such as orthography, morphology, grammar) required to comprehend the target words is not explicitly or adequately explained, it causes difficulty in word comprehension. For example, students are often confused by the grammatical function of Chinese function words. Even advanced learners may still not feel confident to use the participle 了 in their writing. They are not sure where they should use it and where they should not use it.

语言学因素。如果为理解目的词所需要的语言学知识（如缀字知识、构词知识、语法知识）没被讲清楚、讲透彻，那么就会给学生的字词理解带来困难。例如，学生经常对汉语虚词的语法功能感到困惑，即使是高级学习者，也可能仍然没有信心在写作中用好“了”，因为他们不确定什么时候应该用“了”，什么时候不应该用“了”。

Communication factors. Meaningful learning requires multi-level communication between the instructor and students and between students. Communication factors refer to the time and quality of the instructor and students using the target language in the class during their communication. There are two levels of communication that directly affect meaningful vocabulary learning. One level is teacher-student communication. The following is a story from the author of this book:

交际因素。有意义学习要求课堂上师生之间和生生之间能进行多层面的交流。交际因素指的是教师和学生在课堂上使用目的语进行这种交流的质和量。课堂交流分两个层面，第一个层面是教师与学生之间的交流。下面是作者遇到的一个教学实例：

Once I attended a beginning level Chinese class. The teacher spoke English most of the class time. After class, I asked why. The teacher answered: "If I speak Chinese, students would not understand, so I have to speak English." I told her that the problem was that by speaking in English most of class time, the students would have little chance to hear and speak Chinese words in class.

有一次我去听一节初级汉语课，那位老师大部分时间都在用英语教学。下课后我问她为什么说那么多英语，那位老师说："如果我说汉语，学生都听不懂，所以我只好说英语。"我对她说问题在于，如果大部分时间都在说英语的话，学生就很少有机会在课堂上听到和说出汉语词了。

With very limited practice, how can students learn words? On the other hand, if the instructor speaks Chinese, which students cannot understand, students would get lost in the class, and learning will become meaningless. The other level of communication that affects vocabulary learning is student-student communication. In a big classroom setting, pair or small-group work may provide more opportunities for students to practice words; however, it may be difficult for the instructor to monitor individual students' learning quality and provide appropriate guidance and feedback. In order to reduce ineffectiveness during classroom communication, the instructor should try to speak in

Chinese at a level comprehensible to the students and should provide enough opportunities for students to speak using previously and newly learned words at a mutual understanding level, which, in turn, would facilitate meaningful learning.

学生在课堂上练习目的词的机会如此少，他们又怎么能学会呢？从另一方面说，如果教师在课堂上说汉语，学生都听不懂，那么他们就会感到困惑，学习就会变得没有意义了。另一个层面的交流是学生与学生之间的交流。在一个大教学班上，两人一组或两人以上的小组活动可以为学生提供更多练习目的词的机会，但是教师很难监控每个学生的学习质量并给予其适当的指导和反馈。为了减少无效的课堂交流，教师应该尽量用学生能够理解的汉语与其交流，还应该提供足够的机会让学生运用以前学过的或新学的词语在共同理解的水平上进行小组交流，从而促进有意义学习。

How can classroom instructors identify or eliminate the negative effects of these four factors to ensure meaningful character and word learning? For the cognitive factor, the teacher could use methods of surveys, interviews, and class observations to find appropriate cognitive loads for students in a given class. This will equip instructors with the knowledge of how many words should be introduced per week and the appropriate level of extra class assignments. For communication effectiveness, the instructor can use pictures, gestures, actions, and PowerPoint slides to assist verbal expression to help the students to understand the target language. In addition, new instructors may observe experienced instructors' classes and learn how to use simple target language to communicate with students and get their message across.

教师在课堂教学中怎么做才能消除上述四种因素对有意义字词学习造

成的负面影响呢？就认知因素来说，教师可以通过问卷调查、访谈、课堂观察等方法确定某一班级的学生认知负荷量多少比较合适。这样，教师就能知道每星期应该教多少个生词以及布置什么难度的课外练习。为了提高交流的有效性，教师还可以利用图片、手势、动作、幻灯片等辅助语言表达，帮助学生理解目的语。另外，新手教师还可以通过观摩有经验的教师上的课学习如何使用简单的目的语与学生进行交流，以及如何理解学生所表达的信息。

For the linguistic and cultural factors, although it is impossible for instructors to predict all possible problems that students may encounter in learning new words in a particular class, preparation to provide "organizers" to help students in linking new words with their existing knowledge is an effective way to facilitate meaningful learning. The concept "organizer" was proposed by Ausubel (1977) and it refers to special introductory materials that take account of the relevant background knowledge already established in a learner's cognitive structure to provide anchoring ideas for the new materials to be learned. As Ausubel stated, "the principal function of the organizer is to bridge the gap between what the learner already knows and what he needs to know before he can successfully learn the task at hand" (Ausubel, 1977:168). The organizer usually is introduced in advance of the new learning task; therefore, it is also called an advance organizer. To give an example, 国营企业 is a phrase that is not familiar to students in the U.S. and may cause a comprehension problem. Prior to introducing 国营企业, the instructor designed some warm-up activities to serve as an advance organizer for introducing 国营企业. The instructor first asked students to name a few things owned by the U.S. federal government. Students then named post offices, interstate highways, etc.

The instructor then asked students to discuss the advantages and disadvantages of federal government ownership of these things. After that, the instructor asked the students to think about what would happen if all private companies were owned by the government. With all of this foreshadowing, the instructor then presented them with the phrase 国营企业 and asked students to explain the meaning of the phrase and to discuss possible benefits and problems of 国营企业 that may occur in China. With those advance organizers, students then were able to successfully comprehend the phrase 国营企业.

就语言学因素和文化因素来说，教师虽然无法预测学生在一堂课上会遇到的所有困难，但是可以提供“组织者”帮助学生将新词与他们已有的知识联系起来，促进对新词的理解。“组织者”这一概念是由Ausubel（1977）提出的，指的是教师特别准备的引导性材料。这种引导性材料能将学习者认知结构中已经存在的相关背景知识与将要学习的新材料联系起来。就像 Ausubel 所说的，“组织者的主要作用是缩小学习者已知知识与正要学习的知识之间的差距”（Ausubel，1977：168）。一般来说，“组织者”是先于学习任务介绍给学习者的，所以我们也称它为“先行组织者”。例如，“国营企业”对美国学生来说是一个新短语，因为美国社会高度私有化。教师觉得美国学生对这个短语的理解可能会有困难，所以在介绍这个短语之前，设计了一些热身活动作为“先行组织者”：教师先让学生说一说美国联邦政府都拥有或管理哪些服务性企业，学生回答出了邮局、州际高速公路等；然后，教师让学生讨论一下美国联邦政府拥有或管理的这些企业的优缺点；讨论完了，教师让学生思考一下，如果美国的所有企业都让美国联邦政府管理，情况会怎么样。有了这些铺垫之后，教师再把“国营企业”这个新短语展示出来，让学生自己解释这个短语的意思，然后组织学生讨论中国国营企业的利和弊。有了这些“先行组织者”，学生对“国营企业”的理解就水到渠成了。

6.1.2 Promoting skill automatization 促进技能的自动化

In Chapter 1, we explained that full word knowledge included five aspects of knowledge, four of them are definitional, syntactical, pragmatic, and network knowledge. Therefore, to learn word knowledge is to learn the four aspects of knowledge. However, traditionally, in teaching Chinese as a first language, knowing a word is defined as "四会": 会认 is recognizing the word, 会说 is using it in speech, 会写 is using it in writing, and 会用 is using the word in context (张田若, 陈良璜, & 李卫民, 2003, 2nd edition). The 四会 criteria impose mastering word knowledge more from the procedural knowledge perspective than from the declarative knowledge perspective.

在第一章，我们提到了词语知识一共包括五个方面，其中四个是词的定义知识、词的句法知识、词的语用知识和词的网络知识。学习词语知识就是学习这四个方面的知识。但是在传统的汉语作为母语的教学中，掌握一个词是以"四会"为标准的，也就是"会认、会说、会写、会用"（张田若、陈良璜、李卫民，2003）。"四会"标准对词语知识的掌握更多的是从程序性知识的角度定义的，而不是从陈述性知识的角度。

The discussion of declarative knowledge and procedural knowledge initially emerged in Ryle's work (1949). In his book, *The Concept of Mind*, Ryle distinguished two types of mental activities: knowledge remembering and knowledge executing. The former is considered to be declarative knowledge; the latter belongs to procedural knowledge (Anderson, 1982; 2005). From the CSL vocabulary learning perspective, **declarative knowledge** is about the facts of words—the definitional, syntactical, pragmatic, and network knowledge of the words that can be memorized and stored in mind. **Procedural knowledge** is the knowledge of how to use the stored four aspects of word knowledge to complete language tasks. If a learner can automatically use declarative knowledge to fulfill real-life tasks, then the learner has acquired procedural knowledge. That is, the knowledge has been converted into skills. Since the ultimate goal of CSL character and word instruction is to help learners transform their knowledge into skills, then, pedagogically, instruction should take into consideration the integration of character/word knowledge learning and four-skill training at each stage of character/word learning. In the initial stage, instruction may pay more attention to speaking and listening over reading and writing skills, due to students' limited character/word knowledge. In real life, students need all four skills to handle daily life and job-related communication; therefore, a balanced training on the four skills will lead to better character and word acquisition. Another important fact of the four-skill training is that learning will be more effective if multiple modalities participate in character and word learning, because listening, speaking, reading, and writing require cooperation of different physical and mental modalities, which also facilitates procedural knowledge learning.

关于陈述性知识与程序性知识的讨论最早见于Ryle（1949）的 *The Concept of Mind* 一书中。在这本书中，Ryle区分了两种思维活动：知识记忆与知识应用。前者被称为陈述性知识，后者被称为程序性知识。（Anderson，1982，2005）从汉语二语词汇学习的角度看，**陈述性知识**是关于词的事实性知识——词的定义知识、句法知识、语用知识和网络知识，可以记忆并储存在大脑中。**程序性知识**是关于怎么运用词的这四方面知识完成交际任务的知识。如果学习者能够自动运用陈述性知识解决生活中的语言问题，那他其实已经习得了程序性知识。也就是说，知识已经被转化为了技能。既然汉语二语字词教学的最终目标是帮助学习者把知识转化为技能，那么从教学的角度看，教师应该在字词学习的每个阶段都考虑把字词知识的学习与听、说、读、写四项技能的训练结合起来。在初级阶段，由于学生的字词知识有限，教学应该更注重听、说技能的训练。但是在实际生活中，学生需要综合运用听、说、读、写四项技能应付日常生活和工作中的交际活动，因此，只有听、说、读、写四项技能得到均衡的训练才能更有效地促进字词习得。另一方面，均衡地训练听、说、读、写四项技能能使多种感官共同参与到字词学习中，帮助学生取得更好的学习效果，因为听、说、读、写需要身体的和心理的多种感官之间相互合作，这有利于促进学生程序性知识的习得。

How can instruction help students learn declarative knowledge and meanwhile develop their procedural knowledge? At the beginning stage of word learning, "information transformation" is an effective method to help integrate word knowledge acquisition and skill development. Information transformation refers to transformation of one type of information into another, such as transforming visual information into acoustic information. This method allows students to practice word with different modalities, while at same time keeping students interested in the learning activities due to the variation in methods. Please see Teaching Example 4 for detail。

怎样让学生在习得陈述性知识的同时也获得程序性知识呢？在词语学习的初级阶段，"信息转换"是一种能将词语知识的习得与语言技能的发展结合起来的有效方法。信息转换指的是把一种信息形式转换成另一种信息形式，如把视觉信息转换成听觉信息。这种方法可以让学生的多种感官都参与到词语学习中来，同时，教学方法上的多变也能保持学生对学习活动的兴趣。具体请参看教学示例4。

Teaching Example 4 Information transformation

教学示例 4 信息转换

Task 任务

Introduce a friend (Pair work)

介绍一位朋友（两人一组）

Target words to be learned 要学习的生词

高、矮、喜欢、开朗、内向、害羞、好吃懒做、胆小怕事、活泼可爱、普通、心地善良、风趣、幽默、爱管闲事、体贴温柔、聪明好学、诚实坦白、脾气、暴躁、小心谨慎、追求刺激、热心助人

Requirement 要求

Please use as many words as you can from the above list to describe a friend of yours.

请从上面的生词表中选用尽可能多的词语描述你的朋友。

Step 1: Roles A and B take turns introducing one of their friends to each other. They take notes when the other party is speaking.

步骤1：A和B轮流向对方介绍自己的朋友。一方介绍时，另一方做笔记记录。

Step 2: Roles A and B write a paragraph about each other's friend based on the notes.

步骤2：A和B根据各自所做的笔记写一段话描述对方的朋友。

Step 3: Roles A and B take turns reading their own writing to the other party. While one is reading, the other can ask questions for clarification or can comment on the correctness of the description. Necessary revision is then made based on feedback.

步骤3：A和B轮流读出自己所写的内容，聆听的一方可以向对方提问做进一步的确认或评论对方描述的准确性。根据反馈，双方再做必要的修改。

Step 4: Roles A and B exchange their writing. Each reads the other party's writing. During reading, they mark how many words from the list are used in the writing and also mark errors in the writing if there is any.

步骤4：A和B交换稿子并朗读对方所写的内容。在朗读过程中，他们要标出对方所使用的生词表中的词，还要标出对方的用词错误，如果有的话。

Step 5: Roles A and B exchange their opinions on each other's writing.

步骤5：双方互相点评彼此的文稿。

Note: This activity requires information transformation between speaking, listening, reading, and writing.

说明：该活动要求信息在听、说、读、写间相互转换。

(Teaching Example 4 is contributed by Helen H. Shen, The University of Iowa)

After having accumulated a certain amount of vocabulary, using simulated real life tasks such as theme-based activities is another approach for promoting skill acquisition. This approach could be used in the classroom and beyond. For example, if the lesson is about hospital information and students have learned a certain amount of vocabulary about hospitals, the instructor can give a task to ask students to collect information about a Chinese hospital using their learned words after class. This task requires students to read certain articles on Chinese hospitals or to interview people who have visited a Chinese hospital. Based on the information gathered, the student would need to write up a report about what he/she knows about a Chinese hospital using the learned target words.

等学生积累了一定数量的词语后，教师还可以通过模拟真实生活的语言任务，如主题活动促进学生的技能习得。这种方法课内课外都适用。例如，如果课文内容跟医院有关且学生已经学了一定数量的相关词语，那么教师就可以给学生布置一个课外任务，让学生运用所学词语收集有关中国医院的信息。这个任务需要学生阅读一些关于中国医院的文章或者采访那些去过中国医院的人。学生最后要基于自己收集的信息，用所学的目的词写一篇关于中国医院的报告。

6.1.3 Adopting a three-tiered instructional approach 采用三层次的教学途径

In a classroom learning situation, meaningful learning cannot be realized without effective instructional approaches. In order to guide meaningful learning progress from comprehension stage to integration stage, the instructional method design should be in line with the cognitive process of meaningful learning. We propose a three-tiered instructional approach to realize meaningful learning. The first tier is a decontextualized approach; the second tier is a semi-contextualized approach, and the third tier is a contextualized approach. The decontextualized approach refers to the instructional methods and activities designed to teach target characters and words detached from their communicative and linguistic contexts. The semi-contextualized approach refers to teaching target characters and words with incomplete communicative and linguistic contexts. The language materials are excerpts from a full linguistic context or real-life communication. The contextualized approach refers to teaching characters and words using simulated or real-life communicative contexts or a full linguistic context (Oxford & Crookall, 1990).

在课堂学习中，没有有效的教学途径是无法实现有意义学习的。为了引导有意义学习从理解阶段发展到整合阶段，教学方法的设计应该符合有意义学习的认知过程。为了实现有意义学习，我们在这里提出了一个三层次的教学途径：第一层次是非语境化途径，第二层次是半语境化途径，第三层次是语境化途径。非语境化途径是指教学方法和教学活动都是脱离语境而设计的，学习字词不是为了完成交际任务。半语境化途径是指在不完整的语境中教授目的字词，语言材料是从完整的语境中或真实的语料中节选的。语境化途径是指在模拟的或真实的交际活动中教授目的字词，学习的目的不仅仅是学会字词，而且还要完成交际任务。（Oxford and Crookall，1990）

• The decontextualized approach 非语境化途径

The purpose of using a decontextualized approach is to direct students' attention to the target characters and words and make the target a focal point at the initial stage of learning. Thus, students can concentrate on the form, meaning, and sound of the target characters and words without being distracted or confused by other information from linguistic contexts. This approach will help (1) establish internal connections among sound-shape-meaning of the target characters and words; (2) establish a connection between the character and the radicals within. It must be pointed out that "decontextualized" means to extract the target characters and words from a meaningful communicative linguistic context. It does not mean to teach every individual character or word without using any linguistic segments or context such as a word, a phrase, or a sentence. However, the focus of introducing target items by relating them to a word or a sentence is to assist in understanding the target characters and words. Therefore, the linguistic contexts provided for the target characters and words should be familiar to students. For example, we introduce the character 喝 by presenting students the word 喝水. 水 should be a learned character so that it will be easy for students to connect the new word 喝 with the known word 水. The decontextualized approach is more suitable for gaining definitional knowledge of target words. Teaching Examples 5-14 illustrate how this approach is used in instruction for beginning CSL learners.

采用非语境化途径是为了在学习的初始阶段就让学生将注意力集中在目的字词上，让它们成为学习的焦点。这样，学生就可以专心地学习目的字词的音、形、义而不受语境中其他语言因素的干扰。非语境化途径能够帮助学生：（1）建立目的字词音、形、义之间的内部联系；（2）建立部首与所含该部首的合体字之间的联系。需要特别指出的是，这里的“非语境”指的是把字词从有意义的交际语境中分离出来，不是说在教字词的时候不使用任何语言片段和上下文，如与目的字词有关的词、短语或句子。将目的字词和与和其有关的词、短语、句子联系起来可以帮助学生理解目的字词，因此，我们所提供的语言材料应该是学生所熟悉的。例如，我们教授汉字“喝”时先向学生展示“喝水”这个词，因为“水”是学生已知的汉字，所以他们很容易就能将“喝”与“水”联系起来理解。非语境化途径比较适合帮助学生学习词的定义知识。教学示例5—14具体展示了这一途径在汉语初级二语教学中的运用。

Teaching Example 5 Illustrate the character

教学示例 5 画汉字

The goal of this activity is to encourage students to think deeply about a character's graphic form and meaning. I have each student select a few new characters from the lesson to illustrate. They must turn the character into a picture that relates the form of the character to its meaning.

这个活动的主要目的是引导学生深入思考汉字字形与字义的关系。我让每个学生都从课文中选出几个汉字，每个汉字都让学生用一幅图展示字形与字义之间的关系。

In the first example (see the pictures below at the end of this method) 喝 (*to drink*), the student has combined the meaning of the radicals within the character, and her own creative interpretation of the shape 匃, to create a story about what the character means. In her picture, the sun 日 is shining down on a man 人 in a field 勹, which is making him thirsty, so he drinks with his mouth 口. By making this story, she has come up with a way to remember the radical of this character, as well as the part of the character whose component she has not yet learned, 匃. In the second example, rather than telling a story that combines elements of the character, the student has simply turned the foot radical 足 into an image of a walking man.

在第一个例子中（请看下面的插图），学生结合汉字“喝”的部首义和自己对“匃”的创意性诠释，编了一个故事阐述该字的意义。在她画的图中，太阳照射着在田地“勹”中劳作的“人”，他感到很口渴，于是用“口”来喝水。通过编这个故事，该生找到了一种既可以记住该字的部首，又可以记住其中没学过的部件“匃”的方法。在第二个例子中，学生不是把汉字中的各个部件串成一个故事，而是把“足”这个部首直观地用一个行走的人表现出来。

For this activity, I require that students trace the character in a thick dark color, so the character is highlighted within the illustration. Second, the illustration must be very detailed or in color, which requires that students pay attention to the detail of the components, and the role of the components in the compound character. Finally, students must include the meaning and pronunciation of the character at the bottom of the picture to help establish the connection among sound-shape-meaning.

在这个活动中，学生首先要用深色的粗笔勾勒汉字的笔画，凸显汉字的整体轮廓；接下来，学生要描绘汉字中的细节或者给图上色，这要求他们仔细观察各部件的细节并明晰其在该合体字中的作用；最后，学生需要在图的下方标注出汉字的发音和意义，这样可以帮助他们建立汉字音、形、义之间的联系。

Teaching Example 6 Make a story about the character

教学示例 6 给汉字编故事

For this activity, students are divided into groups. Each group can have 2–4 members. Students will need to develop memory-aid stories that relate the meaning and the form of the character. For example, one group of students took the character 忙 (*busy*) and described it as a man with two arms 忄 at a desk with a lamp 亡 who is very busy doing homework. Obviously, this is a student's idiosyncratic story that is quite different from the common knowledge of thinking it is a phonetic-semantic compound and 忄 is a heart radical meaning a person's heart is engaged when he/she is busy, while 亡 (wáng) hints at the pronunciation of the character 忙 (máng). However, if students think their personalized story can help memorize the character better than other explanations, it should be encouraged. We should understand that as more orthographic knowledge is introduced, students will voluntarily use the radical knowledge in their personalized character stories.

在这一活动中，学生每2～4人为一组，每组编一个能将汉字字形与字义联系起来的故事。例如，拿到“忙”字的这组学生将其理解为一个正忙于完成家庭作业的男生，他双臂（忄）倚着桌子，桌上有一盏台灯（亡）。很显然，这个故事带有强烈的个人特点，因为通常来说，我们会将“忙”解释为一个形声字：“忄”是部首“心”，是形旁，表示一个人很忙的时候，他/她的心是全情投入的；“亡”（wáng）是“忙”（máng）的声旁，提示其发音。如果学生认为自己编的故事更有助于记忆汉字，我们也应该予以鼓励。不用担心学生会理解错部首的意义，因为随着学生缀字知识的增加，他们会自觉地将部首知识融入自己编的故事中。

I usually ask students to come up with stories for five to ten characters. After ten minutes, I have each group choose their best stories. One student representative from each group comes up and tells one of their group’s stories to the entire class. I encourage students to do a quick sketch of their character and story on the board to clarify their ideas. After each group has had a turn to tell one story, the group representatives go back to their seats and a new set of representatives come up to share another set of stories.

我一般会让学生先花10分钟的时间给5～10个汉字编一个故事，然后各组选出那个最好的故事，派一个代表出来向全班介绍这个故事。在讲故事的同时，我鼓励学生在黑板上简要地勾画出所描述的汉字与故事情节之间的联系。每组轮流讲完一个故事后，代表们回到座位上，新一轮的代表上台讲新的故事。

Students work in groups for several reasons. First, multiple students can come up with more stories than a single student working alone. Second, when group members listen to a memory-aid story, they evaluate and improve it before presenting it to the class. This process of evaluating a story encourages students to think more deeply about the character and its meaning, and so it helps students memorize the character. Finally, students are more likely to share their stories with small groups than with the entire class.

让学生分组活动有以下几个优点：首先，比起单个学生，多个学生在一起能想出更多的故事。其次，在向全班学生介绍故事前，组员们之间可以先聆听、评价和改进彼此的故事。评价这一过程有助于学生更深入地理解汉字字形与字义之间的联系，并深化记忆。最后，学生更愿意在小组内分享他们的故事，而不是在全班学生面前。

This activity can be conducted as an informal competition to increase student involvement. I never announce a winner, compare the quality of stories, or offer criticism, so it is not a real competition. However, when generating stories, the idea that they could come up with the most original or entertaining memory aid helps motivate students' engagement in the learning activity. During presentations, the students quietly judge each group's stories, and so they pay greater attention to the presenter's ideas.

为了调动学生的积极性，这个活动可以以一种非正式比赛的形式进行。在活动过程中，我不宣布比赛的胜出者，不比较故事的好坏，也不对故事进行评论，因此它本身不是一种真正意义上的比赛。但是，这种比赛性质的活动会让学生在故事构思阶段更积极主动地去创造最具独创性的故事和最有意思的助记方式；而在故事展示阶段，因为学生会在心里默默评判每组故事的好坏，所以他们会集中注意力听别人的故事。

Teaching Example 7 Find your partner

教学示例 7 找朋友

This activity helps students recognize the characters in disyllabic words. For each disyllabic word in a lesson, I make two flash cards—the first character on one card and the second character on another card. I mix all of the cards together and then hand them out to the class, so that each student holds one character. The goal of this game is for each student to find their partner—the student who is holding the second character of their word. Thus, if one student is holding 友, he/she should look for the student holding 朋, to make the word 朋友. To complete this activity, students must recognize the character in their hand, recall which word contains that character, and find their partner. Students usually seek out their partner by calling out the entire word as they wander about the room. After every student has found their partner, I have all the students stand in a circle with their partners beside them. Each pair shows their cards together and says their word aloud. This way, every student gets a chance to see the characters and hear every disyllabic word from that lesson.

这个活动主要是为了帮助学生识别双音节词中的汉字。我先将课文中的每个双音节词都写在两张卡片上，每张卡片上只写其中的一个汉字，然后打乱顺序分发给学生，学生人手一张。这个活动的目的是让学生找到与自己手中字卡能组合成词的另一张字卡的持有者。如果学生手中的字卡是“友”字，那他/她就需要找到持有“朋”这张字卡的学生凑成“朋友”这个词。要完成这个任务，学生必须先识别出自己持有的字卡上的汉字，回想哪个词包含这个汉字，然后再去寻找另一张字卡的持有者。学生一般会在教室里一边来回走动，一边喊出整个要找的词。等所有学生都找到自己的同伴后，我让学生站成一圈，组合成词的字卡持有者站在一起，每组依次展示他们的字卡并大声读出该词。这样，每个学生都有机会看到该课所要学习的汉字并听到每个双音节词的发音。

Teaching Example 8 Word relay race

教学示例 8 听词找词

For this activity, I use the same set of cards I used in the 找朋友 activity. The characters from a disyllabic word are written on two cards, the first character on one card, and the second character on a second card. I affix magnets to the back of the cards, so that I can stick the cards onto the whiteboard. Then I hang all of the first-syllable characters on the left side of the board, and all of the second-syllable characters on the right side of the board. In the middle of the board, I draw two squares, one for the first syllable, and one for the second syllable. I divide the class into two teams. One team is responsible for the first syllables. They sit on the left. The other team is responsible for the second syllables. They sit on the right. One representative comes up from each group. These two students stand behind a starting line, like runners in a race. They take action immediately after I call out a word such as 电话. The student on the left races to find the 电 card and put it in the square I have drawn in the center of the board; the student on the right side finds the 话 card and put it in the square. The student who puts the correct character in the square first wins a point for their team. Their team members can call out clues, such as "It's on the top right!" or "It's the one with the speech radical!", but they cannot get out of their seats to help. After each member of the group has had a chance to compete, I have the groups switch sides, and we play another round. I do this because it is generally easier to find the first character of a disyllabic word than the second character, so that each team has a fair shot at scoring points.

这个活动使用的字卡和上个活动"找朋友"使用的是同一套。每个双音节词中的两个汉字都分别写在两张背后粘有磁条的卡片上。我将写有第一个音节的汉字的字卡和写有第二个音节的汉字的字卡分别贴在白板的两边，中间画两个正方形，分别用于放置每个词的首字和尾字。我将全班分为两组，坐在左边的一组负责找出每个词的首字，坐在右边的一组负责找出每个词的尾字。每轮活动每组各派出一名代表，就像赛跑选手一样，站在起跑线后。我每说出一个词后，他们就开始行动。例如，我说出“电话”一词后，左边一组的学生代表找到字卡“电”并放入白板中间对应的正方形内，右边一组的学生代表找到字卡“话”并放入对应的正方形内。最先将字卡正确放入正方形内的那一组得1分。其他组员可以给出提示，如“在右上角”“是有言字旁的那个字”，但不能起身帮忙。每组成员轮流进行一次后，两组交换场地再来一轮。因为识别双音节词的尾字通常比识别首字耗时要长，交换场地可以确保双方的得分机会均等。

Teaching Example 9 Review race: Character/word grabbing

教学示例 9 抢字/词竞赛

This is a review activity for midterms, finals, or after returning from a long break. For this activity, I select 50–70 words the students have learned. I collect note cards in four colors—white, yellow, orange, and pink. I select the common or simple words, such as 我, and write these on the white cards. I write the more complex or uncommon words on the yellow cards (i.e., 岁). The words that are even more rare or difficult, I write them on the orange cards (i.e., 做菜). I write those difficult words on the pink cards (i.e., 跳舞). I stick a magnet to the back of each card, and then hang all the cards on the board. Two or three students come to the white board. They have 30 seconds to grab all the characters/ words that they recognize. They must move quickly because the other student is grabbing characters/words, too. After time is up, the students read the cards to me in Chinese. Each white card (easy) character/word they recognize is worth one point. The yellow card is two points, orange three, and pink four. We add all their points together. Whichever of the two/three students earns the most points wins. If a student grabs a card and then reads it wrong, or can’t remember the pronunciation, then they lose points accordingly. By taking points off for wrongly read characters, I ensure that students will not just run up, and grab all of the cards indiscriminately.

这个活动适合用在期中、期末或者长假结束后的词汇复习课上。我先选出50～70个学生已学过的词，并准备4种颜色的卡片——白色、黄色、橙色和粉色。白色卡片上写最常见、最简单的词，如“我”；黄色卡片上写复杂一点或不太常见的词，如“岁”；橙色卡片上写更难、更少见的词，如“做菜”；最难的词则写在粉色卡片上，如“跳舞”。每张卡片的背后都贴上磁条，固定在白板上。我叫2～3名学生到白板前来，让他们用30秒的时间取下所有他们可以认读的词。他们的动作必须要快，因为对手同时也在行动。时间一到，学生就要用汉语念出他们所抢到的卡片上的词。每张白色卡片（简单级别）代表1分，黄色卡片代表2分，橙色卡片代表3分，粉色卡片代表4分。分数累计相加后，得分最高的那名学生获胜。学生如果发音有误或是忘记了词的读音，将被倒扣相应的分数，这样也可以避免学生不加选择地盲目争抢。

Teaching Example 10 Information gap: Paired dictation

教学示例 10 信息差：配对听写词语

This is a pair-work activity to help students practice both reading and writing words. I divide students into pairs. One student in the pair is 甲. The 甲 students get the sheet 甲. The second student in the pair is 乙 who gets the sheet 乙.

这是一个两人小组活动，主要帮助学生练习词语的认读和书写。我先将学生分为两组，一组为甲组，另一组为乙组，分别得到如下的甲、乙任务单：

甲			
1. ____	2. ____	3. ____	4. ____
5. 开会	6. 帮	7. 时候	8. 练习

乙			
1. 方便	2. 考试	3. 有事	4. 等
5. ____	6. ____	7. ____	8. ____

Students first take a minute to read the words that are written on the sheet that they have got. If they need, they can write the Pinyin above the words. They can also look up the words in theirs books. Next, 甲 asks 乙 "第一个词是什么?", 乙 reads the first word 方便 to 甲 in Chinese, and 甲 writes the words in the blanks. 乙 continues to read the words until 甲 finishes writing all four words in the sheet. If they can't remember how to write the character, I have them write the word in Pinyin, and then look it up in their books after the activity is done. Then 甲 reads 5-8 to 乙, who writes the words in the blanks next to numbers 5-8. After the activity is completed, both partners compare their sheets, to check if they have written the characters correctly. This activity is the traditional 听写 dictation, except the teacher does not have to do the reading.

学生先花1分钟时间读一下他们各自任务单上的词。如有必要，他们也可以标注出词的拼音，或通过查阅课本认读这些词。然后，学生甲问学生乙"第一个词是什么？"，学生乙读出第一个词"方便"，学生甲根据学生乙提供的信息将相应的词依次填入任务单中1—4的空白处。学生如果不知道字该怎么写，可以先写下拼音，等活动结束后再查阅课本。之后换学生甲读出5—8处的词，学生乙依次填空。活动完成后，双方检查各自的任务单，查看是否写对了所有词。该活动与传统的听写活动相似，但不需要教师读生词。

Teaching Example 11 Analyze the characters in the table

教学示例 11 汉字分析表

I have students do this activity as homework. Students need to fill in a character analysis table as illustrated below:

这个活动作为学生的一个课外作业，主要是让学生按照下面的示例填写汉字分析表。

汉字分析表

Number	A Word	B Word meaning	C Highlighted character	D Character meaning	E Radical(s) and/or phonetics
Example	píngfēn **评**分	to grade	píng 评	to judge, to appraise	讠 speech 平 (ping)
1	qǐchuáng **起**床		qǐ 起		
2	shēnghuó 生**活**		huó 活		
3	hǎibiān **海**边		hǎi 海		
4	hǎibiān 海**边**		biān 边		
5	měitiān **每**天		měi 每		

The words 1-7 are target words I have preselected from one lesson. Students will complete the sheet following the steps. Step 1, write the meaning of the whole word (词) in column B, then use an online dictionary to learn the meaning of individual characters (字) within the word. Step 2, write the meaning of the character (字) in column D. The dictionary www.mdbg.net works best for this activity. Step 3, analyze the character (字) into its components (semantic/phonetic radical) to fill in column E. The next day, in class, the students firstly discuss how the meanings of individual characters (字) within the word relate to the meaning of the entire word. For example, in the example 评分—"to grade," the first character 评 means "to judge or appraise." 分 means "points" or "scores." Giving an A grade (评分) is a form of judgment (评). Next, we discuss as a class how the components within the individual character relate to that character's meaning. For example, in the example 评—"judge" —the radical is speech 讠 and judgments are issued in speech. 分 is to use a knife 刀 to divide an object equally, which hints points are equally distributed. In this activity, rather than simply hearing from the teacher what each character and component means, the students must hunt them down and record them on their own. The action of hunting, recording, and discussing requires that students devote more mental effort and time to their word learning, which leads to deeper learning.

词语1—6是我提前从某课生词中挑选出来的。学生可以按照以下步骤完成表格：第一步，在B列写出整个词的词义，然后利用在线词典查找每个单字在该词中的意义；第二步，在D列写出单字的意思，学生可以登录www.mdbg.net进行在线查寻；第三步，将字拆分成部件，并在E列写出其声旁或形旁。次日课上，学生先讨论单字的义与其所构成词语的义之间的联系。例如，表中列出的示例"评分"，它的意思是"给出分数"，首字"评"的意思是"给出判断或评价"，尾字"分"的意思是"分数"或"成绩"，给出成绩"A"就是评判的一种。然后，全班再集体讨论汉字中的部件与整个汉字之间的意义联系。以"评"字为例，"评"字的部首是"讠"，意思是"说话"，评价往往是以言语的形式表达的；"分"字是指用"刀"均匀地切分某物，这也正好喻示了分数的分布是均匀的。在这个活动中，学生不是简单地听教师的讲解，他们必须自己去寻找和记录这些汉字及其部件的意义和作用。而在寻找、记录和讨论的过程中，学生投入了更多的时间和精力，从而促进了学习的深化。

Teaching Example 12 Find the right one: Character-shape differentiation

教学示例 12 找对象：字形辨析

For this activity I choose a character, such as 风. Then, I find three characters that are similar to 风, such as 凤, 冈, and 网. I then mix the characters together and have students select the correct character based on the English meaning on the right. Students circle the character that matches the English meaning, and then give the Pinyin with tone for that character. I usually do this for 5-10 characters. For beginners who only know a few characters, recognition of a character demands only that they recall the general shape. If a student is only required to read 你 and 好, it is an easy task. However, to write the character, the student must recall every detail of strokes for a character. This character-shape differentiation activity requires that students focus on the details, which will help them later to write the character. It also exposes students to a variety of characters, so that they can begin to build a subconscious understanding of character structure.

在这个活动中，我先选择了一个汉字，如“风”；然后找出了三个与“风”形近的汉字，如“凤、冈、网”，将这四个字放在一起，让学生根据右边的英文解释选出正确的汉字；最后让学生圈出和右边英文解释相匹配的汉字，并标注出拼音和声调。每轮活动我基本上将汉字控制在5～10个。对于识字较少的初学者来说，字形识别只要求他们记住汉字的大致结构。如果仅要求学生读出“你”和“好”这两个字，这并不难；但若是让学生写出这两个字，他们就必须回忆起汉字中每个笔画的细节。字形辨析活动可以引导学生关注汉字中的笔画细节，为以后正确书写汉字奠定基础；同时，也可以让学生接触大量的形似字，帮助他们在潜意识中建立汉字的结构体系。

Teaching Example 13 Complete the character

教学示例 13 补全汉字

This activity is a "completing the character" exercise to encourage students to learn the details within a character. I give students a partially written character, as illustrated below, and ask them to fill in missing components.

"补全汉字"这个活动的目的是鼓励学生在学习汉字时多关注汉字中的笔画细节。我给学生提供了如下几个不完整的汉字，让学生将其补全为完整的汉字。

búcuò 不钅　　　　shuìjiào 睡觉

Teaching Example 14 Correct the character errors

教学示例 14 改错字

This activity helps students remember details within a character. First, I write down several sentences. The sentences are all grammatically correct, but many characters within the sentence have errors which I observed from students' writing. Below is an example:

这个活动主要是帮助学生记忆汉字内部的笔画细节。首先，我会在黑板上写下几个句子。这些句子在语法上都是正确的，但在书写上会出现学生作业中常见的错误。如下例：

我看妹妹，没看弟弟。
Wǒ yǒu mèimei, méiyǒu dìdi.　　(7 errors)

Next, students must find and correct the errors. For example, the character 有 (yǒu) above has been written with an extra stroke. It looks as if the writer has confused 有 with 看 (kàn). To correct the error, students cross off the extra stroke. Beginners have a hard time reading characters, even if they are all correct. If I give them this set of characters with errors, they probably could not guess what characters I "meant" to write. I provide them with Pinyin at the bottom, so they will know which words I mean. Having the Pinyin also allows students to look up the word in their dictionary, something they could not do with a flawed character alone. I always provide how many errors the sentence contains at the end of each sentence, so students will know how many errors they need to correct.

然后，学生要找出这些错误并将其改正。例如，上例中的"有"字上部有多余的笔画，书写者似乎把"有"跟"看"混淆了。这时，学生需要通过删掉多余的笔画改正错误。对于初学者来说，能够认读书写正确的汉字已是不易，如果我给出的汉字书写有误，学生就更猜不出要写的正确汉字是什么了。所以，我在汉字下方标注出了拼音，让学生知道我所指的到底是哪个汉字。这也方便学生利用拼音在词典中查找汉字。因为如果学生识别出来的汉字是不完整的，那他们是无法查字典的。同时，我还在句末标出了每个句子中所含错误的数量，这样学生就知道要纠多少个错了。

(Teaching Examples 5-14 are contributed by Ms Catherine M. Fillebrown, Instructor of the Bergen County Technical schools at Paramus)

• Semi-contextualized approach 半语境化途径

The semi-contextualized approach helps students understand how words are used in a simple linguistic context and the relationship between words, phrases, and sentences to acquire syntactic and network knowledge of target words. The instructional efforts are made to direct students to pay attention to how the words are used in the linguistic contexts and what kinds of semantic and syntactic relationships exist between the target words and other words. In order to make our readers understand this approach in a concrete way, we introduce three teaching methods for using the semi-contextualized approach. They are word grouping, using corpora, and creating concept (semantic) maps. We will discuss each of them in detail below.

半语境化途径可以帮助学生了解词在简单语境中是如何运用的，以及词、短语和句子之间的联系，进而帮助其掌握词的句法知识和网络知识。教学应该努力引导学生关注目的词在语境中是如何运用的，目的词与其他相关词在语义上和句法上是如何联系的。为了让读者更了解半语境化途径，我们将具体介绍三种运用半语境化途径的教学方法，这三种方法分别是词分组、使用语料库和构建概念（语义）图。下面我们将一一说明。

Word grouping 词分组

Each lesson has a list of new words for students to learn. Word grouping refers to classifying the list of words into small groups according to their attributes. Grouping makes words learning easier because meaningful relationships will be established between words in the same group, which facilitates incorporation of the target words into existing schemata. Grouping can be based on linguistic features, such as parts of speech, on semantic connections such as meanings of similar or dissimilar words, and on language functions such as words used for greetings, asking for directions or requesting, and on themes such as playing a sports game, or mailing a letter at the post office. Word grouping should also take into consideration the content of the lesson, so that the word study will facilitate subsequent lesson learning. At the initial stage, the instructor may provide models for grouping words. After an initial period of practice, the instructor can ask students to do groupings by providing grouping guidelines. Once students have fully understood the rationales and methods of grouping, the instructor can let students do their word grouping activity creatively. Please see Teaching Examples 15-17 for using the word grouping methods.

一般来说，教材中每一课都会列出该课的生词表。词分组就是根据词的属性或特点将生词表中所列的词进行分类，每类为一组。分组能让词语学习变得更加容易，因为它能在同组词之间建立有意义的联系。这种联系能够促进目的词融入学习者已有的认知图式中。分组可以根据词的语言学特征分，如将词性相同的分为一组；也可以根据词之间的语义联系分，如把意义相近或相反的分在一组；也可以按词的语言功能分，如将用于打招呼、问路或提出请求的词各分成一组；也可以根据主题分，如以一项体育运动或在邮局寄信为主题进行分组。对词进行分组时，我们也应该兼顾课文内容，与课文内容相联系的生词学习才能促进之后的课文学习。在初始阶段，教师可以先进行分组示范，然后再让学生模仿示例进行分组练习。之后，教师可以只提出分组原则，让学生按原则自行分组。等学生完全掌握了分组的基本原理和方法后，教师就可以让学生进行创造性的分组活动。具体请参看教学示例15—17中的词分组方法。

Teaching Example 15 Word grouping: Find the key word

教学示例 15 词分组：找出关键词

Words are grouped together 生词组

电器、电视机、电冰箱、洗衣机、电灯、电话

In this group, 电灯 and 电话 are learned words, but 电器, 电视机, 电冰箱, and 洗衣机 are new words. The purpose of this grouping is three-fold. One is to connect the new words with the learned words based on their similarities. The second is to find out inclusive relationships between 电器 and the other words so that a new schema for this relationship can be established in the learner's brain. The third is to use the key word 电 as a memory peg to link other words.

在这组词中，"电灯"和"电话"是已经学过的词，而"电器、电视机、电冰箱、洗衣机"是生词。如此分组有三个目的：一是基于生词和已学词之间的相似点在二者之间建立联系；二是让学习者发现"电器"和其他词之间的从属关系，并在大脑中建立关于这一关系的新图式；三是让学习者找出关键词"电"，并将之作为记忆支点，帮助学习者记忆和它有关的其他词。

Teaching Example 16 Word grouping: Landlord's story
教学示例 16 词分组：房东的故事

Words are grouped together 生词组

房东、出租、套、公寓、卫生间、厨房、卧室、客厅、楼

Grouping these words together is to establish meaningful connections among the list of words by creating a storyline. The story could be as follows(see below in Chinese):

将这些词归入一组是为了将它们串联成故事，建立它们之间的意义联系，帮助学习者记忆。故事可以是（见下面的中文）：

房东要出租一套公寓。那套公寓有两个卫生间、一个厨房、三个卧室，还有一个客厅。公寓在东大街的98号楼。

Teaching Example 17 Word grouping: Look for similarities
教学示例 17 词分组：找出相同点

Words are grouped together 生词组

跳、唱、打、谈

These four words are grouped for three reasons: (1) The words are all phonetic-semantic compounds. Students can explore the roles of phonetic and semantic radicals in terms of cuing the sound and meaning for the compound characters and generalize rules whereby the phonetic radical is placed on the right within the compound character and the semantic radical is placed on the left. (2) These words are all action words. Students can act out these words to enhance their memorization. (3) The teacher can ask students to give more examples of these types of words by recalling previously learned characters with similar attributes.

将这四个词归为一组，原因有三：（1）这些词都是形声字。学生借此可以认识到形声字中形旁和声旁的不同功能，并归纳出“形旁在左，声旁在右”的规律。（2）这些词都是与动作有关的词。学生可以将它们一一表演出来加强记忆。（3）教师可以启发学生举一反三，让他们回忆起更多的有相似特征的已学词。

(Teaching Examples 15–17 are contributed by Helen H. Shen, The University of Iowa)

Using corpora 使用语料库

Using a corpus can help students develop a depth of word knowledge such as understanding the syntactic and semantic requirement, restriction, and collocation for a target word to be used in a sentential context. The corpus provides comprehensive information about the word usage, which provides great convenience to instructors for preparing vocabulary instruction. We should be aware that meaningful learning occurs only when the instructor guides students to analyze and synthesize the underlining rules of the target word usage, rather than just presents the rules to students and asks students to memorize them. In addition, using corpora means students are required to read certain numbers of sentences extracted from various corpuses. This requires students to have already accumulated a certain amount of vocabulary. Therefore, this method is more suitable for advanced students. Please see Teaching Example 18 for how to use corpora in vocabulary instruction.

使用语料库可以加深学生对词语知识的理解，如理解目的词在句中如何受句法条件和语义条件的制约、如何与其他词语搭配以及搭配上有何限制等。语料库可以提供词语运用的综合性知识，这为教师准备词汇教学带来了极大的便利。需要指出的是，学生只有在教师的指导下自己分析、归纳词语运用规则时才会进行有意义的学习，教师直接把规则展示给学生并让学生去背诵并不会产生有意义的学习。另外，使用语料库意味着学生必须阅读大量的从语料库中选出来的句子，这需要学生已经具备一定的词汇量，因此这一方法更适合高级水平的汉语学习者。具体请参看教学示例18。

Teaching Example 18 Using corpora for semantic differentiation between words

教学示例 18 利用语料库区分语义

Instructional purpose: Understand the semantic scopes for the words 抛弃, 离开, and 丢掉.

教学目的：理解“抛弃、离开、丢掉”的语义范畴。

Step 1: The instructor presents the target word 抛弃 in a sentence (S1) and asks students to discuss the meaning of this sentence in small groups of three or four persons.

步骤1：教师先用S1向学生展示目的词“抛弃”，然后让学生3～4人为一组讨论该句的意思。

S1. 为了留在美国，他居然抛弃了自己的妻子和儿女。

Step 2: The instructor presents another two previously learned words 离开 and 丢掉 which have the similar meaning as 抛弃, but are not identical (see S2, S3). The instructor asks the students to compare the similarities and differences of the three words 抛弃, 离开, and 丢掉. The instructor then asks the students to discuss whether S2 and S3 are correct and to give reasons for their judgment. Lastly, the instructor asks each group leader to present a group opinion based on their discussion. In the original case, the groups were not able to reach a consensus.

步骤2：首先，教师用S2和S3向学生展示另外两个已经学过的词“离开”和“丢掉”，这两个词和“抛弃”意思相近却不相同。然后，教师让学生比较这三个词的异同，判断S2和S3是否正确，并给出理由。最后，教师让各组组长汇报本组的讨论结果。在实际教学中，小组内一般是达不成共识的。

S2. 为了留在美国，他居然离开了自己的妻子和儿女。
S3. 为了留在美国，他居然丢掉了自己的妻子和儿女。

Step 3: The instructor presents the following three groups of words (please see Sentence groups 1–3) and asks students to group as pairs to explore the differences and similarities of using the 抛弃, 离开, and 丢掉 in context. (Note:

The sentence samples are retrieved from http://ccl.pku.edu.cn:8080/ccl_corpus/index.jsp 北京大学中国语言学研究中心CCL现代汉语语料库 with some modifications.)

步骤3：教师给出以下三组句子，学生两人一组探讨“抛弃、离开、丢掉”在语境中使用时有何异同。（注：例句均来自《北京大学中国语言学研究中心CCL现代汉语语料库》，网址为http://ccl.pku.edu.cn:8080/ccl_corpus/index.jsp。为了使例句难度符合学生的语言水平，原句略做了删改。）

Sentence group 1

① 朱德抛弃高官厚禄，寻求救国救民之真理。

② 其实大家从来就没有产生过抛弃小五的念头。

③ 周恩来抛弃了军国主义可以救中国的想法。

④ 人们终于在20世纪初抛弃了原子不可分割的陈旧观念。

Sentence group 2

① 人们吃芹菜习惯把叶子丢掉，这非常可惜，因为叶子很有营养。

② 我担心失去机会，不抓呀，看到的机会就丢掉了，时间一晃就过去了呀。

③ 由于去年年底在英美车队丢掉了饭碗，威廉姆斯只得无奈地选择退役。

④ 在伊拉克发生的事显示出布什在未来的大选中会付出丢掉总统宝座的代价。

Sentence group 3

① 你看，我出生在北京，我就没离开这个海淀区。

② 我其实也舍不得离开她，见她极力挽留我，便留了下来。

③ 我很快地离开了那家地下招待所。

④ 我还不想这么早离开人世。

Step 4: Under the instructor's guidance, the class summarizes their understanding of the three words.

步骤4：在教师的指导下，全班一起总结这三个词在语义范畴和使用上的异同。

① 抛弃：用于抛弃人、地位、思想观念、行为方式，因为不喜欢、讨厌、过时。

② 丢掉：用于丢掉东西、工作，因为不喜欢、过时、不小心、某种原因。

③ 离开：用于离开人、地方，由于某种原因。

Step 5: The instructor asks students to work in pairs and complete the following exercise. Each group reports their work and gives the reason for their choice.

步骤5：学生两人一组完成以下练习，每组分别汇报他们的答案并说出选择的理由。

抛弃　丢掉　离开

① 这本书很旧，已经没有用了，我把它______了。

② 昨天安利找不到车钥匙（yàoshi），他不知道是什么时候_____的。

③ 因为我家很穷，没钱给我上大学，高中毕业后，我不得不____了上大学的念头。

④ 2007年5月，我______了艾奥瓦，去了芝加哥。

⑤ 因为我要去中国，我只好 _____我的父母亲。

(Teaching Example 18 is contributed by Helen H. Shen, The University of Iowa)

Creating concept (semantic) maps 构建概念（语义）图

Concept mapping is an instructional theory predicated on Ausubel's (1963) meaningful learning theory. Initially, this was developed by Novak's research program in 1972 and used in science education (Novak & Musonda, 1991). Now it is widely used in language instruction. The concept maps are graphical tools for organizing and representing an invisible cognitive map that shows the pathways that the learner uses to connect meanings of concepts to form a cognitive schema in their brains (Novak & Gowin, 1984). Concept maps can be presented either in concepts or in propositions. A concept refers to a perceived regularity in events or objects, or records of events or objects, designated by words or symbols. A proposition contains two or more connected concepts to form a meaningful statement. Propositions are therefore statements about an object or event, which can be called semantic units (Novak & Cañas, 2008). For this reason, the concept map is also called the semantic map.

概念图构建作为一种教学理论是在Ausubel（1963）的有意义学习理论基础上提出来的。概念图构建这一说法最早出现在Novak 1972年进行的一个研究项目中，最早应用于科学教育领域（Novak and Musonda，1991）。现在，这一理论已广泛应用在语言教学中。概念图作为一种图式化工具，它能将学习者大脑中内隐的认知图式变成看得见的外显图形，从而反映出学习者在大脑中建立概念间联系并形成认知图式的过程。（Novak and Gowin，1984）概念图可以以概念的形式呈现，也可以以命题的形式呈现。概念指的是以语言或符号的形式对事物或事件进行的规律性总结或是对事物或事件的记录。命题则是由两个或两个以上有联系的概念组成的对事物或事件的有意义陈述，也被称为语义单位（Novak and Cañas，2008）。因此，概念图也称为语义图。

Concept maps used in vocabulary instruction bear several characteristics. First, the concept or proposition represented by words or sentences in the graphic is in an organized fashion with a focused theme. Second, the concepts presented in the map usually demonstrate three types of relationships between concepts or propositions. The Type 1 map indicates hierarchical/parallel relationship. For the hierarchical one, the most inclusive or general concepts are placed at the top of the map and more specific, less general concepts are in a lower position of the map or vice versa; for the parallel one, it indicates either coordinative, mutual overlapping, or exclusive relationships between concepts (please see Figure 6-1). The Type 2 map is organized chronologically based on an event or plot development (see Figure 6-2). The Type 3 map presents spatial relationships between concepts. The arrangement of concepts is based on physical location or spatial movement of the items (see Figure 6-3). Third, the concepts included in the map are cross-linked to reflect the meaningful relationship between the concepts or propositions.

用于词汇教学的概念图有以下几个特点：第一，概念图中的词或句子所代表的概念或命题是有组织的，集中反映一个主题。第二，概念图中显示的概念或命题之间的关系通常有三种。第一种是表示概念之间的从属或平行关系。表示从属关系的概念图把最具包容性或最具一般性的概念放在最上面，把更具体或不具一般性的概念放在靠下的位置，或者反过来以自下而上的顺序排列。表示平行关系的概念图则表示概念之间的并列、交叉或互不包含的关系（请参看图6-1）。第二种是将概念式命题按事件或情节发展的时间顺序进行组织（请参看图6-2）。第三种是按概念间的空间关系进行组织，概念的排列取决于其在空间中的位置或空间运动轨迹（请参看图6-3）。第三，概念图中的概念之间都用线条或其他标志相互连接，以反映概念之间或命题之间的意义联系。

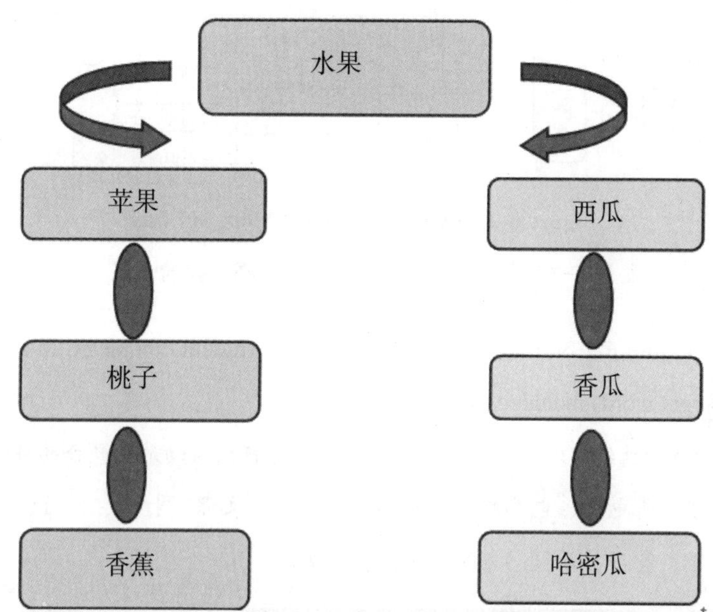

Figure 6-1 Type 1 Hierarchical/Parallel Map: Classification for Fruit

图6-1 类型1 从属/平行概念图：水果的分类

Note: The classification of target words 苹果, 西瓜, 香瓜, 桃子, 香蕉, 哈密瓜, and 水果 in Figure 6-1. Type 1 map is based on our knowledge of 水果 as a general concept and the other items as subordinate concepts. 苹果, 桃子, and 香蕉 grow on trees and 西瓜, 香瓜, and 哈密瓜 grow on the ground; thus, these two groups of concepts are exclusive in terms of their growing conditions, but they share the similarities as fruit.

注：图6-1是对目的词"苹果、西瓜、香瓜、桃子、香蕉、哈密瓜、水果"进行认知加工的概念图。我们一般把"水果"看作最具包容性的概念，而把其他词看作其从属概念。该图就是根据这一认知而绘制成的。其中，"苹果、桃子、香蕉"是长在树上的，"西瓜、香瓜、哈密瓜"是长在地上的，所以从生长环境看，这两组概念是互不包含的，但是它们具有作为水果的共性。

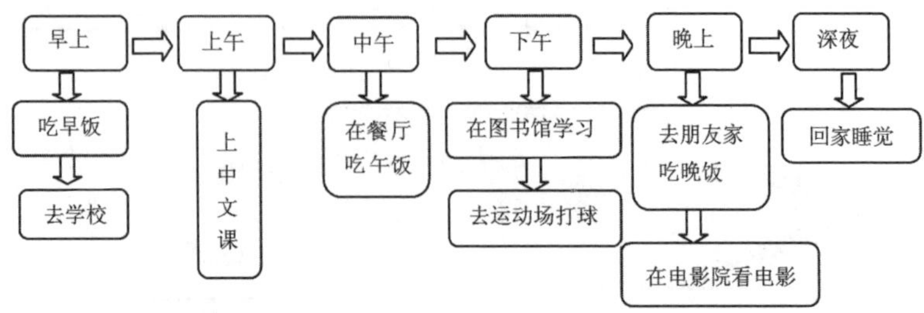

Figure 6-2 Type 2 Temporal Map: My Day

图6–2 类型2 按时间推进的概念图：我的一天

Note: Figure 6-2 outlines the activities that the student completed in a particular day. The target words included in the map are:

注：图6–2总结了学生一天中按时间顺序所进行的活动。所包含的目的词有：睡觉、回家、看电影、电影院、运动场、早上、中文课、打球、学习、深夜、晚上、图书馆、餐厅、学校、午饭、早饭、晚饭。

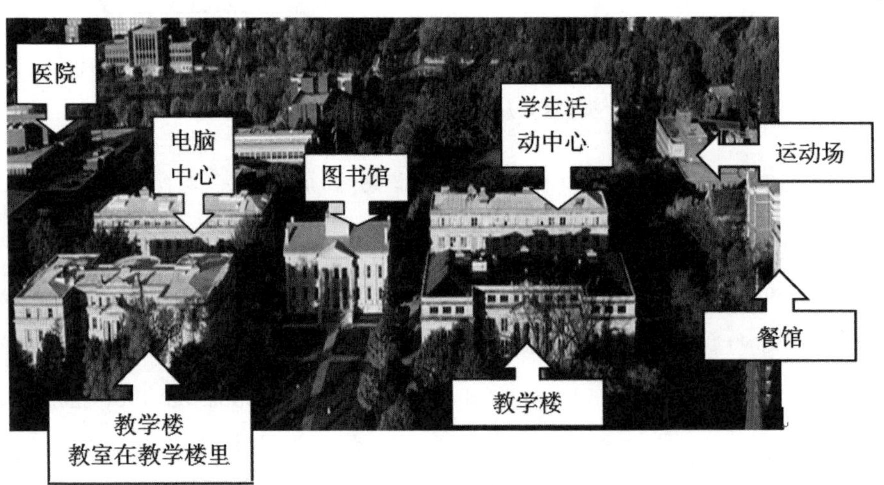

Figure 6-3 Type 3 Spatial Map: My School

图6–3 类型3 按空间位置排列的概念图：我的学校

Note: The target words 图书馆, 电脑中心, 学生活动中心, 教学楼, 教室, 运动场, 医院, and 餐馆 in Figure 6-3 Type 3 map are arranged according to their spatial relationships.

注：图6-3中的目的词“图书馆、电脑中心、学生活动中心、教学楼、教室、运动场、医院、餐馆”是根据它们的空间位置关系排列的。

Based on this concept mapping theory and its application in character/word instruction, the instructor can use internet-based concept map tools such as Web 2.0 tools to have students design different types of concept maps to make meaningful connections between words. Teaching Example 19 illustrates how to use the Web 2.0 tools to develop concept maps for word instruction. The instructor can also have students work out the map by hand. This may save time and also provide opportunity for handwriting words. Incorporating the handwriting mode into instruction can enhance word memorization.

将概念图理论应用到字词教学中，教师可以运用网络工具，如Web 2.0，让学生设计不同类型的概念图，促进有意义学习。教学示例19展示了如何在词语教学中运用Web 2.0设计概念图。教师也可以让学生手绘概念图，这不但节省时间，还能为学生提供手写词语的机会，增强学生对词语的记忆。

Teaching Example 19 Designing a semantic map of family members: Establishing meaningful relations between words

教学示例 19 设计一张关于家庭成员的概念图：建立词语间的意义关系

Words/phrases to be learned 要学的生词/短语

散步、出生、忘不了、确实、年代、曾经、除非、否则、商量、做生意、打听

Instructional tools and materials 教具和材料

PowerPoint, Cacoo online concept mapping tool

幻灯片、Cacoo在线绘图工具

The reason to choose the Cacoo online concept mapping tool for this activity is that it has designed shapes and columns that help students easily analyze relationships. The other reason is that Cacoo supports Chinese input.

之所以采用Cacoo在线绘图工具，是因为该网站提供了现成的图形和符号，方便学生构建概念之间的关系。而且，Cacoo还支持中文输入。

The objective of this activity 活动目的

To review the target words just introduced and to discover meaningful relationships of these words in order to help students make a connection between the target words and their existing knowledge structure.

复习所学的目的词，引导学生发现词与词之间的意义联系，从而帮助学生将目的词融入已有的知识结构中去。

Steps for the activity 活动步骤

Step 1: Present the 11 listed words/phrases and ask students to review these words quickly by using electronic flashcards.

步骤1：教师展示出上面所列的11个生词/短语，并让学生通过抽认电子字卡的方式快速复习一遍。

Step 2: Provide the topic “Introduce my family members” to students and ask them to work in pairs to design a concept map around the topic by using the 11 words/phrases.

步骤2：教师给出话题“介绍我的家人”，学生两人一组围绕这个话题用这11个生词/短语设计一张概念图。

Step 3: After students have completed their designing, a few groups are invited to share their design with the whole class. By assessing each other's work, students reinforce the target words/phrases and their semantic relationships in their memory.

步骤3：学生完成设计后，教师邀请几组上来向全班展示他们的作品。通过评价每组作品，学生可以进一步巩固对目的词/短语及词语之间语义关系的记忆。

Figure 6-4 is an example of the semantic map completed by a student. The central lines and columns illustrate the similarity that father and mother share in the family by using 出生, 年代, 曾经, 做生意, 打听, and 散步.

图6-4是学生完成的一张概念图。图中间用线条和方框标注出了父母之间的共同点，用到了“出生、年代、曾经、做生意、打听、散步”这些词。

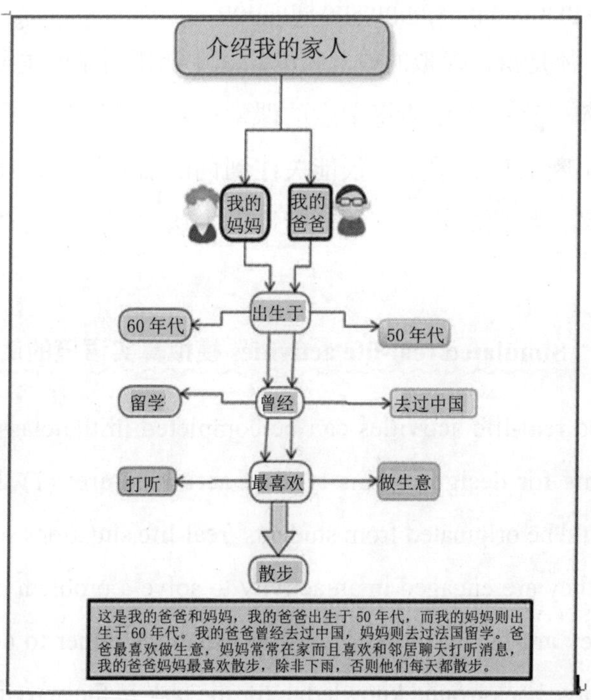

Figure 6-4 Concept Map: Introducing My Family Members

图6-4 概念图：介绍我的家人

(Teaching Example 19 is contributed by Xiaoyuan Zhao, The University of Iowa)

• Contextualized approach 语境化途径

The contextualized approach refers to applying or using learned words in simulated or real-life communicative situations to solve a problem or fulfill a communicative task. This approach bridges the gap of classroom learning with real life communication. By practicing word use in simulated or real-life situations, students will be able to pay attention to both the linguistic form and meaning of the words. It will also help students to notice the pragmatic aspects of word usage in a complex linguistic situation.

语境化途径是指在模拟的或真实的语境中运用所学的词语解决问题或完成交际任务。这一途径能将学生的课堂学习与实际生活联系起来。通过对新词的不断运用，学生不仅能关注到词的语言形式，还能注意到词所表达的意义。除此之外，它还能帮助学生认识到词在复杂语境中是如何运用的。

Simulated real-life activities 模拟真实语境的活动

Simulated real-life activities can be completed in the classroom setting. The key points for designing this type of activities are: (1) the content of activities should be originated from students' real-life situations so that students will fell that they are engaged in an activity to solve a problem or to complete a task that they are facing in their real-life situations rather to do an exercise. (2) students have background knowledge for the task in the activity, so that they will not be distracted or use extra time to familiarize themselves with the task itself; instead, they can focus on practicing words during the task completion. Teaching Examples 20–22 illustrate the use of these types of activities in the classroom.

模拟真实语境的活动是可以在课堂上进行的。设计这类活动要注意：（1）活动内容应该源于学生的真实生活，这样会让他们觉得自己是在解决一个实际问题或完成一个实际任务，而不是在做练习；（2）设置的语言任务应该是学生已有一定背景知识的，这样学生就不需要再花费额外的时间去了解任务本身，也不用分心，可以把全部注意力都放在如何完成任务上。教学示例20—22详细展示了如何在课堂上运用模拟真实语境的活动进行词汇学习。

Teaching Example 20 Simulated real-life activity: IQ contest
教学示例 20 模拟真实语境的活动：智力竞赛

IQ (Intelligence Quotient) contest can often be seen on TV channels in the United States. From elementary school to college, students who are interested or qualified can join IQ groups as an extra class activity. Therefore, students are familiar with this type of activity. The purpose of this activity is to help students review and practice the introduced target words in a linguistic context.

智力竞赛在美国的电视节目上很常见。从小学到大学，对智力竞赛感兴趣的或者有资质的学生都可以加入智力小组这样的课外活动中，因此学生对这类活动比较熟悉。该教学活动的目的是帮助学生在语境中复习和操练刚学过的目的词。

Target words 目的词

图书馆、瓶、杯、罐、工作、家、打工、学校、喝、好吃、好玩、好看、可口可乐、百事可乐、雪碧、汽水、矿泉水、水、咖啡、饮料、茶、啤酒

Task sheet 任务单

Intelligence Quotient Contest 智力竞赛

1. What are the three most popular drinks in the U.S.?
   在美国哪三种饮料最流行？
2. What are the three places that you spend most of your time every week?
   你每周常去哪三个地方？
3. What are the two most common packaging formats for drinks?
   哪两种饮料包装形式最常见？
4. How many drink names are you able to speak and write in Chinese?
   你能用汉语说出并写出哪些饮料的名称？

Procedures 活动步骤

Step 1: Students are grouped in pairs. Each pair is required to write out the answers to the questions listed in the task sheet by using the target words. They then practice orally by asking questions to each other.

步骤1：学生两人一组。每组都要用所给的目的词写出任务单上的问题的答案，然后互相进行口头问答。

Step 2: Students are asked to perform a simulated intelligence contest, either orally or written (to write out the answer in the white board) in the class without looking at the answers.

步骤2：学生参加模拟智力竞赛，在不看答案的情况下，以口头或者书面的形式（在白板上写出答案）回答任务单上的问题。

Then, the class is divided into two groups. The testing rules are worked out based on mutual agreement between the two groups, such as the time to be used to answer questions, and the score for each correctly answered question. During the contest, for the first round, group A sends a person to act as an interrogator and group B sends a person to answer as the interrogatee. The interrogator can ask any question listed on the sheet. The interrogatee must answer the questions quickly and accurately. For the second round, group A and group B exchange roles. The activity continues until each person in the group has an opportunity to serve either as an interrogator or an interrogatee. Finally, scores are added up to decide the winner.

接下来，全班分为A、B两组。两组协商确定具体的比赛规则，如回答问题的时限、每道题的分值。第一轮，A组派出一个人作为提问方，B组派出一个人作为答题方。提问方可以问任务单上的任何问题，答题方必须快速、准确地做出回答。第二轮，A组和B组交换角色。直到小组里每个成员都扮演过提问方或答题方时，活动才可以结束。最后，计算分数，决出胜者。

(Teaching Example 20 is contributed by Helen H. Shen, The University of Iowa)

Teaching Example 21 Simulated real-life activity: Open house
教学示例 21 模拟真实语境的活动：样板房开放日

Opening house events are held by real estate companies to sell houses and apartments in the U.S.. An open house activity is usually arranged during weekends. Students usually are familiar with this type of activity. The purpose of this activity is to review the new words that have just been introduced.

美国的房地产公司经常在周末举办样板房开放日活动来销售住宅和公寓。学生对这类活动也比较熟悉。该教学活动的目的是帮助学生复习刚学过的生词。

Procedures 活动步骤

Step 1: The teacher presents the task to the class.

You are an agent of a real estate company. Your goal is to sell apartments. Your job is to provide an honest introduction to one of the apartments listed below to your potential customers. In your description, please use your knowledge of the apartment to provide complete information. Your description should be based on the picture provided and must include the words and phrases listed on the card on the right.

步骤1：教师向全班布置任务。

现在你是房地产公司的经纪人，要出售下面三套公寓。在样板房开放日活动中，你需要向你的潜在客户介绍其中一套公寓的真实情况。在介绍公寓时，请你根据对该公寓的了解，提供尽量完整的信息。你需要根据下面提供的图片进行描述，并用上右边卡片上的生词或短语。

一号公寓：

楼梯 走廊 地毯 租金/房租 稍微 有点儿贵

二号公寓：

隔壁 体育场 篮球 比赛 激动 大喊大叫

三号公寓：

一室
一厅
包水电
安静
受影响
厨房

Step 2: Each student chooses one of the three new word lists to work out a written description of the house based on the photo.

步骤2：每个学生从三张生词卡中选择一张，然后根据提供的相应图片为该套公寓写篇情况介绍。

Step 3: Each student finds a partner and takes turns acting as the agent and the customer for the open house activity.

步骤3：每个学生找一个搭档，两人轮流扮演样板房开放日活动中的房地产经纪人和客户，分别介绍和参观公寓。

Step 4: The teacher asks each pair to perform in front of the whole class. Students and the teacher provide comments on the language and word use after each pair's performance.

步骤4：每组都要在全班学生面前扮演房地产经纪人和客户进行对话。表演结束后，教师和其他学生就该组的用词和语言表达情况进行点评。

(Teaching Example 21 is contributed by Xiaoyuan Zhao, The University of Iowa)

Teaching Example 22 Designing a simulated online store

教学示例 22 设计虚拟网店

Target words 目的词

衣服、T恤衫、毛衣、牛仔裤、样子、名牌、洗衣粉、牙膏、香皂、卫生纸、杯子、浴巾、化妆品、减价、打折、纯棉、质量、物美价廉、好看、现金、信用卡

Instructional tools and materials: Online diagram tool, the task sheet

教具及材料：在线绘图工具、任务单

The objective of this activity is to help students review and practice target words by describing clothing items, daily necessity items, and money in Chinese. This activity will help to establish vocabulary networks and to use the target words in a simulated real-life situation. Students work individually and design a simulated online store by using online graphing tools. They can also use an online dictionary to look for new words to be used in their design. For example, one student designed a clothing store and described each of her items using learned words and marked a price for each item. After completion of the design, we assess the students' learning outcome by letting them invite each other to visit their stores and provide feedback. The teacher also visits the store and provides feedback.

这个活动的目的是通过用汉语对衣物、日用品和钱等进行描述帮助学生复习相关的目的词，并在大脑中形成词汇网络图，同时帮助其在模拟真实生活的语境中使用这些词。具体来说，这个活动是让学生独立运用在线绘图工具设计一家虚拟网店。学生可以借助在线词典查阅网店设计过程中需要用到的生词。例如，有个学生设计了一家网上服装店，并用所学词语对所售商品进行了描述，标出了价格。网店设计完成后，学生

互相访问彼此的网店页面并给出反馈。教师也可以访问学生的网店页面并给出反馈。

(Teaching Example 22 is contributed by Xiaoyuan Zhao, The University of Iowa)

Real-life activities 真实语境活动

Real-life activities usually are extended beyond the classroom. These types of activities allow students to focus on meaningful communication, which is very helpful for expanding the depth of word knowledge. The real-life activities can be of two types. One type is theme-based social activities, and the other type is reading/writing-based vocabulary activities. The theme-based social activities have three characteristics: (1) the activities has a theme so that students can use the words related to this theme; (2) the activities has a goal and students are required to reach the goal by engaging in the activities; (3) the activities are intended to provide students with opportunities to practice learned target words. Therefore, this type of activity is a guided activity, which is different from natural activities happening in students' daily lives. Teaching Examples 23−27 are examples of theme-based social activities.

真实语境活动大部分是在课堂外进行的。这类活动能让学生将注意力集中在有意义的交流上，这对拓展学生的词语知识深度很有帮助。真实语境活动一般有两类：一类是主题型社交活动，另一类是读写型词汇活动。主题型社交活动有三个特点：（1）活动有一个主题，学生能围绕这个主题练习相关的词语；（2）活动有一个目标，学生可以有目的地参与活动；（3）活动旨在为学生提供练习目的词的机会。因此，这类活动是在教师指导下进行的活动，不同于学生真实生活中自然发生的活动。如何在教学中组织这类活动，请参看教学示例23—27。

Teaching Example 23 Theme-based social activity: Chinese conversational corner

教学示例 23 主题型社交活动：汉语会话角

The instructor can hold a weekly gathering for CSL learners with native Chinese to practice conversation. In order to help students get maximum benefits from this activity, the instructor needs to develop topics and questions based on students' interests and their word knowledge as guidelines for the activity. The instructor also should give a training session to the native Chinese speakers regarding how to communicate with students with limited Chinese word knowledge, so that the CSL learners can use and practice their target words learned from the lessons during the activity.

教师每周可以组织一次汉语二语学习者与汉语母语者的会话活动。为了让学生从活动中最大化地受益，教师可以根据学生的兴趣和词语知识水平提前设计好会话的主题和问题作为活动指南。教师事先也应该对汉语母语者进行有针对性的培训，传授他们一些与汉语词语知识有限的学生进行交流的经验，这样一来，汉语二语学习者才能在活动中有效地运用和操练刚学过的目的词。

Teaching Example 24 Theme-based social activity: Language partner

教学示例 24 主题型社交活动：语伴

The purpose of the language partner activity is to provide an opportunity for CSL learners to be paired with native Chinese speakers (they could be students who are studying at the same institute or other institutes) to practice

Chinese in a natural environment on a regular basis. For vocabulary practice purposes, the instructor can design vocabulary learning tasks beforehand and ask students to complete the tasks during their meetings with their language partners. The vocabulary learning tasks could be to find out what words are used for greeting a person or to express gratitude; or how a word such as 规定 can be used in different contexts.

开展语伴活动的目的是让汉语二语学习者与汉语母语者（可以是在同一学院或其他学院学习的学生）结成语伴，给汉语二语学习者搭建一个交流平台，让他们能在较为自然的语言环境中定期练习汉语。为了更好地操练词汇，教师可以提前设计好词汇学习任务，让学生在与语伴交流时完成这些规定的任务。词汇学习任务可以是与主题有关的，如找出表达问候或感谢时常用的词；也可以是关于某个词的，如弄清楚“规定”在不同语境中的使用规则。

Teaching Example 25 Theme-based social activity: Group online chatting

教学示例 25 主题型社交活动：小组网上会话

In this activity, CSL learners are paired with Chinese students in China or other Chinese-speaking regions through video-conferencing. The instructor-guided online chatting is an effective way to practice and expand vocabulary. The chatting can be arranged in a computer lab or via students' personal electronic devices. The instructor should give students a task on what words should be practiced during each chat. The instructor could also inform the native speakers about the purpose and theme prior to the activity, so that the Chinese partners can do some preparation prior to the chat. At the initial stage, the instructor should supervise the chatting and provide on-site help whenever a student has difficulty in finding the right words to complete the task (see the sample chatting task sheet below).

在这一活动中，汉语二语学习者与中国学生或其他汉语使用区域的学生配对成组进行视频会话。在教师指导下进行的网上会话是一种有效的操练和拓展词汇的方法。网上会话既可以安排在机房进行，也可以通过学生自己的移动电子设备进行。对于汉语二语学习者，教师每次会话前都要给出会话所需使用的词语（参见下面的“会话任务单”）；而对于中国学生或其他汉语使用区域的学生，教师则需要提前告知他们每次会话的意图和主题，使其有所准备。在初始阶段，教师要在旁边监督和指导着学生，并在学生遇到表达困难时及时提供帮助。

会话任务单

Conversation Topic: Sports 会话主题：体育活动

1. Ask your Chinese partner whether they like the following sports by using 你喜欢……吗？
   请用“你喜欢……吗？”这个句式问你的语伴是否喜欢下列体育活动：
   打篮球、踢足球、打乒乓球、跑步、爬山、游泳、拳击、滑冰
2. Tell your partner about the popular sports in your country and also ask your partner to tell you the popular sports in his/her country.
   请告诉你的语伴自己国家流行的体育活动有哪些，也请你的语伴告诉你他/她的国家流行的体育活动有什么。
3. Tell your partner about your favorite sports and also ask your partner about his/her favorite sports.
   告诉你的语伴你最喜欢哪些体育活动，也请你的搭档说说他/她最喜欢的体育活动是什么。

4. Please write out the new sports words that you have learned from your partner during the chat.
请写出你从语伴那儿新学来的有关体育活动的词。

Teaching Example 26 Theme-based social activity: Vocabulary weblog
教学示例 26 主题型社交活动：词汇博客

Students can create a weblog for vocabulary learning purposes. In the weblog, students can post a vocabulary question and ask other students to answer it. The question could be a character/word riddle or puzzle, could ask others for an explanation of a certain word and its usage or could ask others to describe an object or event using specific words. Communication by visiting each other's weblog will greatly stimulate students' interest in learning and practicing vocabulary.

学生可以开通一个专门用于词汇学习的博客。在博客上，学生可以提一些与词汇有关的问题并让其他学生回答。这些问题可以是关于字谜或词谜的，可以是要求对方解释某个词的意义和用法的，可以是让对方用规定的词描述一个事物或事件的。因访问他人博客而产生的交流活动能大大激发学生学习和运用词汇的兴趣。

Teaching Example 27 Theme-based social activity: News report
教学示例 27 主题型社交活动：新闻报道

This type of activity is designed based on individual lesson content. For example, if the lesson is about earthquakes, the instructor could ask students to collect news from the internet about earthquakes to read and identify the words about earthquakes that they have learned, and also to identify a few words that they have not learned and to find out the meaning and pronunciation for these new words. Students could also visit their friends who have first-hand experience about earthquakes. After this, students are required to report to the class about the news they have read and the old and new words they have identified in the news.

设计这类活动应基于每课的教学内容。例如，如果这一课的教学内容与地震有关，教师可以让学生在网上收集与地震有关的新闻阅读，标注出新闻中已学过的与地震有关的词，并对新闻中出现的尚未学过的词进行注音和释义。学生还可以从经历过地震的朋友那里获取第一手资料。完成这些之后，教师再让学生向全班汇报所读到的新闻以及所标出的已学词和新词。

(Teaching Examples 23–27 are contributed by Helen H. Shen, The University of Iowa)

---

word learning can take place in two forms—intentional learning and incidental learning. Intentional learning occurs when learners are clearly aware of their learning goals during the learning process. Incidental learning refers to word learning that is a by-product of a language activity. The learners acquire word knowledge from an activity that is not a pre-planned goal (Hulstijn, 2001). Reading/writing-based vocabulary activities are designed to have learners acquire words incidentally through reading and writing activities. Pleasure reading is an excellent approach to gain new words. The instructor can recommend that students read graded books and articles, which allow students to review previously learned words through repeated exposure during reading or writing, and to learn new words through guessing from the reading contexts. The instructor could also ask students to report their reading content by writing a summary and reporting it to the class. In addition to pleasure reading, the instructor can create theme-based reading/writing activities to help students expand their vocabulary. In designing this type of activities, the instructor should carefully control the difficulty-level of the activities. The activities should be based on class lessons and students' language proficiency level, so that the activities will be challenging yet within the reach of the students' efforts. Please see Teaching Examples 28-30 for designing this type of activities.

词语学习有两种形式——有意识的学习和无意识的学习。有意识的学习是指学习者在学习过程中清楚地知道他们的学习目标；无意识的学习是指词语的习得是某种语言活动的副产品，学习者虽然在活动中掌握了词语知识，但这并不是他们事先计划好的。（Hulstijn，2001）读写型词汇活动旨在让学习者在阅读和写作过程中无意识地学会词语。娱乐性阅读是一种很好的习得词语的途径。教师可以推荐学生阅读一些经教师挑选的分级的课外书或文章，让学生在阅读或写作过程中通过反复接触复习以前学过的词语，并通过阅读上下文猜测新词的意思。教师还可以让学生在读完文章后写一份内容摘要，然后以书面或口头的形式向全班学生汇报自己阅读的内容。除了娱乐性阅读外，教师还可以设计一些主题型读写活动帮助学生扩大他们的词汇量。在设计这类活动时，教师应该控制好活动的难度。活动内容应以课程内容为基础，难度应适合学生现有的汉语水平，可以具有一定的挑战性，但是必须在学生的能力范围之内。如何设计这类活动，请参看教学示例28—30。

Teaching Example 28 Reading/writing-based vocabulary activity: Compare menus

教学示例 28 读写型词汇活动：比比招牌菜

The instructor asks students to conduct an investigation about the dishes provided by a number of Chinese restaurants in the city and to find out the featured dishes from each restaurant for comparison. Then students report the findings to the class. During this activity, students have the opportunity to review dish words learned in class and also to learn new dish words from the menus.

教师让学生对市内多家中餐馆提供的菜肴进行调查，找出各家餐馆的招牌菜并加以比较，然后向全班学生汇报结果。在这一活动中，学生既有机会复习课堂上已学过的有关菜肴的词汇，也能从各种菜单中学到更多的新菜名。

Teaching Example 29 Reading/writing-based vocabulary activity: Class newspaper

教学示例 29 读写型词汇活动：班报

The instructor can ask students to run a regular class Chinese newspaper (either online or offline). The topic for each issue should be related to the lesson content so that students can use the learned words in their writing. Students should elect an editor and an editorial board to be in charge of the newspaper. Each student in the class should contribute stories or news to the newspaper using the target words learned.

教师可以让学生筹办定期出版的中文班报（线上、线下皆可）。每一期的主题都应该与课文内容有关，这样学生就可以在班报写作中使用刚学过的新词。学生应该自行选出一名编辑和一个编委会管理班报。班上的每个学生都要用学过的目的词撰写故事或新闻向班报投稿。

Teaching Example 30 Reading/writing-based vocabulary activity: Writing diaries about the Chinese class

教学示例 30 读写型词汇活动：中文课周记

The instructor can ask students to write a diary once a week to record the things that have happened in the Chinese class and then exchange their diaries with other students in the class. Since the weekly diaries are about the Chinese class, the students can use the words learned from the Chinese class in their diaries writings. The instructor may also encourage students to share their diaries with their Chinese-learning/speaking friends outside of the class.

教师可以让学生每周写一篇中文课笔记，记录中文课上发生的事情，并与班上的其他学生交换阅读。因为周记的内容与中文课有关，所以在写作中学生可以用到中文课上学过的词。教师还应该鼓励学生在课外与其他学中文或说中文的朋友分享自己的周记。

(Teaching Examples 28-30 are contributed by Helen H. Shen, The University of Iowa)

It should be pointed out that the major focus of the reading/writing-based vocabulary activities is on incidental learning of word and the appropriate use of learned words, rather than on the quality of reading and writing. Therefore, the activity design should make sure that students will be given plenty of opportunities to practice the learned words and also to learn new words. The evaluation should give enough weight to the accuracy of word use.

需要指出的是，读写型词汇活动的主要目的是促进学生的无意识词语学习，让学生学会恰当地运用学到的词语，而不是提高学生的阅读能力和写作能力。因此，教师在设计此类活动时应确保活动本身能够给学生提供足够的机会练习所学的词和学习新词，对活动效果进行评估时也应该充分关注词语使用的准确度。

To summarize, we presented the three-dimensional character and word instruction model for Chinese as a second language: cognitive process of meaningful learning, integration of four language skills for building linguistic proficiency, and adopting the three-tiered instructional approach for pedagogical soundness. Based on the above discussion, the complex relationship among the three dimensions for this model is outlined in Figure 6-5. In pursuit of effective character and word instruction, we must know that high quality learning cannot be realized without interaction of these three dimensions. We believe that effective character and word instruction is an art of seamlessly interweaving the knowledge of the three dimensions to achieve a perfect balance among the three.

综上所述，这一章我们讨论了汉语二语字词教学模式的三个维度：有意义学习的认知过程、为提高语言能力而进行的四项语言技能整合以及为提高教学有效性而采用的三层次教学途径。在上述讨论的基础上，我们把这三个维度之间的复杂关系绘成了图6–5。在追求有效字词教学的过程中，我们必须牢记，高质量的字词学习离不开三个维度间的相互作用。只有在三个维度上达到了完美的结合与平衡，高质量的字词学习才能实现。

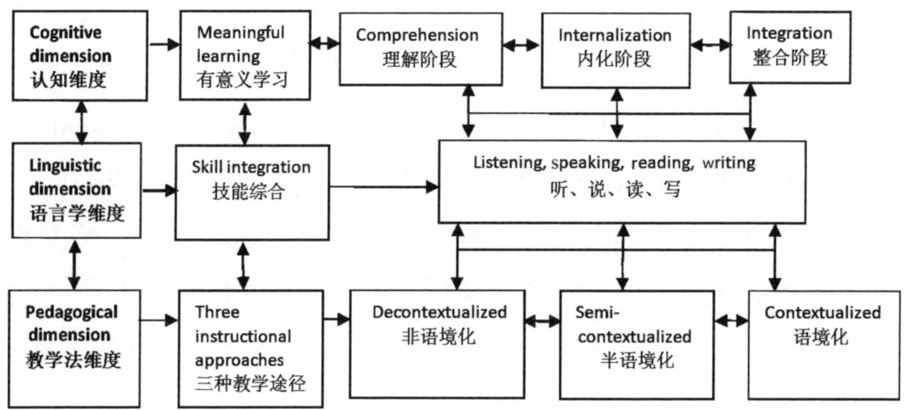

Figure 6-5 Three-Dimensional Character and Word Instruction Model for Chinese as a Second Language

图6-5 三维度汉语二语字词教学模式

The realization of meaningful learning and skill acquisition initiates from effective implementation of appropriate instructional approaches. The instructional approach proceeds from the first tier of decontextualized activities to the second tier of semi-contextualized activities and to the final tier of contextualized activities to support each stage of meaningful learning from comprehension to internalization to integration. At each stage of meaningful learning, the instruction must balance the four language skills in character/word acquisition. The training in four skills should be manifested in the teaching activities in each tier of instructional approach. That is, at each meaningful learning stage, instruction should consider integrating listening, speaking, reading, and writing skills to facilitate the transformation of word knowledge into skills. However, the acquisition of word knowledge from unknown to known and the development of four language skills from controlled to automatic are a gradual process. Due to complexity of cognition and individual differences, the progression is not linear. We should anticipate regression and focalization at any stage. In learning reality, character/word acquisition is not as simple as finding that today students learn 60 new words and tomorrow they learn another 60 words. Rather, we observe that on the second day, students only remember half of the words or fewer introduced the day before. We should expect that some words that have reached the internalization stage may have bounced back to comprehension stage. Therefore, instruction should not be rigid and fixed; rather, it should be flexible and adjustable based on learning reality.

有意义学习的实现和语言技能的获得离不开恰当教学手段的有效实施。在字词教学中，教学途径有序地从第一层次的非语境化活动推进到第二层次的半语境化活动再到第三层次的语境化活动，与此同时，有意义学习也相应地从理解阶段上升到内化阶段最后到达整合阶段。在有意义学习的每个阶段，字词教学都要平衡好听、说、读、写四项技能训练之间的关系。这四项技能的训练应该体现在每一层次的教学活动中。也就是说，在有意义学习的每个阶段，教学都必须考虑如何通过听、说、读、写四项技能的整合将词语知识转化为技能。当然，词语知识从无到有，听、说、读、写技能从控制型运用到自动化运用都是一个渐进的过程。由于认知过程的复杂性和个体的差异性，这种发展不是直线式的，我们应该预测到知识和技能的习得在任何阶段都可能出现回归或高原期现象。实际上，字词的习得并不像学生今天学60个生词，明天再学60个那么简单；相反，学生第二天可能只记得第一天学的一半甚至更少。我们应该预计到，有些已经达到内化阶段的字词是会反弹回理解阶段的。因此，教学手段不应该是固定僵化的，而应该根据实际情况灵活地进行调整。

6.2 Beginning level character and word instruction model for promoting active learning 促进主动学习的初级汉语字词教学模式

In an earlier chapter, we mentioned that word recognition automaticity is prerequisite for reading comprehension. Thus, improving efficiency of character and word instruction in an early stage of learning is a primary factor to facilitate learners' reading skill development at later stages of learning. In this section, we present the beginning level character and word instruction model for promoting active learning which is designed for beginning Chinese L2 classrooms. The model is predicated on the theory of active learning.

在前面的章节中我们提到，字词辨认自动化是阅读理解的先决条件，因此在汉语学习的初级阶段，提高字词教学的效率是促进学生后续阶段阅读能力发展的主要动力。在这一节，我们提出了一个适合初级阶段汉语二语课堂教学的教学模式——促进主动学习的初级汉语字词教学模式。顾名思义，这一模式的理论基础就是主动学习理论。

6.2.1 Active learning theory 主动学习理论

Active learning emerged as a new learning theory in the 1980s for science education but quickly extended to humanities and social science education (Bonwell & Eison, 1991). It is not only applied to classroom learning but also to all areas of learning. The core concept of active learning involves engaging learners not only in actively exploring knowledge but also in reflecting on their own learning process to become more effective learners (Shen & Xu, 2015). Active learning is defined as "providing opportunities for students to talk, listen, read, write, and reflect as they approach course content through problem-solving exercises, informal small groups, simulations, case studies, role playing, and other activities—all of which require students to apply what they are learning" (Meyers & Jones, 1993: 6). From its definition, we can understand that active learning makes learning an ongoing process for students to apply what they have learned in acquiring new knowledge. Thus, knowledge learning and knowledge application are integrated through the entire learning process.

主动学习作为一种新的学习理论出现于20世纪80年代，最初应用在理科教育中，后来很快就被应用在人文社会科学教育中。（Bonwell and Eison，1991）它不仅适用于课堂学习，还适用于其他所有领域的学习。这一理论的核心理念是不仅让学习者积极主动地探索知识，而且让其有意识地反思自己的学习过程，使自己成为一个更有效率的学习者。（Shen and Xu，2015）主动学习的定义是"在课程学习过程中通过问题解决型练习、非正式小组活动、模拟、案例分析、角色扮演，以及其他需要学生应用他们已经学到的知识和技能的活动给学生提供听、说、读、写和反思自己学习方法的机会"（Meyers and Jones，1993：6）。从这一定义中我们可以领悟到，主动学习是将学习过程看作学生应用学到的知识和技能去获得新知识和新技能的过程。这里所说的"学习过程"，是"学"与"用"始终交织在一起的过程。

A comprehensive qualitative study used the active learning theory lens to examine instructors' teaching strategies, methods, and activities in beginning level Chinese L2 character and word instruction were conducted in a one-semester period in an American university (Shen & Xu, 2015). In this study, the first author, Shen, following the principle of the active learning theory, developed a set of criteria for identifying effective teaching strategies, methods, and activities (SMAs) (see Table 6-1), and then observed one semester teaching conducted by the second author of the study, Xu, who was familiar with the active learning theory. Based on classroom observation combining with other qualitative analysis methods of documentation, interview, and survey, Shen finally identified SMAs which were congruent with active learning guidelines. The model presented in this section is based on Shen and Xu's study (2015).

Shen和Xu（2015）进行的一项为期一个学期的综合定性研究，从主动学习的理论角度探讨了美国初级汉语二语课堂字词教学的策略、方法和活动。这篇论文的第一作者，Shen，依据主动学习理论制定了一系列判断教学策略、方法和活动有效性的标准（策略、方法和活动在该研究中简称SMAs，请参见表6-1），并根据制定的标准对初级汉语字词教学课进行了一个学期的观察。初级汉语字词教学课的任课教师是非常熟悉主动学习理论的Xu，也是该论文的第二作者。Shen在课堂观察的基础上又结合了文献综述、访谈和问卷调查等定性分析法，最终提出了一个符合主动学习准则的初级汉语字词教学模式。本节提出的教学模式就是基于Shen和Xu（2015）的研究。

Table 6-1 Guidelines for Identifying Active Learning

表6-1 识别主动学习的准则

Number 序号	Guidelines 准则
1	The instruction should make clear about learning goals prior to learning so that students can actively gauge their learning toward goals 教学应该让学生在开始学习之前就清楚地知道学习目标，这样学生可以为达到目标而努力
2	The instructional activities should stimulate students' learning interest and curiosities so that they will actively engage themselves in learning activities 教学活动应该激发学生的学习兴趣和好奇心，这样他们才会积极地参与到学习活动中去

（续表）

Number 序号	Guidelines 准则
3	The instruction must situate in students' prior knowledge and personal experience so that students can actively make connection/association between new materials and existing knowledge, experience 教学必须立足于学生已有的知识和生活经验，这样学生可以主动地将新知识与他们已有知识和生活经验联系起来
4	The instruction should gear toward developing students' mental model for learning by modeling and by providing opportunities for students to create learning and thinking strategies through problem-solving-based activities so that students will actively learn how to learn 教学应该致力于构建学生的心理学习模式，通过示范及问题解决型教学活动，为学生提供创造学习策略和思维策略的机会，让学生主动学会如何学习
5	The instructional activities must provide opportunities for students to use more than one of speaking, listening, reading, and writing modes, so that students can actively transfer learned knowledge into skills 教学活动必须为学生提供使用一种以上技能（听、说、读、写）的机会，这样学生才可以主动地把学到的知识转化为技能
6	The instruction should provide opportunities for peer interaction and cooperation so that students will learn how to reach group decision based on positive interdependence, individual accountability, and constructive interaction 教学应该为学生提供与同伴互动和合作的机会，这样学生才能在小组中学会如何通过正向互相依赖、个体负责和建设性交流做出小组决定
7	The instruction should present learning materials in an organized fashion and also model how to organize learning materials to let students understand how this can reduce intrinsic cognitive load and facilitate cognitive processing of learning materials 教学应该对学习材料进行有效的组织，同时向学生示范如何有效地组织教学材料，使学生懂得对材料的有效组织能减少其内在认知负荷，有利于其对学习材料的认知加工
8	The instruction should make review as part of learning so that next step learning can be grounded on known concepts 教学应该让复习成为学习的有机组成部分，这样新的学习就可以建立在已知的内容上

（续表）

Number 序号	Guidelines 准则
9	The instruction must guide students to assess their own learning process and result, so that students will learn how to monitor their own learning and move toward goals based on feedback from assessment 教学必须引导学生学会评估自己的学习过程和结果，这样学生就能学会如何监控自己的学习，并通过反馈让自己的学习达到既定的目标

6.2.2 Seven major components 七大要素

The beginning level character and word instruction model for promoting active learning consists of seven major components to be carried out in a character/word instruction class: goal-driven, material grouping, four types of instructional activities, peer interaction and cooperation, built-in systematic review, practicing with four linguistic modes, and performance-based assessment. These seven components are outlined in Figure 6-6. We will explain each of the seven components in the model below.

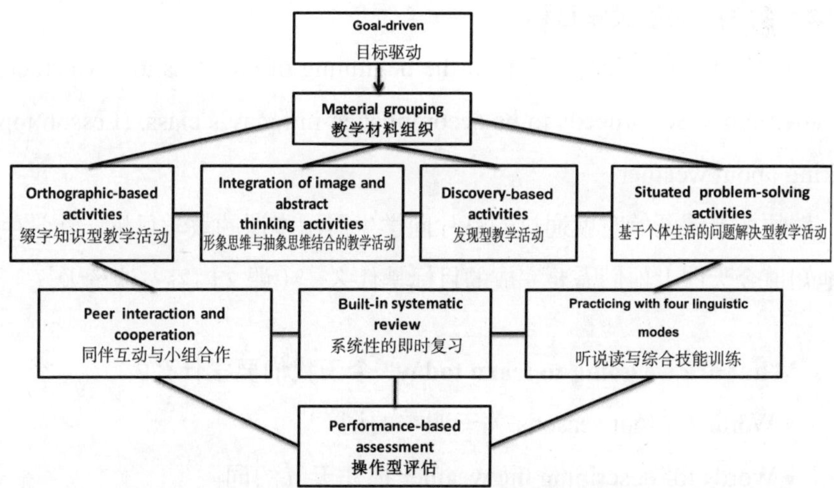

Figure 6-6 Beginning Level Character and Word Instruction Model for Promoting Active Learning

图 6–6 促进主动学习的初级汉语字词教学模式

促进主动学习的初级汉语字词教学模式由七大要素构成，它们分别是目标驱动、教学材料组织、四类教学活动、同伴互动与小组合作、系统性的即时复习、听说读写综合技能训练以及操作型评估，请参看上图 6-6。下面我们将详细阐述这七个要素。

• Goal-driven 目标驱动

The instructor presents a clear goal to students about what to learn at the beginning of the class, so that learning activities can be goal-oriented, and students have a clear focus on what they will learn and how to gear their learning toward goals.

教师在上课伊始就向学生说明该课的学习目标，让学生清楚地了解他们在这一课中要学什么，这样学习就有了目标。

Teaching Example 31 Clarifying goals for learning
教学示例 31 明确教学目标

The teacher provides a slide at the beginning of the class to have students pay attention to what needs to be accomplished in today's class. (Lesson topic: Talking about weather)

教师在上课开始时就通过幻灯片向学生展示本课的教学目标，让学生清楚地知道今天课上他们需要完成的目标是什么。（课文内容：谈论天气）

What are we going to learn today? 今天我们要学什么？

- Words for four seasons 关于四季的词
- Words for describing the weather 描述天气的词
- Words for making comparison 进行比较的词
- Conjunction words 连词

• Material grouping 教学材料组织

Before learning new words, the instructor or student make cognitive grouping of the new words. The purpose of material grouping is to increase interactivity of learning materials to reduce intrinsic cognitive load for the purpose of enhancing short-term memory.

在学习新词之前，教师或学生应该先对新词进行认知分组。对教学材料进行认知分组是为了强化学习材料之间的内在联系，减轻学生的内在认知负荷，提高短时记忆的效率。

Teaching Example 32 Grouping learning materials
教学示例 32 教学材料分组

In this lesson, the teacher grouped new words into six groups by using three types of grouping concepts. The first is semantic grouping (Groups 1, 2, 5, and 6). In these groups the words are grouped based on their relation to an activity of daily life. The second is linguistic grouping (Group 3). Words in this group are of the same part of speech, i.e. measure words. The third is concept grouping (Group 4). Color words are grouped together based on the logical relationship between the concept of the word 颜色 (color) and related words for colors.

教师将这一课的生词分成6组介绍给学生，主要是基于：（1）意义，如第1、2、5、6组。这4组都是根据词与日常生活中某种活动的关系确定的。（2）语言学特点，如第3组。这组词词类相同，都是量词。（3）概念之间的关系，如第4组。在这组词中，具体的颜色词与“颜色”一词所表达的概念之间是从属关系。

Group 1	售货员、买、卖、东西（selling- and buying-related words）
Group 2	穿：衣服、衬衫、裤子、鞋（items we wear）
Group 3	件、条、双（words with similar or the same linguistic function）
Group 4	颜色：黄色、黑色、红色、咖啡色、白色（color and related words）
Group 5	大小、号、一样、合适（words for describing dress etiquette）
Group 6	付钱、块、毛、分、多少、一共、找、便宜、贵（payment-related words）

• Four types of instructional activities 四类教学活动

The instruction mainly uses the four major types of activities. The first one is orthographic-based activities. The instruction requires students to explore and understand the relationship between characters and radicals within. The second type is integration of image and abstract thinking activities to allow dual-coding and multi-modality processing of learning materials. The third type is discovery-based activities in which the instructor encourages students to self-discover the sound, meaning, shape of the new characters, as well as various relationships between words. The fourth type is situated problem-solving activities in which students practice words by relating to their own personal life experiences and by solving real-life problems. These four types of instructional activities, as core components of active learning, stimulate students' learning interest and promote mental activities, which, in turn, increases the level of cognitive, affective, and metacognitive functions during learning. Please see the examples below:

字词教学主要采取四类教学活动：第一类是缀字知识型教学活动，它要求学生主动探索和了解语素与词、部首与汉字的关系；第二类是形象思维与抽象思维结合的教学活动，它可使学生对学习材料进行双编码并运用多条感知通道加工学习材料；第三类是发现型教学活动，即教师鼓励学生自己去发现新字的音、形、义以及词与词之间的多种关系；第四类是基于个体生活的问题解决型教学活动，它要求新词的操练需与学生的个人生活经历和解决现实生活问题紧密联系起来。作为主动学习理论的核心组成部分，这四类教学活动能够激发学生的学习兴趣，活跃他们的思维，提高他们在字词学习中的认知、情感、元认知加工水平。具体参见下面的教学示例：

Teaching Example 33 Orthographic-based activity

教学示例 33 缀字知识型教学活动

The instructor first gives four pictographs of the four characters and asks students to place them under the corresponding characters. Then, the instructor asks students to find out the connections between each pair of ancient and modern forms, which helps students visualize the meaning of the characters. Next, students are encouraged to talk about how to memorize the new characters based on their pictographic forms and explain the meaning of components within the two compound characters. (Lesson topic: Talk about weather)

教师首先出示四个象形文字，要求学生将它们放到对应的现代汉字下面，并找到每组象形文字与现代汉字之间的字形联系，帮助学生直观地理解汉字的字义。然后，教师要鼓励学生探讨如何根据象形文字的字形记忆现代汉字，并解释两个合体字中部件的意思。（课文内容：谈论天气）

气（air）	雨（rain）	春（spring）	冬（winter）

Teaching Example 34 Integration of image and abstract thinking activity

教学示例 34 形象思维与抽象思维结合的教学活动

The instructor presents the picture with three short-sleeve shirts in three different sizes and also purposefully writes the three words 大号, 中号, and 小号 in different font sizes. These visual pictures are to evoke students' image thinking to aid processing the abstract concepts. Next, the instructor asks students to draw an object with three sizes and write in the corresponding words: 大号, 中号, and 小号.

教师首先出示一张画有三件不同型号的短袖衬衫的图片，同时有意识地在图片上用不同的字号将“大号、中号、小号”这三个词写出来。这些视觉图像可以激活学生的形象思维，帮助学生记忆这三个抽象概念。接下来，教师让学生自己选择一个物品，画出三种不同的型号，并且在每个型号下面写出相应的词。

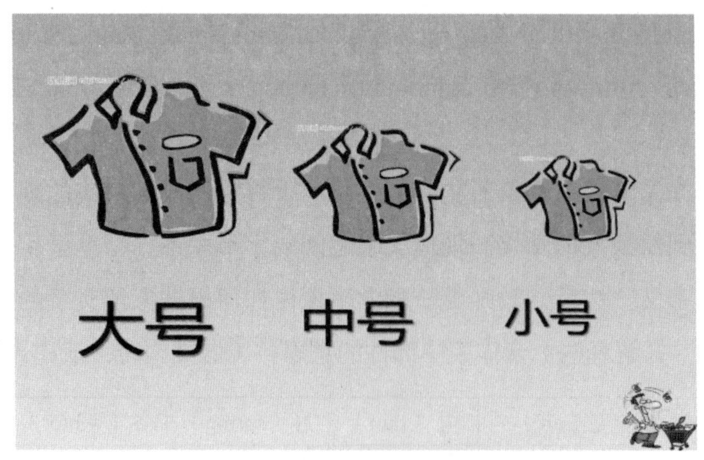

Teaching Example 35 Discovery-based activity
教学示例 35 发现型教学活动

The instructor presents a blueprint of an apartment on a PowerPoint slide (left picture below) and asks students to identify the function of each room and to find out the corresponding words from the new words list that explain the function of each room (the middle picture was made by a student). The instructor then presents the same blueprint (left) and asks students to name each room based on its function. Students must find appropriate words from the new words list to complete the task. The right picture below is the completed version. (Lesson topic: Rent an apartment)

教师先用幻灯片展示一张公寓设计图（见下左图），要求学生识别出每个房间的功能，并从生词表中找出相应的词进行说明。学生完成以后（见下中图），教师出示同一张设计图（即下左图），要求学生根据每个房间的功能，从生词表中找出合适的词给房间命名（见下右图）。（课文内容：租公寓）

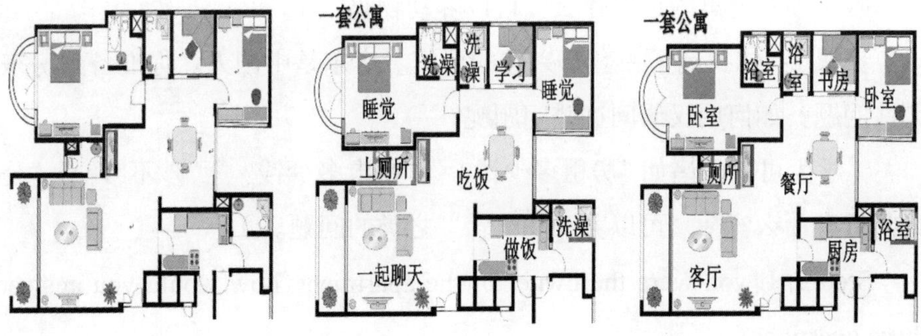

Teaching Example 36 **Situated problem-solving activity**

教学示例 36 **基于个体生活的问题解决型教学活动**

The instructor asks students to complete a simulated real-life task: To rent an apartment. (Lesson topic: Rent an apartment)

教师要求学生完成一个模拟真实语境的任务：租一间公寓。（课文内容：租公寓）

Task 任务

Next semester, you decide to move out of the student dorm and to live in an apartment.

下学期你决定搬出学生宿舍，住到一个公寓里。

Step 1: You have found an apartment that interests you. The owner is Chinese. What kinds of questions are you going to ask and how will you ask those questions in Chinese?

(Students may come up with questions such as 房租多少钱？水电多少钱？吵不吵？公寓附近有什么？可以养动物吗？)

步骤 1：你找到了一套感兴趣的公寓。房东是中国人。你准备问房东哪些问题？如何用汉语问这些问题呢？

（学生可以问诸如"房租多少钱？""水电多少钱？""吵不吵？""公寓附近有什么？""可以养动物吗？"之类的问题。）

Step 2: If you were the owner of the apartment, how would you answer these questions?

步骤 2：如果你是房东，你会如何回答这些问题？

Step 3: Walk around and find a partner to do role play.

步骤 3：在教室里找到你的搭档，你们俩分别扮演房东和租房者进行对话。

• Peer interaction and cooperation 同伴互动与小组合作

The four types of instructional activities proposed above can be better carried out through pair and group learning in which group members actively interact with each other and work cooperatively to solve learning problems based on positive interdependence and individual contribution.

上面提及的四类教学活动在两人或多人的小组中进行能获得更好的教学效果，因为在两人或多人的小组中，学生既可以积极地相互依靠，又可以根据个人能力的不同为问题的解决贡献自己的那份力，积极互动，相互协作，共同解决学习问题。

• Built-in systematic review 系统性的即时复习

Review activities in this model are regarded as part of active learning, because the review activities provide ways and means of practicing with newly learned words in new linguistic situations. The major types of review activities that the instructor applies during instruction are decontextualized review, semi-contextualized review, and contextualized review. The three types of review activities should be grounded in the four types of instructional activities discussed above.

这种教学模式下的复习活动被视为主动学习的一部分，因为它为目的词在新语境中的运用提供了练习的方式和方法。教师在教学中运用的复习活动主要有非语境化复习活动、半语境化复习活动和语境化复习活动。这三类复习活动都应以上面讨论的四类教学活动为基础。

Teaching Example 37 Decontextualized review activity

教学示例 37 非语境化复习活动

Write out the words based on the photos and the questions. Then interview your classmate by asking questions on using the transportation indicated by the photos and take notes for answers.

请根据图片和问题填出相应的词，然后结合图片所示的交通工具和左边的问题采访你的同学并记录答案。

问题				
根据图片填词	（汽车）	（飞机）	（火车）	（地铁）
你想买什么票?	（汽车票）	（飞机票）	（火车票）	（地铁票）
应该在哪坐?	（汽车站）	（飞机场）	（火车站）	（地铁站）

Note: Students are required to fill out the words in the parentheses based on the questions.
注：学生需要根据问题填出括号内的词。

Teaching Example 38 Semi-contextualized review activity

教学示例 38 半语境化复习活动

Read the road map, and tell us how to take the subway to school. Please use the conjunction words 先, 然后, 再, and 最后.

看下面的路线图，然后告诉我们怎么坐地铁去学校。请用上连词“先、然后、再、最后”。

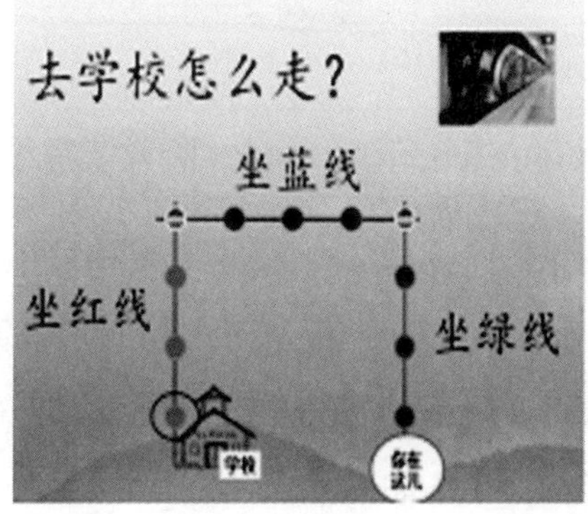

Teaching Example 39 Contextualized review activity

教学示例 39 语境化复习活动

<table>
<tr><td colspan="3">Task: You will be interviewed by an officer from a local department of transportation tomorrow. Please prepare to answer the following questions by using the words learned.
任务：明天本地交通管理局的工作人员要采访你，下面是他们要问的问题，请你提前准备好答案并用上学过的词。</td></tr>
<tr><td colspan="3">你常常乘坐哪种交通工具？为什么？</td></tr>
<tr><td>Transportation means</td><td>*Advantages</td><td>*Disadvantages</td></tr>
<tr><td>火车</td><td rowspan="5">很快，很方便
去……站（机场）很方便
……票很便宜
不用花很多钱</td><td rowspan="5">很慢，有点儿慢
很麻烦
票很贵
得花很多钱</td></tr>
<tr><td>飞机</td></tr>
<tr><td>地铁</td></tr>
<tr><td>公共汽车</td></tr>
<tr><td>出租汽车</td></tr>
<tr><td colspan="3">** 你常常自己开车吗？为什么？</td></tr>
<tr><td>开车</td><td></td><td></td></tr>
<tr><td>不开车</td><td></td><td></td></tr>
</table>

*The words and patterns provided in the middle and right boxes must be used to answer the questions.
请用中间和右边单元格中的词语和句式回答问题。

** This is an optional step that may be done by groups who have time after completing the first activity.
如果有些小组提前完成了第一个活动，那他们可以继续做这个活动。

• Practicing with four linguistic modes 听说读写综合技能训练

In designing the four types of instructional activities, the instructor must consider using two or more linguistic modes for a single activity and alternatively use the four linguistic modes in different activities. This will allow active involvement of multi-modality processing of new words during learning, thereby, to make learning fun and effective.

在设计四类教学活动时，教师必须确保：在每一个活动中，学生都能运用两种或两种以上的语言技能；在不同的活动中，学生能交替练习听、说、读、写这四项语言技能。这样才能使多条感知通道参与学习，保证学习的有效性和趣味性。

• Performance-based assessment 操作型评估

Different from criteria-based assessment, performance-based assessment requires students to perform a task rather than select an answer from a ready-made list. It requires students to actively demonstrate what they know and apply their own understanding of the concepts into variety of contexts. The strengths and weaknesses of students demonstrated during their performance will allow instructors to diagnose the appropriateness and feasibility of instructional SMAs applied during the teaching and make necessary adjustments for next round instruction. Please see the example below.

与标准参照型评估不同，操作型评估要求学生完成一项语言任务而不是从已有选项中选择一项。它要求学生主动地展示自己所学的知识，并将自己对概念的理解应用在不同的语境中。学生在操作过程中表现出来的优缺点可以帮助教师诊断出所使用的教学法的可行性与有效性，以便调整下一轮的教学计划。具体请参见下面的教学示例。

Teaching Example 40 Performance-based assessment

教学示例 40 操作型评估

Procedures 步骤

Students work in pairs to write a short paragraph about their favorite or not so favorite season(s) in their hometown based on the sheet provided. They are encouraged to use as many learned words as possible. Then, individual students report to the class what they have prepared by either pointing to or writing the key words on a board as they speak along. At the end of each report, both the teacher and the students provide feedback about errors in the report.

学生两人一组，根据下面提供的内容写一段关于他/她最喜欢的或不太喜欢的家乡季节的话。教师要鼓励学生尽可能多地使用已经学过的词。之后，每个学生要向全班汇报他们所准备的内容，可以一边说一边在黑板上指出或写出关键词。学生汇报结束后，教师和其他学生可以就报告中用词的准确性进行点评。

Which season(s) do you like/dislike about your hometown? 你喜欢或不喜欢你家乡的哪个（些）季节？

我喜欢/不喜欢_____（春/夏/秋/冬）天，因为_____不但_____（很舒服/暖和/凉快/热/冷/闷），而且_____（常常/不常常/下雨/下雪/刮风）。

(Teaching Examples 31–40 designed by Xu Wenjing and modified by Helen H. Shen, The University of Iowa)

Teaching and learning are a very dynamic process. The two models for

CSL character and word instruction presented in this chapter outlines the dynamic of the character and word learning reality. Although they are still sketchy, and many details need to be ironed out and enriched through further empirical studies, we hope the models can serve as a pilot light for the CSL character and word instruction. At the end of this chapter, we would like to share a traditional Chinese saying with our readers: "There are ways of teaching, but there is no fixed way of teaching." Teaching is very dynamic; we need theories and methodologies to guide our teaching practice, but we also need continuous testing, verification, and development of theories and methods that best describe and fit the ever-changing teaching current. We hope our educators will never consider theories as orthodox beliefs, but rather, in the teaching practice, they will challenge, testify, revise, and develop theories to make the theories full of vitality like evergreen trees.

教与学是一个动态的过程，本章中提出的两种汉语二语字词教学模式大致勾画出了字词习得的动态过程。虽然这些模式还是粗线条的，许多细节还有待于之后的实证研究来完善和丰富，但我们仍希望这两种模式能对汉语二语字词教学产生一定的指导作用。在本章的最后，我们想与读者分享一个中国的传统说法——"教学有法但无定法"。教学是动态的，我们需要教学理论和教学法指导我们的教学实践，也需要不断地检验、验证和发展教学理论和教学法，使之适应不断发展变化的教学潮流。因此，我们希望教育工作者不要把理论当作不变的信条，而要在教学实践中挑战理论、验证理论、修正理论并发展理论，使理论能像生命之树一样常青。

References 参考文献

张田若，陈良璜，李卫民. 2003. 中国当代汉字认读与书写[M]. 成都：四川教育出版社.

Anderson J R. 1982. Acquisition of cognitive skill[J]. Psychological review, 89(4): 369–

406.

Anderson J R. 2005. Cognitive psychology and its application [M]. 6th ed. New York: Worth Publishing.

Ausubel D P. 1962. A subsumption theory of meaningful verbal learning and retention[J]. The journal of general psychology, 66(2): 213–224.

Ausubel D P. 1963. The psychology of meaningful verbal learning[M]. New York: Grune and Stratton.

Ausubel D P. 1977. The facilitation of meaningful verbal learning in the classroom[J]. Educational psychologist, 12(2): 162–178.

Bonwell C C, Eison J A. 1991. Active learning: Creating excitement in the classroom. ASHE-ERIC Higher Education Report, Washington DC: School of Education and Human Development, George Washington University.

Hulstijn J H. 2001. Intentional and incidental second language vocabulary learning: a reappraisal of elaboration, rehearsal and authomaticity[M]. Robinson P. Cognition and second language instruction. Cambridge, UK: Cambridge University Press, 258–286.

Meyer L M. 2000. Barriers to meaningful instruction for English learners[J]. Theory into practice, 39(4): 228–236.

Meyers C, Jones T B. 1993. Promoting active learning: strategies for the college classroom[M]. San Francisco: Jossey-Bass.

Novak J D. 1991. Clarify with concept maps: a tool for students and teachers alike[J]. The science teacher, 58:45–49.

Novak J D, Cañas A J. 2008. The theory underlying concept maps and how to construct and use them[R]. Technical report IHMC Cmap Tools (2006-01)[2008-01]. http://cmap.ihmc.us/publications/researchpapers/theorycmaps/theoryunderlyingconceptmaps.htm.

Novak J D, Gowin D B. 1984. Learning how to learn[M]. New York: Cambridge University Press.

Novak J D, Musonda D. 1991. A twelve-year longitudinal study of science concept learning [J].

American educational research journal, 28:117–153.

Oxford R, Crookall D. 1990. Vocabulary learning: a critical analysis of techniques[J]. TESL Canada Journal, 7(2): 9–30.

Ryle G. 1949. The concept of mind[M]. New York: Barnes and Noble, Inc.

Shen H H, Xu W. 2015. Active learning: qualitative inquiries into vocabulary instruction in Chinese L2 classrooms[J]. Foreign language annals, 48(1): 82–99.

Shuell T J. 1990. Phases of meaningful learning[J]. Review of educational research, 60(4): 531–547.

Stahl S A. 1983. Differential word knowledge and reading comprehension[J]. Journal of literacy research, 15: 33–50.

Stahl S A. 1985. To teach a word well: a framework for vocabulary instruction[J]. Reading world, 24(3): 16–27.

Thelen J N. 1986. Vocabulary instruction and meaningful learning[J]. Journal of reading, 29(7): 603–609.

Appendix A　附录A

Modern Chinese Character Stroke Chart
现代汉字笔画表

基本笔画（6） 笔画、名称、例字	十 一：横	中 丨：竖	人 丿：撇	主 丶：点	大 ㇏：捺	江 ㇀：提	日 ㇕：横折	
派生笔画（24） 笔画、名称、例字	又 ㇇：横撇	写 ㇖：横勾	月 ㇆：横折勾	记 ㇊：横折提	朵 ㇍：横折弯	凹 ㇅：横折折	风 ⺄：横折斜勾	公 ㇜：撇折
	九 ㇈：横折弯勾	队 ㇌：横撇弯勾	及 ㇋：横折折撇	乃 ㇡：横折折折勾	凸 ㇎：横折折折	民 ㇙：竖提	山 ㇗：竖折	戈 ㇂：斜勾
	小 亅：竖勾	酉 ㇄：竖弯	己 ㇟：竖弯勾	专 ㄣ：竖弯撇	鼎 ㇞：竖折折	马 ㇉：竖折折勾	女 ㇛：撇点	家 ㇁：弯勾

注：该表引自《现代汉字教程》第31-32页，张静贤著，现代出版社，1990。（编者注：基本笔画应该是7，但原文是6，疑似笔误）

Appendix B　附录B

Rules for the Character Stroke Order

汉字书写规则

笔顺规则	例字	笔顺
1. 先横后竖	十	一 十
2. 先撇后捺	人	丿 人
3. 从上到下	三	一 二 三
4. 从左到右	做	亻 估 做
5. 从外到里	月	丿 月 月
6. 先外后里再封口	日	丨 冂 月 日
7. 先横后撇	厂	一 厂
8. 先中间后两边	小	亅 小 小
9. 点在上方或左上角，先写点后写主体	文	丶 亠 文
10. 点在右下角或下方或里边，先写主体后写点	术	木 术
11. 上左下包围结构，先写上、里，后写左下	区	一 又 区
12. 上右包围结构，先写上右，后写里边	司	𠃌 司 司
13. 左下右包围结构，先写上边，再写左下、右	凶	㐅 凶 凶
14. 左下包围结构，当左下是辶和廴时，先写右上，后写左下；当左下是其他部件时，先写左下，后写右上	进	井 进

注：该表引自《现代汉字教程》第38-39页，张静贤著，现代出版社，1990。

Appendix C 附录C

Types of Graphic Structure of Compound Characters
汉字间架结构

部件书写顺序：先写红色部分（标“1”处），再写蓝色部分（标“2”处），最后写黑色部分（标“3”处）。

1. Left-Right Structure 左右结构

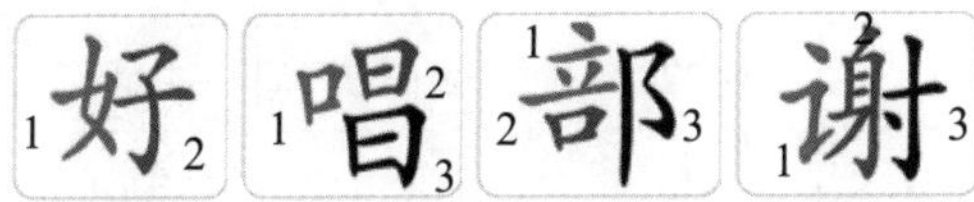

2. Top-Bottom Structure 上下结构

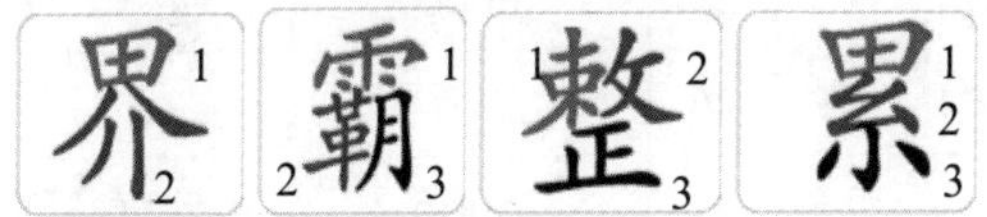

3. Half Encircled Structure 半包围结构

4. Encircled Structure包围结构

Appendix D　附录D

100 Radicals According to Their Frequency
按频率排列的前100个部首

1	shuǐ	水（氵 氺）
2	cǎo	艹（艸）
3	kǒu	口
4	mù	木（朩）
5	shǒu	手（龵 扌）
6	rén	人（亻 入）
7	jīn	金（钅）
8	xīn	心（忄 ⺗）
9	tǔ	土（士）
10	yuè	月（⺼）
11	mì	糸（纟）
12	chóng; huǐ	虫
13	yán	言（讠）
14	nǚ	女
15	zhú	竹（⺮）
16	huǒ	火（灬）
17	wáng; yù	王（玉）
18	rì	日（曰）

19	shí	石
20	yú	鱼（魚）
21	shān	山
22	zú	足（⻊）
23	niǎo	鸟（鳥）
24	nè	疒
25	chuò	辵（辶）
26	yī	衣（衤）
27	quǎn	犬（犭）
28	mù	目
29	dāo	刀（刂 ⺈）
30	yì	邑（阝在右）
31	mián	宀
32	hé	禾
33	mǎ	马（馬）
34	bèi	贝（貝）
35	chē	车（車）
36	fù	阜（阝在左）

（续表）

37	shì	示（礻）
38	shí	食（饣）
39	y6u	酉
40	bā	八（丷）
41	xié; yè	页（頁）
42	jīn	巾
43	mén	门（門）
44	yǎn; guǎng	广
45	dà	大
46	mǐ	米
47	tián	田
48	shí	十
49	chì	彳
50	gé	革
51	pū	攴（攵）
52	gē	戈
53	shī	尸
54	xué	穴
55	lì	力
56	zhōu	舟
57	wéi	囗
58	yǔ	雨
59	hàn; chǎng	厂
60	yòu	又
61	niú	牛（牜 ⺧）
62	mǐn	皿

63	bīng	冫
64	yǔ	羽
65	yáng	羊
66	gōng	弓
67	è; dǎi	歹（歺）
68	xiǎo	小（⺌）
69	qiàn	欠
70	zǐ	子
71	zhuī	隹
72	ěr	耳
73	bái	白
74	gǔ	骨
75	lì	立
76	jiàn	见（見）
77	sī	厶
78	máo	毛
79	bǔ	卜
80	chǐ	齿（齒）
81	fāng	方
82	hēi	黑
83	shū	殳
84	rén; ér	儿
85	shān	彡
86	qì	气
87	bāo	勹
88	zhǎo	爪（爫）

（续表）

89	wǎ	瓦	95	cùn	寸
90	zǒu	走	96	zhǐ	夊
91	fāng	匚	97	shǐ	矢
92	hù	户	98	jīn	斤
93	gōng	工	99	shé	舌
94	zhǐ	止	100	shēn	身

注：该表引自《汉字部首教程》（*Learning 100 Chinese Radicals*）第16页，沈禾玲、王平、蔡真慧编著，北京大学出版社，2009。